PRISONS IN CONTEXT

PERSONS IN CONTEXT

PRISONS IN CONTEXT

Edited by

Roy D. King
Mike Maguire

CLARENDON PRESS · OXFORD
1994

Oxford University Press, Walton Street, Oxford OX2 6DP
Oxford New York Toronto
Delhi Bombay Calcutta Madras Karachi
Kuala Lumpur Singapore Hong Kong Tokyo
Nairobi Dar es Salaam Cape Town
Melbourne Auckland Madrid
and associated companies in
Berlin Ibadan

Oxford is a trade mark of Oxford University Press

Published in the United States
by Oxford University Press Inc., New York

This is a special issue of the
British Journal of Criminology

British Library Cataloguing in Publication Data
Data available

Library of Congress Cataloging in Publication Data
Data available
ISBN 0–19–825865 8

1 3 5 7 9 10 8 6 4 2

Typeset by Cotswold Typesetting Ltd, Gloucester

Printed on acid-free paper by Alden Press Limited,
Oxford and Northampton, Great Britain

CONTENTS

INTRODUCTION

Contexts of Imprisonment: An International Perspective

ROY D. KING and MIKE MAGUIRE*

This volume was conceived at the time of Lord Justice Woolf's inquiry into the riot at Strangeways prison in Manchester (Home Office 1991). It was anticipated—judging from the tenor of the public seminars which formed part of the inquiry—that Woolf would move well beyond the investigation of immediate events, eschewing the search for scapegoats and troublemakers, and seek to put what happened in Strangeways and the several other riots that occurred in its wake into a broader context. In the event those expectations were amply rewarded. In marked contrast to Mr Justice May's inquiry 12 years earlier (Home Office 1979), which had been predicated upon the unruliness of staff, Woolf managed to open out the questions surrounding the behaviour of people in prison into a fundamental re-examination of the structures on which relationships are based—not just internally within the prison system but externally in regard to the rest of the criminal justice apparatus.

There has been no shortage of commentaries on Woolf, and Player and Jenkins (1993) bring together many contributions analysing different aspects of the Woolf agenda in Britain. But even before Woolf had reported it was decided to take a wider and more distanced perspective on 'prisons in context' for this volume: to ask questions not merely about the relationship between imprisonment and the criminal justice system as a whole, but also whether, and in what ways, the use of imprisonment and the treatment of prisoners reflect economic and political structures as well as what Winston Churchill once called the 'mood and temper' of the society which generates them.

Woolf's achievements should not be underrated. If nothing else it will never again be possible, in Britain at least, to consider prison disturbances without reference back to the conditions in which they occur. Such conditions include not only the physical facilities, but the quality of the regime and the nature of the relationships between staff and prisoners. Above all they include the sense of justice or injustice which underpins and 'legitimates' (or not) the whole penal edifice. But at one level many of the ideas expressed in Woolf were not new. The development of standards for the

* Respectively University of Wales, Bangor and University of Wales, Cardiff.

1

prison services of the United Kingdom, for example, had long been canvassed (see, for example, Casale 1985) and even briefly embraced by William Whitelaw when Home Secretary; effective grievance procedures, including a specialist prisons Ombudsman, had been called for many times (Wener 1983; Maguire 1985); and community prisons had their antecedents in the call for a loosening of the distinction between local and training prisons and the development of more multifunctional institutions genuinely serving their localities (King and Morgan 1980). What was new was the context in which such ideas were expressed. By the early 1990s these were ideas whose time had come, their somewhat surprising resonance with the political doctrines of measured performance in the public sector and with the citizen's charter becoming irresistible. Moreover, at another level, the political context was changing even faster, so that the transition from Prison Department to Prison Service Agency and the rapid application of privatization to the process of imprisonment— topics scarcely touched on in Lord Woolf's report—raised further questions of accountability and legitimacy for the prison system even as Woolf appeared to be setting them at rest.

It was also readily apparent that the problems experienced in Britain were by no means unique. In the face of a string of adverse court decisions and the holding of some complete jurisdictions to be in breach of the constitution, the American Correctional Association had long since voluntarily adopted a code of standards and established the Commission on Accreditation for Corrections for monitoring them, apparently on the principle that attack is the best means of defence (see Morgan and Bronstein 1985). But whatever bulwark these may have provided against poor conditions, it was being swamped by some of the most dramatic increases in prison population growth ever seen. And in the familiar setting where the willingness to increase public expenditure on prisons does not match the demand for punishment, the Americans were the first to re-invent private prisons, particularly in the Southern states. How far did recent developments in the American use of imprisonment reflect intended changes in policy? And are they a portent for what might happen in Britain?

Extending the context of imprisonment from a purely British one to an international one immediately raised other issues. Though there are important social, economic, and cultural differences between Britain and the United States of America there are at least two reasons for supposing that penological differences might be more matters of scale rather than matters of substance. First, there has long been a history of interchange on matters concerning imprisonment which can be traced—at least on this side of the Atlantic—from William Crawford's (1834) report on American penitentiaries to Terry Platt's report (Home Office 1985) on new generation prisons. Second, the increasing convergence of political ideas during the Thatcher–Reagan years provides many contextual resemblances. But what if the international dimension were extended wider—to Western Europe, with a different cultural and political heritage and a radically different system of criminal justice? Or to the societies of Eastern Europe or the former Soviet Union, trying to reconcile old institutional frameworks with newly emerging fledgling democracies? In such a context how far is it possible to make meaningful comparisons of the use of imprisonment in different countries? How helpful is it to think in terms of international standards for imprisonment, independently of those prevailing for other aspects of social life, and if it is, how might they be enforced?

2

Might different societies have quite different problems and procedures for legitimating their prison systems, from those adopted by Woolf? Would such considerations suggest that Lord Justice Woolf's solution is a recipe for all—or might it be the case that it is insufficient even for the United Kingdom?

It is easy to raise questions and set an agenda, but quite another to provide answers—especially within the confines of one slim volume. Even with much more space at our disposal we would have had to be very selective, and we must be the first to recognize that the limitations of the exercise have produced arbitrary inclusions and omissions. There is probably no need to catalogue the latter because they are sufficiently obvious, although we are particularly conscious of the lack of a Third World perspective (a glaring gap in the literature generally, though Whitfield (1991) provides some welcome new data). However, we should say something about what is included. As editors our strategy was to discuss the above issues with some of the leading experts in their respective fields and then to invite them to contribute in the way they thought most appropriate to the theme of 'prisons in context', bearing in mind an international audience. We chose to opt for fewer papers, raising important matters in reasonable depth, rather than to attempt more comprehensive, but inevitably more superficial, coverage. All of the first nine authors (and co-authors) we approached embraced the idea with immediate enthusiasm. There was no need for arm twisting, and there was a minimum of hassling over deadlines. There was no shortage of ideas for other contributions, nor of potential other contributors—but there was a finite amount of space and the editorial search stopped almost as soon as it began. The result, we trust, is a collection of papers with an appropriate mix of theoretical, empirical, descriptive, and analytical concerns: in short there is something here for everyone with an interest in contemporary imprisonment.

A number of themes stand out. Perhaps the most fundamental concerns the question of legitimacy. The paper which addresses this most directly is by Sparks. In a comparatively rare, but welcome, attempt to place official, popular, and radical thinking about prisons into the context of central and long established theoretical concerns within sociological and political thought, Sparks argues that 'legitimacy is not an abstruse concern . . . (but) . . . is intimately and practically implicated in every aspect of penal relations'. The conceptual power of the notion of legitimacy, he goes on, 'lies in the connections which it illuminates between the interior life of penal systems . . . and the larger economic and political settings in which penal institutions are embedded'. Woolf's report is seen as 'seeking to restore the legitimate basis of the system in the face of a near terminal crisis of order and moral credibility'. In that sense any shortcomings in Woolf's specific policy recommendations are less important than his posing the question of whether 'the failure of the Prison Service to fulfil its responsibilities to act with justice created in April 1990 serious difficulties in maintaining security and control in prisons' (Home Office 1991, para. 9.2). Conceptually, Sparks contends, this breaks with the past official assumptions that the maintenance of legitimate authority in prisons is '*essentially* unproblematic, albeit *practically* difficult at times'. It renders the technical, quick, repressive fix to prison problems, which are so often defined in official discourse as separate, contingent, and individual matters, that much harder to sustain. It ushered in 'a significant extension of the scope of formal legality in prison management'.

In the light of that analysis, it seems all the more surprising that privatization, until then a comparatively minor sub-text of debates on imprisonment, should abruptly re-emerge as a dominant concern so shortly after the appearance of the Woolf Report. Sparks argues that, using enabling powers 'buried deep in the Criminal Justice Act 1991 (s.84[3])', the Home Secretary was able 'to present the large scale contracting out of both new and existing prisons as a *fait accompli* whose legitimacy was already established'. Whereas Woolf was at pains to justify what went on in prison as an extension of the intention of the courts, advocates of private prisons express their arguments essentially in consequentialist terms—lower costs, better regimes, and so on—concentrating solely on the *delivery* of penal services as though this were completely independent of the *allocation* of, and *demand* for, imprisonment itself. By such devices the debate over legitimacy is arbitrarily truncated.

A review of this most controversial policy development—the re-emergence of private prisons in the United States, the United Kingdom, and Australia—is provided in the contribution by McDonald. The growth of private prisons in the USA appears to have been driven first and foremost by financial arguments, the huge increases in prison populations compelling correctional authorities to look for cheaper and more efficient ways of coping with them. In England and Wales, while efficiency arguments are superficially prominent, there are different political agendas that need to be taken into account, including the long-standing desire of the Conservative Government to reduce the power of the Prison Officers' Association, as well as the symbolic ideological value of prisons as a vehicle for demonstrating that even the most obviously 'public' of the public sector's functions can be successfully privatized.

McDonald has made a valuable start on the comparative analysis of privatization and provides British readers with important evidence about the privatization experience, particularly in relation to service delivery. However, there clearly remains much to be done in developing a theoretically integrated account of how and why privatization of prisons has taken such a sudden and strong hold in these jurisdictions. Such an account will have to include analysis of the role played by international private security companies on the one hand (see Lilly and Knepper 1992) and of the specific local conditions within which they have operated on the other. It will be an account in which the central issue raised by Sparks, the legitimacy of the undertaking, will have to be comprehensively addressed.

Sparks's eventual answer to his own general question 'can prisons be legitimate?' is more positive than Mathiesen's (1965, 1974, and 1990) evolving view that any attempt to discover a legitimate basis for the distribution of power and authority in prisons is inevitably *post hoc* rationalization. He is more persuaded by Garland's (1990) 'tragic' conclusion, seeing punishments as 'both endlessly straining after an ever-receding legitimacy on the level of theory or principle and yet retain[ing] an entrenched cultural and emotional presence which enables them to be represented as self-legitimating'. Following Held (1987), he notes that the most tempting course of action for systems in crisis is to seek a 'weak' restoration of legitimacy, sufficient to fend away the visible features of the problem for the time being: Woolf went further than that, and ultimately Sparks recognizes that while all prison systems confront severe legitimacy deficits, such deficits are not always total, or equally severe. It is possible, therefore 'to distinguish clearly between better and worse, preferable and less preferable, stronger and less strong justifications' for the prison and its internal practices.

The question of legitimacy lies also at the heart of Pavarini's paper, which sets out the Italian version of penal politics in a state of crisis. In Italy, according to Pavarini, the criminal justice system is characterized by unusually severe sanctions, often protecting not a natural order but an artificial order dating back to the fascist era of Mussolini. Such sanctions are quite lacking in political legitimacy. Indeed their very provenance had rendered 'virtually legitimate' the widespread practice of 'softening' their implementation by the courts. Until recently, Pavarini argues, recurrent 'law and order' campaigns promoted by conservative political forces had little effect, partly because the crime problem has been construed more as a problem of power relations and therefore susceptible to political solutions, than as a problem of individual deviance requiring penal repression. In Pavarini's enchanting and memorable phrase, it has been a case of 'a prince paying lip service to severity, an indulgent judge, and a populace 'distracted' by politics'. As a result Italy was a comparative 'penitentiary paradise', with one of the lowest prison populations in Europe.

In Italy, as elsewhere, a process of divergence has occurred whereby 'soft' (non-custodial) social control measures have been applied to 'appropriate' lesser offenders whilst prison, increasingly stripped of its justificatory rehabilitative rhetoric, has been reserved for incapacitating the more dangerous. But it took a unique kind of economic and socio-political crisis to produce in the two-year period 1991–2 a doubling of the Italian prison population. In those two years the proportion of those confined for drug abuse rose from 20 per cent to 60 per cent of the prison population; and that for persons from outside the EC (i.e., black immigrants) rose from 5 per cent to 20 per cent. According to Pavarini the old collective perception of 'political danger' has given way to one of 'social danger'. Primarily, he argues, this is because the collapse of any prospects for real social change by any political party, but especially by those of the left, has turned people away from politics into a search for moral scapegoats. One example of this has been the campaign of judicial repression against dishonest politicians in league with the mafia, who together have conspired to rob the nation of its wealth. A new consensus has appeared which accords a hitherto unequalled degree of legitimacy to the police and judicial apparatus ('previously as highly feared as they were little respected') and for the first time defines the mafia as 'only' a criminal issue. But this consensus, argues Pavarini, has rendered legitimate a much wider repression and an indiscriminate rise in the levels of punishment that has led to 'paradise lost'.

Sparks quotes de Tocqueville, and subsequently Sykes, in addressing the irony of the modern prison—that it operates as an autocracy within a democratic polity, and that this powerfully affects the nature of the legitimation problems which it confronts. That was clearly not the case in Mussolini's Italy, or in the countries of the former Warsaw pact, or indeed in many a regime throughout the contemporary world—though it may well be contended that such systems felt (or feel) little need to seek legitimacy of authority for so long as they could (or still can) rely on the straightforward use of power. In any event, as King reports, the corrective labour system of the Russian Federation, which was once formally legitimated by reference back to Lenin's insistence on the replacement of prisons by institutions intended for labour re-education, has been struggling to re-legitimate itself first in the context of communist perestroika and now against the backdrop of emergent democratic institutions. Although some strides had been taken towards making Russia what Kudryavtsev called 'the Socialist Rule-of-Law State', the autocratic structures and relationships remain largely intact. Thus reforms are expected to be implemented through the promulgation of new codes and the issuance of new instructions to carry them out. Yet the criminal justice system continues to be staffed by the same judges, the same procurators, the same Ministry officials and the same prison officers who served the old Gulag. It would, of course, be premature—to say the least, given the wholesale upheaval in Russian society—to have expected a Woolf-type inquiry into the riots at Krasnoyarsk and elsewhere which occurred in the autumn of 1991. But it is remarkable that there appears to have been no inquiry of any kind with officials being content to deal with the matter largely through propaganda. It is hardly surprising that human rights activists see the system as merely seeking a veneer of respectability. But in a society which has freed its political prisoners, has long become accustomed to severe sanctions for criminality, and now faces a potential real explosion in levels of crime, the kind of legitimacy afforded in Italy may not be far off.

The prison population in Russia is currently (June 1993) rising at the rate of 4,000 a month—about 6 per cent per annum—and this points to a second general theme that underpins several papers, the sudden growth in prison populations and its interpretation. In Italy the prison population *doubled* in a mere two years between 1991 and 1992. But in the preceding decade, a period when Italy's prison population declined from 30,373 in 1980 to 26,150 in 1990, the prison population in California *quadrupled* from 24,569 (a little over half that for England and Wales) to 97,309 (more than double that for England and Wales). By the latest Italian standard the growth in California's prison population was slower, though still phenomenal, and long sustained: it doubled between 1980 and 1985 and then doubled again between 1985 and 1990. Such astonishing rates of growth almost beggar belief—the more so, clearly, as explanations for what happened in California cannot be found in socio-political crises of the scale apparent in Italy, let alone Russia. They demand the most searching investigations to understand them.

In their case study of the Californian situation Zimring and Hawkins argue that about half the growth in the prison population in California could be accounted for by the general growth in imprisonment across the United States over the same period—though that itself requires explanation. Furthermore, a 30 per cent growth in the California state population (which might have been expected to account for a 30 per cent rise in prisoners, had imprisonment rates been stable) undoubtedly interacted with the national trends to produce a proportionately greater use of imprisonment in California. But California's rate of growth, which enabled it to jump from twenty-fourth to fifteenth in its use of imprisonment relative to other American states, was 'singular in both its pace and its magnitude'.

Zimring and Hawkins argue that the growth in imprisonment in California cannot be traced either to significant increases in (non-drug) crime or—despite the determinate sentencing laws of 1977—to overt government policies or legislative initiatives. Instead, they conclude, it was caused by 'a revolution of practice rather than theory'. Quite simply, individual sentencers, presumably in response to a new public 'mood or temper', began to use imprisonment more often in 'threshold' cases, the numerous unremarkable cases of theft, burglary, assault, and drug related offences which form the 'bread and butter' work of the courts and in which the decision whether or not to imprison is a marginal one.

The effect of this shift in sentencing practice was multiplied by a further key factor; an explosive increase in drug arrests, arising from the 'war on drugs' launched at a national level in the mid-eighties. The combination of the two produced an acceleration of the prison population that had been totally unforeseen by policy makers or those responsible for prison population projections.

Zimring and Hawkins assert that the Californian experience holds many important lessons and implications for prison systems across the world. In particular, it demonstrates that a state's or country's prison population can be massively altered over a short period, without any major changes in crime rates, in legislation or official sentencing policy, or in social or political stability, simply by what they have called elsewhere 'contingency factors' (Zimring and Hawkins 1991). A shift in public mood towards reduced tolerance of offending, reflected in marginal changes in the practice of individual sentencers, can be sufficient to set in motion an almost uncontrollable surge in prison numbers. Such contingencies, moreover, are not easily predictable, and this has implications for resource planning and statistical projections: Zimring and Hawkins illustrate starkly the deficiencies of standard straight line projections of prison populations, which can be wildly wrong even over the relatively short term. Finally, they argue, it would be quite unforgivable if the extraordinary 'natural experiment' which has taken place in California were to go by without yielding decisive answers to questions about the relationships between crime rates and sentencing policy, including whether locking up several times more people has any effect—be it deterrent, incapacitative, or rehabilitative—upon the level of criminal behaviour in the community.

The contribution by Tonry focuses upon a different—and even more disturbing—feature of American, and other, prison populations, namely the gross over-representation of ethnic minorities, especially black people, amongst those serving sentences. This matter goes to the core of the theme of this volume, the social context of imprisonment.

Tonry begins his essay by noting that American incarceration rates, using prison population per 100,000 residents, are between four and 15 times higher than those in other developed countries. Moreover, blacks, who make up 48 per cent of the prison population, are four times more likely to be in prison than would be predicted from the fact that they constitute only 12 per cent of the total population of the USA. These figures immediately suggest not only that the United States employs exceptionally punitive criminal justice policies, but that they are implemented with extreme racial bias. But he goes on to argue that the initial tendency simply to use the comparison between the proportion of blacks in prison and their proportion in the American population, as evidence of black–white disproportion, is 'understandable but wrong'. It considerably understates that disproportion because it ignores the under-representation of whites. It is more appropriate, Tonry argues, to make comparisons on the basis of racially disaggregated incarceration rates—that is, the number of confined persons of a given racial group per 100,000 population of that group. By that measure black incarceration rates are *six-to-seven* times higher than for whites.

The importance of using racially disaggregated data can hardly be overstated. First of all, it allows more realistic comparisons to be made between countries. Tonry's analysis demonstrates that the common view, that the level of racial disproportion in prisons is greater in the USA than elsewhere, is fundamentally mistaken: on the contrary, it is almost as high in Canada and Australia and, if anything, is worse in England and Wales. Secondly, such data seem to show that what crucially influences

7

the overall size and structure of a prison population is the proportionate size of the most visible minority group in the total population. Thus, Tonry is able to show that if the proportion of blacks to whites in the general population of England and Wales were the same as it is in the United States—and vice versa—and yet each country continued to imprison at its own racially disaggregated rates, then the differences in the size of prison populations in these jurisdictions would greatly diminish. To wit, the prison population of England and Wales in 1990 would have included 30,732 whites (instead of 36,300) and 32,748 blacks (instead of 4,910), with an overall incarceration rate of 140 per 100,000 (instead of 89). In the United States the result of such a thought experiment would be that the combined black and white prison population would have fallen from 1,133,820 to 759,632 and the incarceration rate from 474 to 315 per 100,000.

In other words, disproportionate black incarceration in England and Wales is much more of a problem than is commonly and complacently acknowledged, hidden only by the small number of blacks in the general population. Similar conclusions may be reached in relation to Canada, Australia and, one suspects, many other countries with white majorities. And, in the course of intriguing comparisons between American states, Tonry echoes the earlier findings of Hawkins (1985) and Blumstein (1982) that Minnesota and Wisconsin, which are generally considered amongst the most enlightened in criminal justice terms, actually have some of the most racially disproportionate incarceration rates in America. Moreover, when allowance is made for America's higher crime rates (in admittedly limited cross cultural comparisons) as well as racial disproportion, then America's overall incarceration rate turns out to be somewhat closer to those of other countries than might have been expected.

Finally, Tonry's analysis of racial disproportion will, it is hoped, make more of us face up to the crucial question of why there should be such a consistent tendency for countries with white majorities to lock up so many of their black citizens. It focuses attention sharply upon the behaviours of, and the policies towards, the most visible minority groups for any understanding of what drives prison populations. Tonry cites the evidence from Blumstein (1982) for the United States, and Hood (1992) for England and Wales, which appears to suggest that up to 20 per cent of the disproportion results from discriminatory discretionary decisions in sentencing, whilst up to 80 per cent results from the fact that blacks are more likely to appear before the courts for crimes which are likely to attract imprisonment. But this pushes the question about the reasons behind the apparently high black involvement in crime back to prior considerations about internationally reproduced levels of racial discrimination. These may be manifested in relative poverty and unemployment, and in the concentration of black people in the most deprived, the most criminogenic, and the most intensively policed areas of large cities. It also raises questions about the nature and impact of educational and social policies to redress these problems. On one point Tonry is unequivocal: the scale of the phenomenon has been greatly exacerbated by the 'war on drugs', a factor similarly stressed by Zimring and Hawkins, which targeted black dealers and black communities relentlessly. Given that drug offences were actually in decline when the 'war' began, Tonry charitably argues that for the officials who launched it, the blackening of the American prison population must have been 'a foreseen but not intended consequence'. Less charitably, he claims, it has to be seen as the 'product of malign neglect' and he outlines a number of policy solutions to redress the racial imbalance.

8

Just as Tonry questions the standard interpretations of one widely quoted form of comparative data (the proportions of blacks in custody compared to their proportions in the general population), Pease questions conclusions which are commonly drawn from another—prison populations expressed as rates per 100,000 of the general population.

Both Tonry and Pease force us to look more deeply behind the superficial assessments of 'punitiveness' which are part of a shorthand which too often passes for penological debate. We use the term 'punitiveness' in quotation marks here, following the usage by Pease, because any attempted measurement of the concept is at best a rather poor proxy. Many writers have observed that what Sykes called the pains of imprisonment may vary considerably from time to time, prison to prison, and circumstance to circumstance: Downes (1988), for example has examined what he calls the 'depth of imprisonment' in his comparison between English and Dutch prisons, and King and McDermott (forthcoming), distinguish between different English prisons in terms of the 'weight of imprisonment'. Similarly, Pease draws attention to differences in the stigma of imprisonment in different societies.

Such considerations are also relevant to Carlen's contribution, in which the author expresses concern at the extent to which the literature on women's imprisonment has concentrated upon highlighting differences in regimes for male and female prisoners, and on showing how women experience custody differently from men. Focusing upon such issues, she argues, leads many writers into voluntary or involuntary collusion with prison administrators in offering merely liberal, reformist critiques. In her view, it blinds them to the much more important ways in which imprisonment is a common experience for all prisoners and, hence, to deeper questions about its 'punitiveness' as a social institution. However, it has to be said that the alternative agenda she wishes to see—the investigation of prisons as 'deliberate and calibrated mechanisms of punishment inflicting state-legitimated pain'—is by no means a straightforward one, given Pease's warnings. It becomes especially difficult if a comparative approach is adopted. How, for example, can one convincingly determine the extent to which the 'horrendous' conditions in British prisons deliver more or less pain than prisons elsewhere? Or how much more or less pain is delivered (or is intended to be delivered—and if so, by whom) by present-day prison regimes than by those of previous periods?

Be that as it may, Pease makes a compelling case for the futility of continuing to use incarceration rates of prisoners per 100,000 of the general population with any pretence that this has any serious meaning in comparing the 'punitiveness' of different jurisdictions. Such a measure 'has meaning only in showing the effects of some combination of national differences on rates of crime, rates of clearance of crime and identification of putative offenders, processing of those offenders, and choice of final sanction. Any of those variables, singly or in combination, will produce differences in indices of prison use'. However, Pease notes that the kinds of league tables published by the Council of Europe have become the common currency of debates on penal reform, usually to shame one or another administration into changed practices: the descriptive 'more than elsewhere' slides all too easily into the moral 'too many'. Yet, he points out, 'fewer prisoners than elsewhere' could still be too many; and 'more prisoners than elsewhere' could still be too few.

In fact, the few studies which make national comparisons with an appropriate degree of circumspection yield results which are counter-intuitive. Pease cites the work of

Lynch (1987), whose comparisons of imprisonment were related to arrest rates rather than general population, on the basis of which the apparent difference between the United States on the one hand and Canada, England and Wales, or the Federal Republic of Germany on the other, largely disappears. The work of Tonry on racial disproportion, just discussed, of course, has similar implications. After consideration of the possible alternatives Pease concludes that the least flawed measure of the 'punitiveness' of different jurisdictions, at the point of sentencing, would involve analysis separately by offence category and use prison admissions as the numerator and convictions as the denominator. Substituting prison population as the numerator would convert the measure to one of 'punitiveness' that also takes account of discretionary release. Even then the measures are more convincing for the more serious offences, where one can be more confident that pre-trial diversion has not removed a significant proportion of offenders from the picture.

Pease also reports data from the attempt by the Criminal Law Committee of the International Bar Association to assess severity of sentencing by asking legal practitioners in member countries to indicate the range of sentences which should be imposed in respect of case information supplied for certain offences. England and Wales emerged as more 'punitive' than the international median towards the offences of rape, serious assault, and tax fraud—and the 'punitiveness' lies in the length of sentence imposed rather than the threshold of imposing custody. On the other hand, in a further analysis, Pease uses United Nations data to try to assess the 'punitiveness' of the *penal system*, as distinct from 'punitiveness' of *sentencing*, bearing in mind that the 'bark' of the judge in passing sentence may be more severe than the 'bite' of the sentence actually served. On this basis England and Wales and Scotland come out less 'punitive' than France for rape, and less 'punitive' than either France or West Germany for robbery.

If forced to a conclusion, then, Pease believes that England and Wales may be marginally more severe than elsewhere in Europe at the point of sentence, but less severe when discretionary release is taken into account. It should be noted that the distinction drawn here between bark and bite sentencing is somewhat different from the distinction drawn in Pavarini's discussion of 'punitiveness' in Italy where the full weight of the legally available sentence was actually eschewed by the judges (which also, of course, happens in England and Wales).

In passing, Pease makes an important point in relation to comparative statistics relating to remand populations. It is commonly argued, on the basis of superficial interpretations of the Council of Europe statistics, that Britain keeps too many people in prison, but that the problem rests more with sentenced than remand populations. But if British remand prisoners were counted in the same way as in Europe, where they are still counted as being on remand, even after sentence, until the last possible date for appeal has passed, then this view could not be sustained. Remand prisoners would make a greater contribution to the total and sentenced prisoners correspondingly less, thereby further reducing the comparative severity of the system in England and Wales.

Pease, in his discussion of 'punitiveness', argues that what invites opprobrium is some combination of the offending person and the offending act and that there are bound to be international differences in what is seen to merit punishment. This rather nicely raises additional questions as to which context it is appropriate to employ when making judgments about criminal justice or penal systems in different jurisdictions. Are these matters to be raised purely in the context of the 'mood and temper' of the immediate society and the specific nature and extent of the problems to which criminal justice and penal systems are a response? Or is there some more universal international rubric within which, ultimately, all such judgments have to be made?

The matter is raised explicitly by King who observes that while it is clearly the case that on many matters the conditions in the prisons and colonies of the Russian system of corrective labour fall below those required by international standards, in other respects the 'contextual gap' between conditions obtaining inside and outside such institutions in Russia may be smaller than that obtaining in Britain. Sometimes this contextual gap benefits Russian prisoners compared to their British counterparts, for example with regard to wages. Sometimes, as in the case of space provision, it benefits British prisoners. In such circumstances the pressure towards international standards can present us with a new version of the familiar problem of 'less eligibility': to what extent does it make sense, *in pursuit of international standards*, to hold out norms for prisons which are above those generally prevailing in the outside society? Or, in terms of cultural relativism, is it appropriate, say, to hold out a norm of single-celling in prisons for societies where individualism and privacy are less highly prized than collectivism and sharing?

No answer to those questions is attempted here although they are likely to be increasingly addressed as more becomes known about prison systems outside the familiar European and Anglo-American context, especially Third World systems (see Maguire 1991), and as they come increasingly within the purview of international agencies. However, some useful insights can already be gained from studies of the work of international bodies—both inter-governmental and non-governmental—whose role in monitoring or inspecting prisons is already well established. Morgan and Evans provide an overview of the main international mechanisms and inspection agencies— the United Nations, regional inter-governmental organizations, the International Committee of the Red Cross, Amnesty International, and the various Human Rights Watch Organizations—before presenting their case study of the work of the Council of Europe Committee for the Prevention of Torture and Inhuman or Degrading Treatment or Punishment (CPT).

Morgan and Evans note that organizations such as Amnesty International rightly concentrate their campaigning activities on the relatively clear cut issues surrounding the imprisonment of people for their political or religious beliefs and the use of torture and the death penalty, and generally avoid the 'open-ended' 'cultural relativity' of questions concerning prison conditions. On the other hand CPT has, for the most part, been less concerned with torture than what constitutes inhumane or degrading treatment and has quickly become a body whose work is 'critical . . . for the ongoing debate about what constitute acceptable conditions in custody'.

Finally, one of the most intriguing aspects of the contribution by Morgan and Evans is their discussion of the way in which penal politics has become a critical dimension of a much wider political agenda: without denying the honourable human rights intentions of politicians and administrators, ratifying the Torture Convention and embracing the inspection visits of the CPT is a price well worth paying for countries seeking membership of the EC. Although Turkey was the first member of the Council of Europe to ratify the Torture Convention it has been the subject of more visits than any other country and is the only country so far to have been on the receiving end of a public statement—'extraordinarily damning' in that it makes explicit reference to

11

findings consistent with the practice of torture. Elsewhere the normal procedure has been for the CPT to provide confidential reports to the governments concerned, although they are written in a form suitable for publication. So far most governments have permitted publication of CPT reports, and all have taken the trouble to produce responses. Although the process is slow, it seems to have had some effect. The British Government rejected the CPT appellation of 'inhuman and degrading treatment' with respect to Brixton, Leeds, and Wandsworth but it speedily took action to end the practice of holding prisoners three to a cell. Unfortunately, as Morgan and Evans wryly observe, it is doubtful whether CPT would have approved the method by which this was done—transferring the prisoners to police cells. A perfect demonstration, perhaps, of Held's 'weak' restoration of legitimacy.

REFERENCES

BLUMSTEIN, A. (1982), 'On the Racial Disproportionality of United States Prison Populations', *Journal of Criminal Law and Criminology*, 73: 1259–81.

CASALE, S. (1985), 'A Practical Design for Standards', in M. Maguire, J. Vagg, and R. Morgan, eds, *Accountability and Prisons: Opening up a Closed World*. London and New York: Tavistock.

CRAWFORD, W. (1834), *Report of William Crawford, Esq., on the Penitentiaries of the United States, Addressed to His Majesty's Principal Secretary of State for the Home Department*. Parliamentary Papers, 1834 (593), vol. 16.

DOWNES, D. (1988), *Contrasts in Tolerance: Post-war Penal Policies in the Netherlands and England and Wales*. London: Oxford University Press.

GARLAND, D. (1990), *Punishment and Modern Society*. London: Oxford University Press.

HAWKINS, D. F. (1985), 'Trends in Black–White Imprisonment: Changing Conceptions of Race or Changing Conceptions of Social Control?', *Crime and Social Justice*, 24: 187–209.

HELD, D. (1987), *Models of Democracy*. Cambridge: Polity Press.

HOME OFFICE (1979), *Report of the Committee of Inquiry into the UK Prison Services* (May Report), Cmnd. 7673. London: HMSO.

—— (1985), *New Directions in Prison Design: A Report of a Home Office Working Party on American New Generation Prisons* (Platt Report). London: HMSO.

—— (1991), *Prison Disturbances April 1990* (Woolf Report), Cm. 1456. London: HMSO.

HOOD, R. (1992), *Race and Sentencing*. London: Oxford University Press.

KING, R. D., and McDERMOTT, K. (forthcoming), *The State of Our Prisons*. London: Oxford University Press.

KING, R. D., and MORGAN, R. (1980), *The Future of the Prison System*. Farnborough: Gower.

LILLY, J. R., and KNEPPER, P. (1992), 'An International Perspective on the Privatisation of Corrections', *Howard Journal*, 313: 174–91.

LYNCH, J. P. (1987), *Imprisonment in Four Countries*. Washington, DC: Bureau of Justice Statistics.

MAGUIRE, M. (1985), 'Prisoners' Grievances: the Role of the Boards of Visitors', in M. Maguire, J. Vagg, and R. Morgan, eds, *Accountability and Prisons: Opening up a Closed World*. London and New York: Tavistock.

MAGUIRE, M. (1991), 'The Indian Prison', in D. Whitfield, ed., *The State of the Prisons—200 Years On*. London: Routledge.

MATHIESEN, T. (1965), *The Defences of the Weak*. London: Tavistock.

—— (1974), *The Politics of Abolition*. Oxford: Martin Robertson.

—— (1990), *Prison on Trial*. London: Sage.

MORGAN, R., and BRONSTEIN, A. (1985), 'Prisoners and the Courts: the US Experience', in M. Maguire, J. Vagg and R. Morgan, eds, *Accountability and Prisons: Opening up a Closed World*. London and New York: Tavistock.

PLAYER, E., and JENKINS, M., eds (1993), *Prisons After Woolf*. London: Routledge.

WENER, G. (1983), *A Legitimate Grievance*. London: Prison Reform Trust.

WHITFIELD, D., ed. (1991), *The State of the Prisons—200 Years On*. London: Routledge.

ZIMRING, F. E., and HAWKINS, G. (1991), *The Scale of Imprisonment*. Chicago and London: Chicago University Press.

CAN PRISONS BE LEGITIMATE?

Penal Politics, Privatization, and the Timeliness of an Old Idea

RICHARD SPARKS*

> The ideas whose time has come are old, familiar, well-tested
> ones. (It is the new ideas whose time has passed.)
> Timothy Garton Ash

This paper seeks to follow some of the twists and turns of recent penal discourse, especially those official rhetorics which support the marketization of the system as a principal means of addressing its problems. I contend that there is a deeply vexed, but generally unarticulated, problem that haunts most discussions of prisons, prison disorders, and other aspects of penal politics, whether these spring from 'official' or 'radical' perspectives. This is what has long been known to sociologists and political theorists as the problem of legitimacy. It is a problem whose practical, theoretical, and normative dimensions need to be much more carefully and patiently examined than is currently usual in penal debates. I want to suggest that in pausing to consider the problem of legitimacy directly, rather than obliquely and implicitly as is more often done, we may be able to organize and attain a critical point of purchase upon a number of otherwise confusing and apparently discrete recent developments. Indeed, just as some commentators propose that legitimacy can rightly be seen as the central problem of political theory (see Beetham 1991: 41, revising Weber (1991) and Habermas (1976)), so I hope to show that it can provide an organizing idea in penal politics, in terms of which both the coherence and justifiability of particular practices and the adequacy of critical and reforming stances upon them can be considered. In particular I want to try to assess the claim embedded in the rhetorics favouring privatization (or contracting out, or proprietary prisons, as the various locutions have it) to have answered many of the key legitimation problems of modern penal systems. I will argue that in fact such concerns are more often evaded or suppressed than answered, and that the arguments over the justification of *any* practice of imprisonment (private or otherwise) need to be more strenuously pursued than contemporary rhetorics allow.

What is Legitimacy?

The problem of legitimacy is an abiding concern of political theory. In that sense it can safely be said to be an old idea. Briefly put, the term legitimacy refers to the claims made by any government or dominant group within a distribution of power to justified authority. Historically such claims have rested on any number of grounds, from divine right of succession to popular election. Beetham in *The Legitimation of Power* (1991)

* Department of Criminology, University of Keele.
I would like to thank David Beetham, Tony Bottoms, Pat Carlen, Nicola Lacey, and Ian Loader for their help in formulating the ideas and arguments contained in this paper.

14

outlines the elements of a post-Weberian approach to legitimacy.[1] He argues that however variable the historical conditions governing the nature of legitimacy claims may be, there are underlying structural constants which are very general in scope. In Beetham's terms:

Power can be said to be legitimate to the extent that:
  (i) it conforms to established rules;
 (ii) the rules can be justified by reference to beliefs shared by both dominant and subordinate;
(iii) there is evidence of consent by the subordinate to the particular power relation.

(Beetham 1991: 16)

Beetham argues that all systems of power relations seek legitimation. Such criteria are almost never perfectly fulfilled, and each dimension of legitimacy has a corresponding form of non-legitimate power. Where power fails to conform to its own rules of legal validity it is *illegitimate*. Where it lacks justification in shared beliefs it experiences a *legitimacy deficit*. Where it fails to find legitimation through expressed consent it may finally experience a crisis of *delegitimation* (withdrawal of consent) (1991: 20).

To talk about the legitimacy of power relations is thus to draw attention to such matters as constitutional legality, the normative principles which are said to underlie any given distribution of power, and the presence or absence of conferred consent amongst subordinate groups. Once we take the issue of legitimacy seriously, Beetham argues, we can no longer ignore the fact that systems of social power inherently generate normative elements (1991: 27; see also Lacey 1988: 14). To the extent that people confer consent they do so for a complex of moral as well as self-interested reasons, and rarely through coercion alone.

On this view, to speak of power is almost in the same breath to raise the question of its need for legitimation, and the presence or absence of legitimacy carries large consequences for all parties in a system of power relations. Only legitimate social arrangements generate commitments towards compliance on moral rather than just expedient grounds. Meanwhile, the need for legitimation constrains the actions of the powerful since, as Giddens puts it, 'to speak of legitimacy in the usual sense implies the existence of standards external to he [*sic*] who claims it' (1977: 92).

One irony of the modern prison, first noted by de Tocqueville and subsequently most pointedly elaborated by Sykes (1958), is that it operates as an autocracy within a democratic polity. This powerfully affects the nature of the legitimation problems which it confronts. As Dahrendorf and others have remarked in other contexts, autocratic structures may stand as greatly in need of legitimation as others but they may encounter great difficulties of inflexibility and justification in responding to their problems (see Dahrendorf 1990: 15–17). Hence, legitimacy is a key term in the analysis of social disorder generally and of revolutions, riots, and other moments of upheaval and rapid social transformation especially.

How do these concepts help us to understand the recent history of and current prospects for British prisons? We have grown used to using the term 'crisis' to describe the scale of the problems afflicting prison systems today. Is it then the case that a

---

[1] Beetham differentiates his approach to the question of legitimacy from that of Weber on the grounds that Weber defines the issue in terms of 'belief in' legitimacy. In Beetham's view this dissolves all the difficult normative questions surrounding the issue in the name of 'value freedom' and moreover disregards those aspects of the matter that are not really about belief but rather about legality or rule-following (Beetham 1991: 7–15).

succession of apparently distinct problems has congealed into something much more akin to a durable 'legitimation crisis' (see also Cavadino and Dignan 1992)? One can readily discern, for example, how different agendas for penal change centre on differing depictions of the nature of the 'crisis'. Abolitionism, for example, views the prison as an unreformable autocracy and its options for change as parallel to those of a Soviet-style regime—it cannot reform itself without subverting its very basis (cf. Elster 1989: 163–4).

Penal Problems as Legitimation Problems

I think it makes a great deal of sense to try to think through many of the current problems of western penal systems in terms of the concept of legitimacy. Indeed I suspect that the tradition of sociological study of 'captive society' can be read very largely in terms of the competing views it throws up of issues of legitimacy and legitimation problems (see also Sparks and Bottoms 1992). Furthermore this has a crucial bearing on our interpretation of such central matters as prison disorders and prisoners' rights campaigns. By the same token legitimacy is also central to the understanding of official discourses generated in response to prison problems.

In principle legitimacy is an issue for every practice of punishment or sanctioning, as it is for all distributions of power and resources (see Beetham 1991, chapter 2). This is true on various levels. These include the endlessly recurrent arguments about which philosophical principles might animate or justify the imposition of criminal sanctions, or about the failure of such principles.[2] Any genuinely full discussion would also have to deal with the equally extensive and contentious problem of the relations between practices of punishment and the sources of social power.[3] I cannot extend or revise the discussion of these big issues here. Rather I will use the concept of legitimacy in an exploratory way to discuss some more particular and topical questions (already quite large enough in themselves). I will attempt:

1. to clarify what we mean when we speak of a prison system as being 'in crisis'; and
2. to review some recent official statements on penal policy by looking at them as attempted solutions to legitimation problems.

Legitimacy is not an abstruse concern. Quite the contrary—it is intimately and practically implicated in every aspect of penal relations. For this reason it has recently begun to attract the attention of commentators speaking from a variety of differing vantage points, such as Cavadino (1992), Sim (1992), Sparks and Bottoms (1992) and arguably Woolf himself (1991). Its conceptual power lies in the connections which it illuminates between the interior life of penal systems, and the social relations that characterize them, and the centrally important 'external' issue of the conditions under which it is judged appropriate to impose prison sentences in the first place. Neither is

---

[2] In modern times this means the still unfinished disputes between the claims of Kantian high retributivism and Benthamite utilitarianism and the various inheritors and critics of these positions. See, for discussions, Walker (1991), Lacey (1988), Mathiesen (1990).

[3] I have in mind here the literature that effectively begins with Rusche and Kirchheimer (1939) and extends through Mathiesen (1974), Melossi and Pavarini (1981) and Ignatieff (1978) to Foucault (1979), Garland (1985, 1990), and others.

this to forget the larger economic and political settings in which penal institutions are embedded. Rather it is to look at the connections between the 'interior' and the 'exterior' aspects of penal problems from a slightly altered vantage point.

A number of recent interventions in penal affairs (notably Lord Justice Woolf's report on the 1990 disturbances) implicitly depend on some such idea but in a way that is generally unspoken, or at least inadequately defined. I suggest that it is right to view Lord Justice Woolf's inquiry and other recent documents as seeking to restore the legitimate basis of the system in the face of a near terminal crisis of order and moral credibility. One of the objectives of such interventions is to prevent the re-emergence of the kind of violent upheavals which prompt them, and in so doing to forestall their delegitimating effects. To emphasize the problem of legitimacy, therefore, is to inspect such attempts through the lens of social and political theory as a way of evaluating their adequacy, their progressive credentials, and their likely success. Ultimately it may also help to refine our general ways of thinking about penal problems and to move beyond certain received ideas and distinctions—for example the tension on the 'radical' side between reforming and abolitionist projects. More immediately, to operate *without* the kind of intellectual grounding which such concepts provide is to continue to allow some versions of official discourse and the claims of other interests to define many prison problems as being separate, contingent, and individual matters, and hence as being open to merely technical and/or repressive 'fixes', whether these be lodged in terms of architecture and hardware or indeed of management technique and ownership (the level at which current debates about privatization often appear stuck).

It would seem that for a host of reasons the resulting questions (which I have summarized in the one question 'can prisons be legitimate?') are not likely to receive an overwhelmingly positive answer. Indeed, the attendant sense of intractability is a part of what has motivated some observers to take the view that to seek any positive answer to such questions is inevitably both futile and collusive. Thus the arguments that Mathiesen sets out in *The Politics of Abolition* (1974) and *Prison on Trial* (1990) in favour of prison abolition are in large measure a radicalized consequence of the conclusions he originally reached in *The Defences of the Weak* (1965). That is, that a legitimate distribution of power and authority in prisons is impossible and that attempts to discover one are inevitably *post hoc* rationalizations for the persistence of the 'prison solution' to social problems. It follows for Mathiesen that any 'positive reform' is open to being seized upon by the prison institution as an opportunity for relegitimation (1974: 174–6). Consequently, Mathiesen argues, the only reforms which should be pursued are those which are 'negating', 'exposing', and 'of the abolishing kind'. They must seek to demonstrate once and for all that the prison solution is a 'fiasco' and to unmask its supporting ideologies (Mathiesen 1990: 141–2).

On the other hand, Mathiesen is also explicit in *The Politics of Abolition* that his concepts of negative reforms within the horizon of 'the unfinished' are precisely intended to cut through any settled reform/revolution dichotomy by keeping the direction and destination of progressive change deliberately open. On my argument, the very generality and open-textured nature of the concept of legitimacy fits it for a similar job. This is because it is double-edged: it is always in question in the present, yet always apparently unrealized. It therefore has an inherent dialectical energy. Yet, I will conclude by arguing, it is thereby also open to rather different and more politically feasible inferences than those which Mathiesen would wish to draw. First, however, we

17

must consider how the problem of legitimation bears upon the state of affairs that we have come to know as the 'penal crisis'.

Legitimacy and the 'Penal Crisis'

It is by now quite generally recognized that the term 'crisis' is in key respects inadequate as a description of the depth and durability of penal problems (see, e.g. Morris 1989; Cavadino 1992). In common parlance the term crisis denotes something severe but usually of short duration: sterling crisis, Suez crisis, and so forth. At the same time it includes an implication of change—if an illness reaches its crisis the patient either dies or begins to recover. More prosaically, the term crisis has become a journalistic commonplace (not so much 'Crisis? What crisis?' as 'Crisis? Oh, that crisis'). It is a term that in its ordinary usage now refers us to the visible symptoms of a problem (in this case overcrowding, insanitary conditions, brutality, riots) rather than the structural properties of the system that generates them. When the word is used in this way a government can announce certain measures (end slopping out, improve visiting arrangements, install some telephones, build some more prisons) and claim, for all relevant purposes, to have averted the crisis, at least for the time being. Yet as King and McDermott (1989) document, the English 'penal crisis' is not of this short-lived kind, but rather a durable state of affairs of deepening severity throughout the 1970s and 1980s.

Cavadino (1992) attempts to clarify our ways of talking about such matters by thoughtfully setting out some possible competing accounts of the origins of the present crisis in British prisons. The 'orthodox account' is, on his reading, an eclectic and mechanistic shopping list of 'factors' such as overcrowding, understaffing, poor security, and inappropriate 'mix' of prisoners which some officials and journalists use to explain the occurrence of trouble. This is analogous to what Thomas and Pooley earlier called the 'powder keg' theory of prison riots (1980, chapter 1). Cavadino proposes an alternative 'radical pluralist' account of the penal crisis. On this view there is a complex interaction between material conditions (both within the prison and in its surrounding environment), and ideological influences (the collapse of the rehabilitative ideal, law and order ideologies) to produce a crisis of legitimacy of which the well-known and familiar array of penal problems (most visibly 'riots') are symptomatic.

Viewed from the more inclusive perspective of the problem of legitimacy within political theory, Cavadino's two models have something in common with competing constructions of the legitimation problems of modern Western political systems generally. Held (1987) distinguishes between theories of 'overload' and theories of 'legitimation crisis'. Broadly speaking, conservatives argue that modern political systems have a strong tendency to become overloaded. They undertake functions they cannot adequately perform and set up expectations they cannot meet by involving themselves more and more in welfare provision and economic management. Their primary options in getting out of this situation are the retrenchment of social programmes and the freeing of market forces, perhaps in combination with the reassertion of their authority in the sphere of law and order in the face of the necessity of containing the transitional social upheaval. Theorists of legitimation crisis on the other hand, most importantly Habermas, contend that the gradual increase in welfare functions and economic intervention by the state results from (rather than causes) the necessity of managing the inherent instability of capitalist economies—though of course nobody now doubts that the capitalist economies have handled their crisis tendencies rather more flexibly than their state-socialist counterparts (Dahrendorf 1990). The point is that the vagaries of business cycles (or in the British case of long-term relative economic decline) may give rise to recurrent crises in public finances but no corresponding improvement in the state's ability to transcend the systematic con-straints it encounters (Held 1987: 235). The greater visibility of the state in this interventionist guise leads to the politicization of ever-greater spheres of life and demands on its competence. Where such demands cannot be met the state may confront a 'legitimation and motivation crisis' (ibid., 236). In such circumstances a move towards authoritarianism and the prioritization of order is likely (see Hall *et al.* 1978), but other and more progressive outcomes, in which the givenness of newly politicized practices and institutions becomes questioned, are also possible.

Considered in this light, Cavadino's 'radical pluralist' reading of the penal crisis moves us in the direction of a 'legitimation crisis' theorization, and away from the short-termism and managerial positivism of the 'orthodox' (or overload) view. But it is still possible that it underestimates the complexity of the question of the prison's legitimacy and the equivocal outcomes of associated problems. David Garland in *Punishment and Modern Society* (1990) seeks to place the matter in a longer perspective. Garland identifies 'a growing sense of doubt, dissatisfaction and sheer puzzlement about modern penal practices' (1990: 4), so deep as to constitute not merely a contingent 'penal crisis' but rather a 'crisis of penological modernism' as a whole (1990: 7). In this sense these are no longer normal times for punishment, and especially for the prison as its central material and symbolic institutional site (1990: 5–6).

For Garland this finally enforces a 'tragic' conclusion. The survival of punishment in its accustomed forms beyond the lifetime of its ostensible rationales requires an effort of understanding of our deep attachment to it and its centrality within our culture, vocabulary, and sensibilities, long before we can safely predict its passing away. In a profound sense punishments may be both endlessly straining after an ever receding legitimacy on the level of theory or principle and yet retain an entrenched cultural and emotional presence which enables them to be presented as self-legitimating.

I find this analysis compelling. Yet, to return to the crisis in its more familiar and immediate manifestations, it may not very obviously help us to find our bearings. For, as Geuss tersely has it, one of the purposes of a critical theory is 'to show us which way to move' (1981: 54). The prison's problems of legitimation may admit of no conclusive resolution. Yet we also feel as a matter of both passion and prudence (Dunn 1990: 200) that every crisis holds out better and worse, reactionary and progressive, preferable and less preferable choices. Indeed as Garland has himself subsequently noted:

But if power is indeed 'legitimated' by such changes, this may be because the newly reformed practices . . . actually represent a small shift in the power balances between the governed and the governing which bring official practice more into line with the sensibilities which currently prevail. (Garland 1992: 411)

How, in the present time, are penal systems likely to respond to their legitimation problems, and with what consequences? After all, as Held points out, the most likely and most tempting course of action is to seek a 'weak' restoration of legitimacy, sufficient to fend away the visible features of the problem for the time being. If, to adapt

Gramsci's eloquent expression, one definition of a crisis is that 'the old order is dying, the new struggling to be born', can one determine in which direction progress might lie, rationally and without falling back on mere emotivism?

Legitimacy and Current Penal Discourse

It is integral to my argument that all penal discourse can be scrutinized (amongst other things) in terms of its orientation towards legitimation problems. Here I can concentrate on only two ways in which such problems have been approached (or rather first raised and then suppressed) in recent policy discussion. I will refer first (and rather briefly) to Lord Justice Woolf's analysis of the 1990 English prison disorders and his general diagnosis for penal change and secondly (at slightly more length) to the sudden re-emergence of the privatization issue as a main strand in current British penal policy.

Tony Bottoms and I have argued elsewhere (Sparks and Bottoms 1992) that a primary source of significance in Lord Justice Woolf's intervention in penal debates lies in his implicit recognition of some entrenched legitimation problems attending the management of the English prisons. In that sense, we argued, any shortcomings in his specific policy recommendations or in subsequent governmental responses to them (for a fuller account see Morgan 1992) are of less lasting importance than his introduction of certain new terms into the lexicon of English official penology. The full implications of these have yet to be worked through. Woolf's general view of the disorders is this:

A recurring theme in the evidence from prisoners who may have instigated, and who were involved in, the riots was that their actions were a response to the manner in which they were treated by the prison system. Although they did not always use these terms they felt a lack of justice. If what they say is true, the failure of the Prison Service to fulfil its responsibilities to act with justice created in April 1990 serious difficulties in maintaining security and control in prisons. (Woolf 1991: para. 9.24)

There is a distinct conceptual development here. Woolf breaks with the assumptions of prior official statements (see for example the Home Office 1964: 2(2) and 1984, para. 16) all of which regard the maintenance of legitimate authority in prisons as *essentially* unproblematic, albeit *practically* difficult at times. By the same token Woolf has no particular attachment to 'rotten apple' or 'powder keg' theories of prison riots (see Thomas and Pooley 1980) which attribute the existence of trouble mainly to the conspiratorial doings of the uncontrollable few (see also King and McDermott 1990; Scraton *et al.* 1991). Rather he identifies a generally shared sense of injustice. What flows from this in policy terms is a significant extension of the scope of formal legality in prison management, especially in relation to grievance and disciplinary procedures (see paras 14.289 *et seq.*). Woolf also uses the terms 'threshold quality of life' and the 'legitimate expectations' (para. 14.32) of prisoners to denote minimum standard in treatment and conditions which cannot, as hitherto, be abrogated for purely discretionary, expedient, or punitive reasons. Hence Woolf moves away from the historically received conception of prisoners' goods and services as 'privileges' and towards a more explicit and formally accountable position.

Of course it is itself eloquently indicative of the prevailing realities of the English prisons that the introduction of such basic commonplaces of liberal jurisprudence into the penal realm should have been greeted as a radical development. This is in part what leads some commentators, notably Sim (1992), to question the progressiveness of Woolf's contribution. Moreover, the Government's dual response of nominally accepting the greater part of Woolf's agenda yet in the same breath creating the new criminal offence of 'prison mutiny' carrying a ten-year sentence did little to reassure sceptics that the fundamental point had been well taken.

Nevertheless, the period immediately following the publication of Woolf's report did appear to betray signs of cultural change within the Prison Service. For example, public statements by the incoming Director General Mr Pilling (especially his Eve Saville Memorial Lecture 'Back to Basics: Relationships in the Prison Service') struck a strongly progressivist tone. Pilling's stance put in the foreground problems of complexity and sensitivity in the human aspects of confinement, and placed particular emphasis on the development of the staff role. It also suggested a strong intuition that the relegitimation of imprisonment depended on the vocabulary deployed to animate and justify its practices. Thus Pilling devotes considerable attention to developing an armoury of rhetorically powerful key words 'respect', 'fairness', 'individuality', 'care', 'openness' (ISTD 1992: 5–8). Moreover, Pilling also returned to the submerged question of the justifications for imprisonment in terms of personal development, behavioural change, and educational opportunities for prisoners (see also Dunbar 1985), proposing in effect a modified rehabilitationist view (p. 9). This renewed preoccupation with justificatory language had other curious consequences also. These included the invitation in June 1992 to tender for consultancies under the heading 'Values and Vision for the Prison Service—Plan 2000' in which senior prison managers turned to external sources for advice on corporate philosophy and objectives. The aims of the consultancy included the attempt to 'Facilitate a searching examination of what the Prison Service is in business for and how to do it better'. The same year also witnessed a discussion document on 'A Code of Standards for the Prison Service' (a notion which, pre-Woolf, had enjoyed a chequered and contentious career in official thinking). This document bore clear traces on the one hand of earlier unofficial attempts (e.g. Casale 1984) and on the other of the European Prison Rules (Council of Europe 1987; see also Neale 1991). For these reasons it seems appropriate to view developments during 1991 and 1992 as being, at least on the rhetorical level, rather self-consciously a period of state-sponsored modernization.

None of these initiatives positions itself very explicitly in relation to the issue of prison privatization, although the Government's known attachment to private sector involvement in service provision provides an animating sub-text. Indeed, Pilling's position can be read as something of a reassertion of the idea of a public service vocation in prison management. Neither did Woolf make more than passing reference to the idea of private sector involvement, and then only in the context of escort duties (1991 para. 12.166). However much Prison Service insiders may have secretly known or foreseen the Government's intentions in this respect, it is nowhere suggested that the fulfilment of the internal reform agenda *required* privatization as its means.

It will have come as something of a surprise to the casual observer, therefore, how abruptly privatization re-emerged as a dominant concern in the dying days of 1992. Indeed, with a curious enabling power buried deep in the Criminal Justice Act 1991 (s.84(3); see Wasik and Taylor 1991: 147–8) it was possible for the Home Secretary Kenneth Clarke in a newspaper article to present the large scale contracting out of both new and existing prisons as a *fait accompli* whose legitimacy was already established (*The Independent*, 22 December 1992).

It is not possible here to outline all the practical, legal, and moral arguments which have been presented on either side of the privatization debate,[4] nor to present a detailed narrative of all relevant developments. Rather I merely want to point out some of the ways in which the advocates of private sector initiatives pose (or avoid) legitimation problems. The dominant position in such advocacy, it seems to me, is one which presents the issue of privatization in purely consequentialist terms. That is, if it could be shown that privately managed prisons would be superior on some or all of various quantifiable indicators of performance (cost, regime services, security, for example) then they are *ipso facto* better prisons, and no further argument is possible. Such a view rests on a sharp separation between the *allocation* of punishment by the state and the *delivery* of penal services by any agency to which the state delegates this function, subject to the satisfaction of contractual conditions. Thus Kenneth Clarke felt able to defend his preference for private sector involvement on the grounds that he had no 'ideological prejudices' as to who should carry out the practical tasks of confinement. From his perspective:

It cannot be more moral to lock up prisoners for long hours a day with little chance to associate, limited opportunities for visits and little access to education, work or PE than to see them unlocked all day with access to a full programme of activities, simply because the poor programme is provided by staff directly employed by the state and the better programme by staff employed by a contractor of the state. (*The Independent*, 22 December 1992)

Of course once one has accepted that the issue of who should deliver punishment is one about which it is legitimate *not* to have 'ideological prejudices' this argument becomes almost impossible to rebut. It calls upon the usual array of assumptions which are taken to buttress the case for privatization in any area of public provision: that the disciplines of the marketplace inherently stimulate efficiency; that the split between the purchasers and providers of services enhances regulation and accountability; that the breaking up of the public sector monolith frees the institution from the dead hand of restrictive practices and vested professional interests, and so forth (see especially Logan 1990; Hutto 1989). It also has the disconcerting purpose of equating criticism of privatization with the defence of the *status quo*, as Ryan and Ward uneasily note (1989). It is a line of argument calculated to neutralize critical commentary, whilst appearing to situate itself outside any possible political controversy. It predefines privatization and progress as identical.

Not all privatization proponents are quite so chary about asserting that their position has anything to do with politics or ideology. For example, Logan (the most scholarly and disinterested of such commentators) explicitly affirms that:

The privatization of corrections, or punishment, is an especially significant part of the broader privatization movement. By challenging the government's monopoly over one of its ostensibly 'core' functions, this idea directly challenges the assumption that certain activities are essentially and necessarily governmental. (1990: 4)

---

[4] For the most convincing exposition of a pro-privatization position see Logan (1990) and, from a less evangelizing stance, McConville (1990). Likewise Pease and Taylor (1989) make out an interesting case for a link between

This has the benefit of greater candour, because it is unabashed about linking the issue of prison privatization with the view of the state characteristic of the New Right. Logan's position thus has the great virtue of at last rendering a normative debate on the legitimacy of private prison management possible.

Privatization, Legitimacy, and the 'New Penality'

Of all the arguments advanced in support of privately managed prisons I will deal here briefly with only two closely related ones. These are:

(i) whether the sharp distinction between the allocation and delivery of punishment which advocates of privatization are compelled to draw is defensible; and

(ii) the assumption on the part of Clarke and others that advocating privatization on technical or managerial grounds does not commit one to a view of the penal realm which is fundamentally altered in other respects.

As we have seen the response of the private prisons lobby to the first of these questions is simple. There is no problem—merely a set of technical issues which can be dealt with by setting up the appropriate systems for regulation and oversight, specifying contractual obligations, retaining state-appointed ombudspersons and inspectors, and so forth. Indeed McConville suggests that those who insist on raising such matters of principle are posing questions which completely escape rational adjudication (1990: 94). (If he is right then of course those who oppose privatization have an argument that is just as strong as those who advocate it.) For Logan the matter is beguilingly simple: private and public prisons face all the same problems:

It is primarily because they are prisons, not because they are contractual, that private prisons face challenges of authority, legitimacy, procedural justice, accountability, liability, cost, security, safety, corruptibility, and so on. Because they face no problems that are both unique and insurmountable, private prisons should be allowed to compete (and cooperate) with government agencies so that we can discover how best to run prisons that are safe, secure, humane, efficient and just. (Logan, 1990: 5)

Of course Logan knows that this view is open to an interpretation deeply uncongenial to, indeed disregarded by, most of his fellow travellers in the privatization camp—namely that privatization in and of itself settles none of the prior questions about the legitimacy of the penalty of imprisonment in any given case. One can turn this logic to the view that neither public nor private prisons were ever likely to be safe, secure, humane, efficient, and just enough to warrant their continued use on anything like their present scale. This is clearly not what is intended, however. Rather, the sharp distinction between allocation and delivery of punishment serves rhetorically to insulate the two areas of discussion from one another. It protects the original act of sentencing (a judicial specialism—one sphere of expertise) whilst at the same time it presents the delivery of imprisonment in a moderated and sanitized language (a

privatization and the reassertion of basic penological aims of a kind likely to appeal to, for example, no small number of disillusioned liberal prison managers. For more sceptical appraisals see Ryan and Ward (1989, 1990), Lilly and Knepper (1992*a*, 1992*b*) and for some of the difficult legal issues Weiss (1989).

RICHARD SPARKS

correctional specialism—another sphere of expertise—nothing to do with the intended delivery of pain).

These manoeuvres serve to nudge the questions which have classically preoccupied political philosophers interested in punishment away from the centre of penal debate. Lacey raises the traditional issues in a sharp form. It is inherent in the definition of punishment that it involves the deliberate imposition of unpleasant consequences. Hence its intrinsic need for the strongest possible justification. Otherwise it could only be a '*prima facie* wrongful exercise by state officials of state power' (Lacey 1988: 14).

This leads us into the second area of concern, namely the ways in which privatization itself alters the contours of the penal realm. I am arguing that the allocation/delivery split tends to sandpaper away the contested and 'dismaying' (Garland 1990: 1) nature of state punishment. In that sense it makes it appear *more* akin to other spheres of ordinary administrative activity (hence 'governmental' in Foucault's sense of the term rather than Logan's). To this extent the delegation of penal service delivery to private agencies only serves to accelerate and intensify tendencies which are in any case characteristic of modern institutions of punishment. These tendencies have been identified with particular clarity by Garland when he writes of the 'rational, passionless terms' increasingly characteristic of modern penality 'wherein moral evaluation is displaced by scientific understanding' (1990: 186). Such developments clearly predate the advent of privatization as such, but the ascendancy of consequentialism and quantification in the language of private correctional management decisively shifts the terrain of debate in this direction. Thus the construction of complex input–output models of correctional efficiency (Garland 1990: 188) and the construction of refined actuarial techniques of risk management (Simon 1988) in criminal justice all bespeak a dominant form of managerialism identified by some as a 'new penality' which tends to displace older normative concerns and anxieties. This in turn corresponds closely to the more general regulation of social life under conditions of modernity by 'expert systems' to which Giddens alludes (1990: 27–8).

Here we can do no more than sketch a couple of the possible consequences of this. First there is the inherent likelihood that expert systems of punishment, whether 'public' or 'private' and however formally accountable, will tend to escape any public sphere of informed debate and decision (with the possible further consequence that lay opinion is left to roam free in a realm of imagination and mythmaking with only the most tenuous connection to what happens inside the system (Garland 1990: 188; Sparks 1992: 160–2)). Secondly, there is the question of the scope and extent of the system itself.

This latter issue returns us very directly to the question of privatization as such. It is unconvincing, indeed even inconsistent, for advocates of privatization to argue that their position is not wedded to growth in the prison system. Logan merely argues weakly that:

Contracting need not always be aimed at increasing the number of available prison cells. If the need for secure confinement should decline, or if a viable alternative is developed, it should be easier to alter contracts or change contractors than to restructure entrenched public bureaucracies. (1990: 10)

There are several reasons why this view is both at odds with observable trends and contrary to the logic of privatization initiatives in general. First, as Lilly and Knepper

24

(1992*a*) point out, privatization has to date only seriously taken root in those jurisdictions with the highest proportionate prison populations amongst Western countries (Britain, the United States, and Canada). Within the United States it is strongest amongst those southern states whose existing prison systems are most decrepit, most overcrowded, and most fiscally overburdened. It begins, that is to say, as an emergency measure. Secondly, Logan's position rests on a naive and falsely transparent conception of elasticities of demand for imprisonment. Both the 'need' for prison places and the 'viability' of alternatives are matters of political decision and ideological preference—and in any case the free market preferences of governments sympathetic to privatization and their high demand for prison places are more than accidentally related (Hale 1989; Pease 1990; Greenberg 1991). Thirdly, serious corporate investors in private prisons will not commit capital to prison construction and management unless there are realistic prospects of growth and long-term returns (Lilly and Knepper 1992*b*), and in any case (as Lilly and Knepper further point out (1992*a*)) the construction of new prisons and the provision of their hardware is by far the most profitable sector of the business. Fourthly, as recent British experience culminating in the sentencing provisions of the Criminal Justice Act 1991 suggests, serious governmental pressure on sentencers to treat prisons as a scarce resource only tends to arise where the existing system has become a real economic and political burden, a circumstance which private investment is precisely designed to obviate. Fifthly, and by no means least, many of the companies most keenly interested in prison privatization are defence contractors experiencing a 'negative peace dividend', whose lobbying skills and ties to government are already strong and whom governments may experience a strong political pressure to assist.

If one takes the strong analogy of private provision of health services, the whole strength of the privatization case turns on the notion of an indefinitely large demand which public provision alone can never in principle satisfy. In examining privatization discourse the term which routinely arises is *supplement* (Fulton 1989; Gardiner 1989; Logan 1990). Private prisons are explicitly conceived as *supplementary to* an existing system which has reached or exceeded even the most permissive estimation of its capacity. They are extremely unlikely, for reasons of economic and political logic, to reduce the overall dimensions of any such system. Moreover, there is a powerful tradition of criminological analysis which suggests that *supplementarity* is precisely the mechanism whereby criminal justice institutions are most likely to extend their scale and their sphere of operations (see e.g. Cohen 1985; Nelken 1989).

For these reasons alone, though there are numerous others, there is reason for extreme scepticism over whether the current preoccupation with privatization in any sense presages a renewed concern with the normative legitimacy of the system, or whether it will in any sense creatively focus public anxiety on the justifications for imposing penal sanctions.

Conclusions—Towards a 'Utopian Realist' Politics of Imprisonment

The problem of legitimacy has received rather short shrift in writing about prisons, despite the central importance which, I have argued, it possesses, or should possess. Too often it has been defined (as at times in Mathiesen's writings—1990: 141–2) as *nothing but* the ruses of statecraft whereby a bankrupt system seeks to perpetuate and protect itself. Of course this negative, ideological sense of the term is important, and examples of it are everywhere to be found.

Yet the idea of legitimacy also carries a deeper and more challenging implication. On a proper understanding of its significance, as a problem that is chronically implicated in all penal practices, it delimits in large measure the very arena within which penological debate must take place. What I have tried to indicate by considering some current prison problems and examples of official discourse in response to them is the growing necessity of reinstating this concern at the centre of penal politics. The concept of legitimacy carries an open and dialectical awareness of change, such that every time an attempt at legitimation (such as Lord Justice Woolf's reform agenda) appears to promise a new settlement one can begin to discern within it the outlines of another emergent set of issues and possibilities and to reach towards them.

In his recent writings Giddens speaks of the inherent 'institutional reflexivity' of modernity, defined as 'the routine incorporation of new knowledge or information into environments of action that are thereby reconstituted or reorganised' (1991: 243). Such a reconstitution is continual and has no necessary stopping point. I am arguing that the debate about the legitimacy of imprisonment must now become of this kind. In a post-traditional social order it is open to us to review our institutional environment in a more sceptical and more thoroughgoing way than may have been possible in the past. In the case of an institution such as the prison we may ultimately come to the conclusion that its intrinsic design faults are such that it rarely or never achieves its stated objectives, or that it routinely produces unintended 'perverse consequences' (Giddens 1990: 152) which may be so severe that it must either be transformed or abandoned.

In such a case the appropriate form of engagement lies in what Giddens terms a stance of 'utopian realism' (or alternatively 'a critical theory without guarantees'—i.e., one grounded in rigorous practical reasoning and without recourse to an implicit teleology or determinism (1990: 154)). On this view it may indeed be open to us to imagine a future without prisons as we currently know them or in which our reliance on them is radically reduced, provided only that we can show that we are not thereby increasing the level of 'high consequence risks' by courting a perverse outcome (say by increasing the public's real risk of exposure to serious victimization or by inviting the substitution of some other more noxious form of social control) and that this course has some grounding in 'immanent institutional possibilities' (1990: 155).

'Power in its broadest sense', Giddens comments, 'is a means of getting things done.' The question of legitimacy focuses our attention on which distributions of power we are prepared to accept and which we come to define as divisive, exploitative, or oppressive (1991: 211) in the light of norms of justice which we regard as valid and with which we hope to persuade other to agree (1991: 212–3). Hence, 'justifiable authority can defend itself against the charge of oppression only where differential power can be shown to be morally legitimate' (1991: 212).

All prison systems confront severe legitimacy deficits, especially from the vantage points of the confined. But such deficits are not always total. Nor are they everywhere equally severe. This being so, for as long as we must have prisons, it is indeed possible to distinguish clearly between better and worse, preferable and less preferable, stronger and less strong justifications both in the conditions which externally govern their use and in their internal practices.

26

REFERENCES

BEETHAM, D. (1991), *The Legitimation of Power*. London: Macmillan.

CASALE, S. (1984), *Measurable Standards for Prison Establishments*. London: NACRO.

CAVADINO, M. (1992), 'Explaining the Penal Crisis', *Prison Service Journal*, 87: 2–12.

CAVADINO, M., and Dignan, J. (1992), *The Penal System: An Introduction*. London: Sage.

COHEN, S. (1985), *Visions of Social Control*. Cambridge: Polity Press.

COUNCIL OF EUROPE (1987), *The European Prison Rules*. Strasbourg: Council of Europe.

DAHRENDORF, R. (1990), *Reflections on the Revolutions in Europe*. London: Chatto.

DUNBAR, I. (1985), *A Sense of Direction*. London: HMSO.

DUNN, J. (1990), *Interpreting Political Responsibility*. Cambridge: Polity Press.

ELSTER, J. (1989), *Nuts and Bolts for the Social Sciences*. Cambridge: Cambridge University Press.

FOUCAULT, M. (1979), *Discipline and Punish*. Harmondsworth: Penguin.

FULTON, R. (1989), 'Private Sector Involvement in the Remand System', in M. Farrell, ed., *Punishment for Profit?*. London: ISTD.

GARDINER, E. (1989), 'Prisons—an Alternative Approach', in M. Farrell, ed., *Punishment for Profit?*. London: ISTD.

GARLAND, D. (1985), *Punishment and Welfare*. Aldershot: Gower.

—— (1990), *Punishment and Modern Society*. Oxford: Oxford University Press.

—— (1992), 'Criminological Knowledge and its Relation to Power', *British Journal of Criminology*, 32: 403–22.

GEUSS, R. (1981), *The Idea of a Critical Theory*. Cambridge: Cambridge University Press.

GIDDENS, A. (1977), *Studies in Social and Political Theory*. London: Hutchinson.

—— (1990), *The Consequences of Modernity*. Cambridge: Polity Press.

—— (1991), *Modernity and Self-Identity*. Cambridge: Polity Press.

GREENBERG, D. (1991), 'The Cost-Benefit Analysis of Imprisonment', *Social Justice*, 17: 49–75.

HABERMAS, J. (1976), *Legitimation Crisis*. London: Heinemann.

HALE, C. (1989), 'Economy, Punishment and Imprisonment', *Contemporary Crises*, 13: 327–49.

HALL, S., CLARKE, J., JEFFERSON, T., CRITCHER, C., and ROBERTS, B. (1978), *Policing the Crisis*. London: Macmillan.

HELD, D. (1987), *Models of Democracy*. Cambridge: Polity Press.

HOME OFFICE (1964), *The Prison Rules*. London: HMSO.

—— (1984), *Managing the Long-term Prison System: the Report of the Control Review Committee*. London: HMSO.

HUTTO, D. (1989), 'Public Agencies and Private Companies—Partners for Progress', in M. Farrell, ed., *Punishment for Profit?*. London: ISTD.

IGNATIEFF, M. (1978), *A Just Measure of Pain*. London: Penguin.

ISTD (1989), *Punishment for Profit?*, M. Farrell, ed. London: ISTD.

KING, R. D., and McDERMOTT, K. (1989), 'British Prisons, 1970–87: the Ever Deepening Crisis', *British Journal of Criminology*, 29: 107–28.

KING, R. D., and McDERMOTT, K. (1990), 'My Geranium is Subversive: Some Notes on the Management of Trouble in Prisons', *British Journal of Sociology*, 41/4: 445–71.

LACEY, N. (1988), *State Punishment*. London: Routledge.

LILLY, J. R., and KNEPPER, P. (1992a), 'The Corrections–Commercial Complex', *Prison Service Journal*, 87.

—— (1992b) 'An International Perspective on the Privatization of Corrections', *Howard Journal*, 31/3.

LOGAN, C. (1990), *Private Prisons: Cons and Pros*. Oxford: Oxford University Press.

MCCONVILLE, S. (1990) 'The Privatization of Penal Services', in Council of Europe, *Privatization of Crime Control*. Strasbourg: Council of Europe.

MATHIESEN, T. (1965), *The Defences of the Weak*. London: Tavistock.

—— (1974), *The Politics of Abolition*. Oxford: Martin Robertson.

—— (1990), *Prison on Trial*. London: Sage.

MELOSSI, D., and PAVARINI, M. (1981), *The Prison and the Factory*. London: Macmillan.

MORGAN, R. (1992), 'Following Woolf: the Prospects for Penal Policy', *Journal of Law and Society*, 19: 2.

MORRIS, T. (1989), *Crime and Criminal Justice Since 1945*. Oxford: Basil Blackwell.

NEALE, K. (1991), 'The European Prison Rules', in J. Muncie and J. R. Sparks, eds, *Imprisonment: European Perspectives*. Hemel Hempstead: Harvester Wheatsheaf.

NELKEN, D. (1989), 'Discipline and Punish: Some Notes on the Margin', *The Howard Journal*, 28: 245–54.

PEASE, K. (1990), 'Punishment Demand and Punishment Numbers', in D. M. Gottfredson and R. V. Clarke, eds, *Policy and Theory in Criminal Justice*. Aldershot: Avebury.

PEASE, K., and TAYLOR, M. (1989), 'Private Prisons and Penal Purpose', in R. Matthews, ed., *Privatizing Criminal Justice*. London: Sage.

RUSCHE, G., and KIRCHHEIMER, O. (1939) *Punishment and Social Structure*. New York: Columbia University Press.

RYAN, M., and WARD, T. (1989), *Privatization and the Penal System*. Buckingham: Open University Press.

—— (1990), 'The State and the Prison System: Is There a Role for the Private Sector?', in R. Light, ed., *Public and Private Provisions in Criminal Justice*. Bristol and Bath Centre for Criminology.

SCRATON, P., SIM, J., and SKIDMORE, P. (1991), *Prisons Under Protest*. Buckingham: Open University Press.

SIM, J. (1992), ' "When You Ain't Got Nothing You Got Nothing to Lose": The Peterhead Rebellion, the State and the Case for Prison Abolition', in K. Bottomley, T. Fowles, and R. Reiner, eds, *Criminal Justice: Theory and Practice*. London: British Society of Criminology.

SIMON, J. (1988), 'The Ideological Effect of Actuarial Practices', *Law and Society Review*, 22.

SPARKS, J. R. (1992), *Television and the Drama of Crime*. Buckingham: Open University Press.

SPARKS, J. R., and BOTTOMS, A. E. (1992), 'Order and Legitimacy in Prisons', Paper presented to the American Society of Criminology Meetings, New Orleans, November 1992.

SYKES, G. (1958), *The Society of Captives*. Princeton NJ: Princeton University Press.

THOMAS, J., and POOLEY, R. (1980), *The Exploding Prison*. London: Junction Books.

WALKER, N. (1991), *Why Punish?*. Oxford: Oxford University Press.

WASIK, M., and TAYLOR, R. (1991), *Blackstone's Guide to the Criminal Justice Act 1991*. London: Blackstone Press.

WEBER, M. (1991; orig. 1918), 'Politics as a Vocation', in H. H. Gerth and C. Wright Mills, eds, *From Max Weber*. London: Routledge (new edition).

WEISS, R. (1989), 'Private Prisons and the State', in R. Matthews, ed., *Privatizing Criminal Justice*. London: Sage.

WOOLF, LORD JUSTICE (1991), *Prison Disturbances, April 1990*. London: HMSO.

PUBLIC IMPRISONMENT BY PRIVATE MEANS

The Re-emergence of Private Prisons and Jails in the United States, the United Kingdom, and Australia

DOUGLAS C. MCDONALD*

Although privately operated imprisonment facilities were commonplace in previous centuries in England and the United States (Holdsworth 1922–4: 397; Crew 1933: 50; McKelvey 1977: 197–216; Feeley 1991), by the twentieth century, governments had assumed responsibility for nearly all imprisonment and most other criminal justices functions. Indeed, the principle of public responsibility for the administration of justice—and especially for imprisonment—has become so well established that imprisonment is seen by many as an intrinsic function of government (American Bar Association 1989: 3; DiIulio 1990: 172–7; Robbins 1988: 44; Howard League for Penal Reform 1990: 3). Beginning in the mid-1980s, however, a debate emerged in the United States, Britain, and in some other English-speaking countries over the propriety of governments contracting with private firms to operate and even own prisons, jails, and other places of imprisonment. This has gone beyond talk, for governments in the United States, Britain, and Australia are now contracting with private, for-profit firms to operate penal facilities of various types, and a private imprisonment industry has emerged (or, taking a longer historical view, re-emerged).

This essay surveys developments in the United States, Britain, and Australia, the only countries that have so far moved to delegate operations of imprisonment facilities to private entities. The first section provides a thumbnail sketch of developments in these countries since the early 1980s, followed with a discussion of why private imprisonment emerged during this period. Some of the principal issues raised by private imprisonment, including some of the important research questions, are identified and discussed briefly.

The Rediscovery of Private Imprisonment in the United States

The contemporary movement to expand private authority over the administration of penal and detention facilities owes its origins to independent developments on both sides of the Atlantic, although there has been considerable cross-fertilization. Whereas in Britain, the earliest proposals came from policy reformers—for example, the Adam Smith Institute (1984) and McConville and Williams (1985)—the stimulus in the United States came largely from business entrepreneurs who were promoting their own ventures. Policy reformers later developed a more elaborate rationale for opening government to business interests (e.g., President's Commission on Privatization 1988; Stewart 1986; Logan 1990).

* Douglas C. McDonald, Ph.D., is a senior social scientist in the Law and Public Policy Area of Abt Associates Inc., a policy research organization based in Cambridge, Massachusetts. He conducts research and writes on criminal sentencing, intermediate sanctions, corrections policy and financing, privatization, and drug abuse policy and treatment.

One of the principal seedbeds for the current wave of private imprisonment firms in the United States was the network of detention centres under the authority of the US Immigration and Nationalization Service (INS). Beginning in 1979, the INS began contracting with private firms to detain illegal immigrants pending hearings or deportation. By the end of 1988, the number of private detention facilities had grown to seven, and they held about 800 of the approximately 2,700 aliens in INS custody (McDonald 1990a: 92). This was an important market for the emerging private imprisonment firms, giving several of the now significant players their early starts. This included the Corrections Corporation of America (CCA), a Tennessee-based firm that incorporated in 1983 and opened its first detention centre in Houston, Texas the following year, and has since grown into one of the dominant forces in the field. CCA has recently expanded its operations into Britain and Australia through subsidiaries (Corrections Corporation of America 1992; Corrections Corporation of Australia 1992). Another of the large enterprises, Wackenhut, Inc., an established private security firm, entered the private prison business by winning the contract to build and operate a detention facility for the INS in Denver, Colorado (McDonald 1990a: 94). There were other smaller entrepreneurs who won some of the early INS contracts and gained attention—e.g., Ted Nissen's Behavioral Systems Southwest—but fell behind when more heavily capitalized firms emerged (Press 1990).

Government officials in the INS 'went private' chiefly because contractors were able to create new detention facilities much more quickly than could the federal government. (Government procurement procedures required long lead times.) Indeed, Wackenhut was able to construct and open a 150-bed facility at breakneck speed: 90 days from the contract's signing. Conveniently, the cost of acquiring this new capacity could be paid for out of the government's operating funds—through per diem reimbursements—rather than requiring the allocation of capital funds for facility construction, which could be a bureaucratically cumbersome process (McDonald 1990a).

In addition to the INS detention centres, the private imprisonment industry also established early sites with various low-security facilities, and in the less visible regions of the adult and juvenile penal systems. For example, the federal government's Bureau of Prisons had been contracting with private firms since the late 1960s to operate community treatment centres, halfway houses to which federal prisoners were transferred prior to being paroled (Bronick 1989: 12–14).

These developments provoked little controversy or even notice. That changed, however, in late 1985 and 1986. Private firms began taking over or building facilities that were closer to the core of the adult penal system, which had previously been the nearly exclusive preserve of government. In the closing months of 1985, CCA contracted with the Bay County (Florida) government to operate its jail. A similar contract was signed in August of 1986 with the Santa Fe, New Mexico county government. In January 1986, US Corrections Corp. opened a 350-bed prison (the Marian Adjustment Center) in St Mary's, Kentucky, and contracted with the state's Department of Corrections to hold sentenced prisoners (Press 1990).

What brought the issue to public attention and ignited a public policy debate, however, were two incidents. One was CCA's audacious offer to take over the entire state of Tennessee's troubled prison system, with a 99-year lease from the state, for which it would pay $250 million. CCA would then house the state's convicted prisoners at a negotiated per diem rate and would guarantee that the system would meet standards set by a federal court judge, who had earlier found the entire system to be in violation of the US Constitution because of inadequate conditions of confinement. The state ultimately turned down the offer after several months of consideration, but the matter became a national news story (Corrections Corporation of America 1985; Tolchin 1985a, 1985b; Press 1990).

The second signal event was the opening of a small privately operated facility, called the 268 Center, by one Philip E. Tack, in rural Cowansville, Pennsylvania. Tack arranged with the District of Columbia authorities to transfer 55 inmates from the District's jails to relieve overcrowding there, but the townspeople were not pleased. Among other things, the inmates were all black, the townspeople all white. Local residents organized themselves and patrolled the streets with shotguns, fearing escapes. This caught the attention of a prison reform group that got the state legislature to declare a moratorium on privately-operated prisons (Joint State Government Commission 1987; Press 1990; Bivens 1986).

In the train of these events, private imprisonment emerged as one of the most salient issues in correctional circles. The National Institute of Justice convened a conference and circulated reports of the proceedings (Peterson 1988), and Congress held hearings (US House of Representatives 1986). Most of the organized bodies in the criminal justice arena took a stand on the issue. The American Federation of State, County, and Municipal Workers and the National Sheriffs' Association opposed contracting for operations; the American Correctional Association gave it guarded support (US House of Representatives 1986), and the American Bar Association asked for a moratorium pending further study (1986), and upon further study, argued that delegating operating authority to private entities posed grave constitutional and policy problems (1989).

The issue remained in the public eye for a few years, prompting a spate of articles, books, and reports (e.g., Robbins 1988; Logan 1990, 1991; Logan and McGriff 1989; Logan and Rausch 1985; Feeley 1991; Keating undated; Mullen 1985; Mullen et al. 1984; National Criminal Justice Statistics Association 1987; Legislative Research Council 1986; McDonald 1990b; Tolchin 1985a, 1985b, 1985c; Urban Institute 1989; Bowman et al. 1992; also see Immarigeon 1987). By the turn of the decade, however, the debate had died down. There had neither been a rush to privatize correctional facilities, nor had the nascent industry been stopped dead in its tracks. Instead, the industry continued to grow slowly, and new facilities were opened, including major maximum security prisons (four in Texas, for example). The large firms have also broadened their reach into other markets—the United Kingdom and Australia.

By the end of 1990, there existed 44 secure adult facilities operated by private firms in the United States, some of these facilities owned by their operators, holding approximately 15,000 inmates (McDonald 1992). This represented only a small fraction of the approximately 4,900 prisons and jails in this country (American Correctional Association 1991), and they held slightly less than 2 per cent of all inmates under custody at that point (McDonald 1992).

Parallel to these developments was another form of privatization: the construction of privately-owned facilities that were leased to governments for direct government operation. This first emerged in Colorado, where an investment banking firm put together a lease-purchase deal for a county government that wanted to build a new jail.

31

A private corporation was formed to build the new jail, and investors bought 'certificates of participation'—what amounted to corporate bonds. The jail was then leased to the county, and the lease payments were used to repay investors (McDonald 1990c). Similar arrangements were developed for prison and jail construction in other places (Chaiken and Mennemeier 1987).

These emerged largely because of constraints on public officials' ability to authorize capital expenditures for new prisons, and have been used to finance other types of public purchases (Leonard 1986, 1990). In the United States, most state governments build prisons by issuing bonds purchased by investors, but must first obtain the approval of voters to incur these debt obligations. Spurred by a tax revolt that spread across the United States in the late 1970s and early 1980s, citizens were voting down these bonding proposals, even though they were demanding at the same time that more criminals be imprisoned in the hopes of making their communities safer. Public officials saw the 'creative financing' techniques such as lease-purchase arrangements as a convenient way out of this dilemma, as a rent payment could be paid out of government operating budgets. How many facilities were built through lease-purchase arrangements is difficult to determine, for lack of a central accounting system in the US's fragmented federal system.

Developments in Britain

Although proposals for privately operated prisons first surfaced in 1984 and 1985, advanced by the Adam Smith Institute (1984) and two academics, McConville and Williams (1985), the Government had already been contracting for immigrant detention services for a decade and a half (Green undated; Rutherford 1990). In July 1970, the Home Office contracted with Securicor Ltd, a private security firm, to administer detention centres at the four principal airports, as well as various escort services associated with them. By the mid-1980s, when the contemporary debate over privately operated prisons began, the largest facility used by the Immigration Service, a detention centre at Harmondsworth, was privately administered. This and a small number of other private detention centres held a substantial proportion of all detained immigrants—nearly half, according to one survey conducted in April 1988 (Joint Council for the Welfare of Immigrants 1988: 13, quoted in Green undated: 4). In January 1989, Securicor lost the contract for these centres to Group 4 Total Security, the operating arm of Group 4 Securitas International, a subsidiary of a large Swedish firm, Securitas International. The parent firm has operating companies in approximately sixteen different countries (Green undated: 4).

It appears that current developments to contract out for prisons began not as a considered extension of this experience with immigrant detention centres (indeed, this experience has been little studied) but resulted from separate initiatives. In 1986, when attention to private prisons was high in the United States, the Home Affairs Committee of the House of Commons, which exercises parliamentary oversight of the prison system, decided to examine private prisons and jails in the United States as part of its broader inquiry into the state of prisons and jails in England and Wales (Rutherford 1990). On that trip, the chair of the committee, Sir Edward Gardiner, became an enthusiastic proponent of privatization, and the short report that resulted from this visit recommended that the Home Office should, as an experiment, permit private firms to tender for the construction and management of custodial institutions. The committee also recommended that priority be given to contracting out the remand centres 'because it is there that the most overcrowding in the prison system is concentrated' (Home Affairs Committee 1987).

This was followed by two reports, one by Peter Young of the Adam Smith Institute, who argued that the 'monopolistic provision' of imprisonment services should be broken to encourage an increase in the supply of beds, improvements in quality, and cost reductions. Young recommended that five existing prisons be privatized as an experiment and that one new private remand prison in London be built (1987: 2). In the same year, Maxwell Taylor and Ken Pease (1987), two liberal academics, wrote a paper supporting privatization because it could serve as a 'springboard for the development of a truly rehabilitative programme'. This could be done by building incentives into the contracts. As *The Independent* declared, this support by the liberal wing of the penal reform lobby 'gave crucial new authority to the campaign' (5 March 1987).

On 30 March 1988, the Government announced that it intended to publish a discussion document (a 'Green Paper') on private sector involvement in the remand system, and that private management consultants would be engaged to consider the details (Gill 1992: 1). The paper was published the following July (HMSO 1988) and the consultants appointed. Their report, published in March of the following year (Deloitte, Haskins, and Sells 1989), offered a number of specific recommendations. It recommended issuing contracts to private firms to design, construct, and operate remand centres, and to turn existing remand centres over to the private sector. It also recommended issuing between four and ten separate contracts for court and escort duties, each corresponding to geographical districts to be designated. (These tasks include escorting prisoners to and from court, guarding prisoners at court, and providing court security.) This separation between remand centre and escort duties was recommended as a means of increasing the efficiency of staff and managers that would result from concentrating specially trained employees on their principal missions, rather than requiring (or permitting) them to do both. This report was followed by the Government, in July 1990, issuing another discussion paper that adopted most of the consultants' recommendations, inviting comment (Home Office 1990).

The consultants indicated that they were not able to conduct a precise cost-effectiveness analysis of their proposal, but declared that 'our analysis of this inform-ation indicates a reasonable prospect of improvements in cost-effectiveness outweighing the additional costs that contracting would cause in contract administration and in monitoring' (Deloitte, Haskins, and Sells 1989: p. iii). They suggested that savings in the remand centres could be generated by expanding the use of clerical services, instituting more flexible work practices, greater use of improved technology, and higher ratios of inmates to staff than currently prevail.

In December 1991, the Government announced its intentions to proceed with contracting out the court escort services, beginning with one newly defined district that would include East Midlands and Humberside. Tenders were received from six firms and a contract was signed in 1993 with Group 4. Service was planned to commence in April 1993 (Gill 1992: 9).

Although the consultants recommended contracting with private firms for the design, construction, and operation of new remand centres, the prison population took 'one of its inexplicable nosedives, such that the urgent need for new places to be built receded' (Gill 1992: 3). The Government decided instead to contract out a new prison that was under construction in the North East of England, the 320-bed Wolds remand prison, in North Humberside. Enabling legislation was needed for this, which was obtained in the Criminal Justice Act 1991. This Act provided the power to contract out the management of new prisons for unsentenced inmates, but was extended once in July 1992 to encompass sentenced prisoners and again in February 1993 to enable contracting out of *existing* prisons. A five-year contract for operating The Wolds remand prison was signed in November 1991, with the Group 4 Remand Services Ltd (Gill 1992: 5).

The second prison to be contracted out was a new one at Blakenhurst, a 650-bed local prison for sentenced and unsentenced prisoners. This contract was awarded in 1992 to UK Detention Services, a consortium of the Corrections Corporation of America and British construction firms John Mowlem and Sir Robert McAlpine (Ford 1992; Corrections Corporation of America 1992). Private operations were scheduled to commence in April 1993 (Clarke 1992).

A frontier of sorts is being crossed in a more recent development: the 'market testing' of the Prison Services' administration of the Manchester prison ('Strangeways'). This prison, originally opened in 1868 as Salford Prison, was the site of a prisoner uprising in April 1990 that lasted nearly a month and left most of the interior destroyed. A refurbishing job was undertaken, and the government invited tenders in October 1992 from private firms to operate the prison. The plan was to make a contracting decision in April 1993, with private operation commencing the following September. Bidders were told to assume that they should anticipate providing the capacity to hold 866 prisoners, but that another 134 cells could be authorized for occupancy, raising the total to 1,000 (Home Office 1992: 13–15).

In contrast to The Wolds and Blakenhurst competitions, the Prison Service was permitted to submit a bid for the Strangeways contract. One apparent purpose of this market testing was to force the Prison Service to reconsider (and perhaps to renegotiate) the labour practices prevailing in its facilities. Kenneth Clarke, at that time the Home Secretary, wrote that 'Market testing will, I believe, cause the prison service to examine its own performance in the light of competitive pressure and encourage the spread of those reforms across public sector prisons much more quickly than would otherwise have been the case' (Clarke 1992). In a briefing paper issued in November 1992 by the Prison Service, the bidding team stated that 'Our aim will be to put forward a winning bid which takes full advantage of the flexibilities available—with the agreement of staff and unions.' However, 'A bid sticking to every detail of a central agreement [between management and labour] dating from 1987 is unlikely to beat the competition . . . Any agreements that hinder the chances of constructing an effective bid will have to be reconsidered in consultation with the unions' (HM Prison Service 1992: 2).

In mid-July of 1993, Derek Lewis, the Director General of the Prison Service announced that the 'in-house bid team'—the Prison Service itself—had won the competition to manage the prison. 'Seven tenders were submitted and there was a very strong field from which to chose', he stated. 'It is quite clear that the spur of competition has generated bids which represent levels of performance and value for money that we have not previously seen in the public or private sector . . . It was a strong and imaginative bid, which offered the best overall value for money' (HM Prison Service 1993*a*). In the absence of a contract, the Government drew up a service agreement for a five-year period, during which time the team would receive £79 million to fund the prison's operation.

In the wake of this decision, in September 1993, the Government announced that it would further stimulate the development of a private correctional industry by seeking contracts for a number of other prisons. 'Our aim is to create a private sector able to provide sustained competition', said Michael Howard, the Home Secretary. '[The] private sector must be large enough to provide sustained competition and involve several private sector companies—a genuinely mixed economy' (HM Prison Service 1993*b*). The strategy for accomplishing this will be to contract, during the 'initial phase', with private firms for the management of about 10 per cent of the prisons in England and Wales (12 prisons in total). Moreover, contracts will be issued for the design, construction, and perhaps even the financing of new prisons. The specific prisons to be 'market tested' are to be chosen by the Prison Board, and priority will be given to those that have most room for improvement.

It is possible that contracting out will advance further in Britain than in the United States, in large part because of the Government's broader commitment to rolling back the public agencies' domain. Unlike the United States, a single national government has authority over prisons and jails, permitting a more rapid implementation of changed policy. In the United States, the growth of the private prison industry is slowed by the existence of separate governments (and, therefore, markets) in 3,400 counties, and 50 states, in addition to the federal government. Conversely, a change in administration in Britain might bring a rapid halt to developments there, whereas the march of the private prison industry in the United States is less likely to be affected by the defeat of a conservative administration at the federal level.

Australia

A 1988 report to the Queensland Corrective Services Commission that provided a blueprint for correctional reform in Queensland called for the development of one prison operated and managed by the private sector under contract to the commission (Kennedy 1988). This, the report argued, would create a competitive market for correctional institutions in Australia and Queensland, speeding reform of the prison system. The commission accepted the recommendation and invited tenders to manage and operate the Borallon Correctional Centre, a new 240-bed facility near Brisbane. The contract was awarded in November 1989 to the Corrections Corporation of Australia, a newly-formed consortium made up of the Corrections Corporation of America, Wormald Security, and John Holland Constructions. Private operations began in January 1990, under a three-year contract that had an option for renewal for another two years. By the end of the first year, the prisoner population was predominantly a medium security one (Macionis 1992: 9).

A second privately-operated prison resulted from the breakdown of negotiations between the commission and the labour union representing staff to be employed at the newly constructed 380-bed Remand and Reception (Arthur Gorrie) Centre at Brisbane. When no agreement could be reached regarding work rules and procedures, the commission informed the Government in October 1991 that it intended to call for tenders for the private sector operation of this facility. This came to pass shortly, and in March 1992, a contract was awarded to Australasian Contract Management (ACM), a consortium of Wackenhut Security and ADT, an Australian-based security company, and the centre went operational in June 1992. This facility is a critical piece of the Queensland correctional system, as it is the main reception centre for the state's 11 facilities; all the initial assessment and classification of prisoners is conducted there (Macionis 1992: 3–4).

The Junee prison in New South Wales, scheduled for opening in March 1993, was the third facility to be contracted out. This 600-bed prison was designed and constructed by ACM, to be operated by that firm for an initial period of five years, with options for renewing a three-year term (Harding 1992: 1). Observing these developments, Harding wrote that 'the momentum seems inexorably to be increasing. Indeed the Wacol contract [for the Queensland Remand and Reception Center] could mean that, for cash-strapped governments, the ideological walls will now come tumbling down. The question is thus not whether privatization will occur; but rather to what extent, in relation to what sorts of institutions and which types of prisoner . . . and above all whether it will improve the overall imprisonment system' (Harding 1992: 1).

Why Contract for Prison and Jail Operations?

It is interesting that the development of privately operated prisons has emerged in a few English-speaking countries. Part of this results from language barriers, making it difficult for American firms to penetrate markets where English is not spoken widely (such as France, where the Mitterand Government held discussions with officials of the Corrections Corporations of America in the 1980s).

Rolling back the state

A deeper explanation, however, is found in the ideological orientation of the governments in power at the time of the nascent industry's development. In Britain, the United States, and Queensland, conservative governments held sway. In the former two countries, these governments launched a concerted attack on the institutional structures and ideology of the welfare state. Certainly the most aggressive programme of cutting back the public sector has been in Britain, following Thatcher's election in 1979, which has continued under John Major's administration. This movement of privatization and contracting out for operations in government-owned facilities has been extensive, cutting across a wide variety of services. In the United States, the movement has been less aggressive, largely because the federal government (which was under divided Republican and Democratic control) holds relatively few assets that can be privatized. Nonetheless, the public landscape was combed in the United States in search of targets for privatization of assets or contracting, and prisons were sighted by those advocating broader private sector involvement in the delivery of public services (e.g., President's Commission on Privatization 1988).

Rising prisoner populations

Another contributing factor to these developments was the increasing demand for prison and jail beds, at least in the United States and in Britain. Between 1973 and 1990 in the United States, the numbers of prisoners under custody at any one time grew nearly fourfold (Bureau of Justice Statistics 1991). At the same time, the federal courts were finding a large number of imprisonment facilities—and even entire state prison systems—to be in violation of the Constitution's prohibition of 'cruel and unusual punishment', largely because of overcrowding and inadequate conditions of confinement. By mid-1991, 40 states were operating prisons found by the courts to have unconstitutional conditions (Bernat 1991). The result of both was strong pressure on governments at all levels to acquire new imprisonment facilities, either by constructing new ones or converting buildings once dedicated to other uses.

Similar pressures were being felt in Britain. During the 1980s, prison populations were rising because of the increasing proportions of convicted persons receiving custodial sentences, the imposition of longer prison sentences, and some lengthening of delays in bringing people to trial. Between 1980 and 1987, the growth of the prisoner population was twice that of the increase in capacity, so that by the end of 1987, a capacity shortfall of about 5,800 beds existed. The government responded by increasing expenditures for prison services substantially: a 72 per cent increase between 1980 and 1987, and a prison building programme projected a 53 per cent increase in capacity between 1980 and 1995. Despite this higher level of expenditure, about 40 per cent of all prisoners in 1986–7 were being held in overcrowded facilities, mostly in remand facilities. Remand prisoners were also backed up into police cells; during 1987, police cells held an average of 530 such prisoners (Rutherford 1990: 44–6).

Speedy expansion of capacity

In the United States, the private sector had a special advantage over government that was appealing to public managers: lengthy procurement procedures could be evaded by issuing contracts with private firms. Moreover, public managers did not have to risk having requests to increase public debt for prison construction turned down at the ballot box, because payments for contracted imprisonment facilities could be made with funds from accounts for operations rather than capital accounts. Because these constitutional constraints do not exist in Britain, the private firms were not so advantaged there.

Lower costs

Certainly an important stimulus to contracting has been the belief—or hope—that contracting will be less costly than direct governmental provision. In the United States, leaders of the private firms have proclaimed this to be a fact. In Britain, this quest for more cost-effective (or, at least, less costly) imprisonment services appears to be a main reason for turning to the private sector (Clarke 1992), although data on private firms' costs are not public because the Government has agreed to consider this information proprietary and confidential. In Australia, one of the principal reasons that the Queensland Corrective Commission resorted to contracting was that it was unable to obtain agreements from the staff regarding work procedures and, therefore, costs (Macionis 1992). Whether private contracting is, in fact, less costly and more cost-effective remains an open question, as discussed below.

Increased managerial control

Although some have argued that contracting with independent private firms weakens the ability of government managers to control the provision of public services (e.g., DiIulio 1990; AFSME 1984), some government officials who have turned to contractors report that they have done so to *increase* control and better ensure performance. In the United States, the need to increase governmental control was a significant factor in some of the earliest contracts. For example, the Bay County (Florida) commissioners turned to contractors because they were unable to gain assurances from the jail administrator (the sheriff) that the conditions of confinement would be improved. They then contracted with CCA and obliged it to meet certain specified standards by a fixed date (McDonald 1990c; Press 1990). Santa Fe (New Mexico) county commissioners also turned to CCA because they were unable to control the costs of a newly constructed jail (Press 1990). Jails in the United States pose a special case because they are typically under the authority of sheriffs, who are independently elected and do not serve at the pleasure of county commissioners or executives. However, even where political control of prisons is not so fragmented, as in the case of England, the need for gaining stronger managerial control over prisons and prison systems is given as a reason for contracting (Gill 1993; Clarke 1992).

The belief that privatization offers enhanced control over public services appears to be based on several different dynamics of contracting. First, the pressure to compete forces a reconsideration and change of work rules that have been built up in the public sector. Inefficient practices will be more difficult to support if one's employment is at risk. Secondly, contracting forces government agencies to establish specific and written performance standards and goals, something that is done less frequently in direct public provision of services. Thirdly, private firms are exposed to more risk for failing to meet these standards, at least compared to public employees who have expansive rights and protections against dismissal. Fourthly, some have argued (e.g., O'Hare *et al.* 1990) that contracting permits managers to focus attention on the quality of output (including services), rather than on the myriad processes by which outputs are produced.

Finally, in instances where higher-level political or managerial authority is unable to control by command the performance of subordinates, turning to contractors may result in higher levels of compliance with policy and performance objectives. For example, in Massachusetts during the early 1970s, a reform-oriented manager was appointed to run the state's correctional services for youth, but failed to get the entrenched and tradition-bound employees of the agency to change their practices. Nearly overnight, he closed the large closed training schools and contracted with a number of smaller private organizations to care for the youths. Although this event has usually been understood as a crucial event in the 'deinstitutionalization' movement, undertaken to supplant a custodial culture with one that gave higher priority to juvenile rehabilitation, contracting was the tool for accomplishing the reform objective (Coates *et al.* 1978).

This finds an echo in Australia, where contracting has just begun. The Queensland Corrective Commission announced its aim of creating a 'more rehabilitative' environment in its correctional centres. 'In order to achieve this, custodial staff would need to adopt a much different approach to their work than that of the traditional stony face guard on a fixed post . . . [It] has been difficult to bring about the type of cultural change required. Private sector involvement has provided an opportunity to establish centres where staff could be recruited with skills and attitudes commensurate with today's philosophy and direction' (Macionis 1992: 7).

The Main Issues and Research Questions

Contracting for imprisonment services raises a number of issues, both normative and empirical. Resolution of the normative questions, posed as either legal or policy issues, turns on choosing values and principles that are to govern practice. Other questions, empirical in nature, can be resolved by observation and, if needed, systematic research.

Is contracting proper?

Probably the central normative issue concerns the proper responsibility of government for imprisonment. In the United States, this has been framed in part as a question of constitutionality: Does government's contracting with private entities for imprisonment conform to the general principles established in the US Constitution? One committee of the American Bar Association has argued that it probably does not: 'there can be no doubt that an attempt to delegate total operational responsibility for a prison or jail would raise grave questions of constitutionality under both the federal Constitution and the constitutions of the fifty states' (American Bar Association 1989). No direct constitutional challenges to private prisons have been brought to the courts, however. Nor are there realistic hopes for such challenges. Since *Carter* v. *Carter Coal Company* (1936), the courts have upheld the federal government's delegation of broad powers to private actors. Delegation by state and local governments has also not been seen to pose federal constitutional issues since the 1920s (Lawrence 1986). Private bail bondsmen's powers to arrest and detain those for whom they have posted bond has been consistently upheld (*Corpus Juris Secundum* undated), as have the detention powers of private security firms (Shearing and Stenning 1981). To be sure, laws in some states regarding private delegation are inconsistent and confusing, so that several legislatures seeking to support privately operated correctional facilities have passed laws explicitly granting these powers.

That private prisons have not been declared unconstitutional does not resolve the question whether delegation of administrative authority over imprisonment is proper and desirable, however. Some have argued that imprisonment is 'intrinsically governmental in nature' (Robbins 1988), but this ignores the historical record. Others argue that governments should retain full and direct control over the administration of criminal justice because not to do so weakens the social compact in a pluralistic society (DiIulio 1990). The contrary view is that what matters most is not the legal status of the service provider—whether public or private employee—but the quality of the service, and whether the service conforms to established standards and law (Logan 1990; McDonald 1990c).

What are the consequences of contracting?

Beyond the question of propriety lie a number of empirical questions. What are the consequences of delegating imprisonment authority to private entities? Are privately operated facilities more efficient (by some measure to be specified) and less costly? If a cost difference is found, from what does it result? Is market provision of imprisonment services inherently more cost-efficient than direct government provision? If there is no inherent superiority, under what conditions are privately operated facilities more efficient or less costly? Are there inherent pressures or incentives for private firms to deliver higher or lower quality services? What are the consequences for inmates of delegating imprisonment administration to private firms? Are prisoners cared for and are their rights safeguarded better or worse than in public facilities? Will public policies be adversely affected by the existence of an organized private imprisonment industry?

Unfortunately, many of these questions have not been studied. Many developments are too recent to have been subjected to systematic evaluation. However, parallel experiences that could be studied profitably have been largely overlooked. For example, much could be learned by studying the private sector's involvement in holding delinquent juveniles and other children in trouble. In both Britain and the United States, the institutions for wayward youths were developed largely by the voluntary charitable organizations in the nineteenth century. Although governments in both countries assumed direct control over many parts of the system (more so in Britain than in the United States), there continue to this day two tracks: privately provided and publicly provided juvenile correctional services (McDonald 1992; Lerman 1982; Rutherford 1990). In the United States, the private sector has grown substantially in recent years; by 1989, 67 per cent of all juvenile correctional facilities were privately operated, and held 42 per cent of all children in custody that year (McDonald 1992). These institutions have been little studied, especially for the purpose of assessing the benefits and costs of public and private management. The same is apparently true in Britain. Rutherford writes that even though the British system for 'youth in trouble' is publicly funded, it remains largely hidden from public view, little information about it is collected systematically, and the number of children being held in it is not even known. (Rutherford 1990: 55–6).

Is private imprisonment less costly?

On this important question, advocates and critics have advanced a number of claims. Proponents of contracting argue that government is inherently inefficient (or, in the less absolute version, tends toward inefficiency), relative to private firms (e.g., President's Commission on Privatization 1988). Some see this as the result of government's 'monopolistic' provision of services, devoid of competition, reinforced by the public manager giving higher value to the expanding power rather than controlling costs or delivering cost-effective services (Stewart 1986; Young 1987). Others argue that the costs are lower and efficiency greater because managers in private facilities have more freedom to manage effectively—that is, without countervailing labour organizations and constraints of negotiated work rules (Tolchin 1985a). Critics argue that contracting is more expensive because the cost to government of contracting and monitoring contracts outweighs any savings that may result (e.g., Keating undated).

Donahue (1990) argues that the technical means of producing the service of imprisonment (consisting largely of people guarding other people) are not susceptible to significant improvements in productivity, so that there is little room for a private firm's cutting costs except by reducing services. The limited labour-saving technologies that do exist (e.g., greater use of electronic monitoring and communications systems) are available to government as well as to private correctional organizations.

Few systematic studies comparing the costs of public and private facilities have been done. These include studies of the privately contracted Ocheechobee School for Boys in Florida (Brown *et al.* 1985), public and private juvenile facilities in the United States (Donahue 1990), a privately operated Hamilton County facility jail in Tennessee (Logan and McGriff 1989), publicly and privately operated detention facilities for illegal immigrants in the United States (McDonald 1990*a*), public and private facilities in Massachusetts and Kentucky (Urban Institute 1989), and the privately operated Borallon centre in Brisbane (Macionis 1992: 22–3).

In the United Kingdom, independent assessments of the relative costs and cost-effectiveness of private imprisonment will be especially difficult because, as mentioned above, financial information is considered proprietary and is kept secret by the government and the firms.

As discussed more fully elsewhere (McDonald 1990*a*, 1992), the findings of several of the published studies of costs are of questionable validity because of inconsistencies and shortcomings in the accounting methodologies employed. Public and private accounting systems are quite different, and the costs that these differing systems identify are not always comparable. For example, public accounts often treat capital expenditures inconsistently, which confuses the estimation of operating costs. Whereas private firms typically include in their operating costs the depreciated value of the physical assets employed, governments rarely know the value of their standing assets, and cannot estimate a comparable cost of capital. Moreover, private accounting procedures are designed for the purpose of cost analysis, whereas public accounting systems are designed to control expenditures of appropriated public funds and to identify unwarranted expenditures, including fraud. Using public accounts to estimate costs of public services is difficult because the costs of a discrete service such as imprisonment are often borne by different agencies or government accounts (departments of utilities, health, transportation, employee retirement benefits, etc.). Using expenditures by the correctional agency alone may consequently underrepresent the true cost. Costs measured on a per inmate basis are also misleading if facilities differ in their utilization rates, suggesting that crowded facilities appear less costly to operate than less crowded ones— which may affect the public/private comparison (McDonald 1980, 1989; Wayson and Funke 1989: Clear, Harris, and Record, 1982). Because so few of the studies have conducted a rigorous and comparable accounting of both public and private costs, it is premature to conclude that we know much about the relative cost advantages of privately-operated facilities.

Further experience with private imprisonment services and systematic studies of those experiences will probably show that there is no inherent superiority of contracting, in terms of cost-effectiveness, but that certain privately operated facilities may be more cost-effective than the available public alternatives. The comparative advantage that a private firm will have probably depends upon the conditions found in the public agency that would operate the facility in the absence of contracting. For example, some

41

jails run in the United States by incompetent and independently elected sheriffs may be operated more cost-effectively by contracted firms, but one cannot assume that this will be true for all jails. Where inefficient work rules or practices prevail in publicly-operated facilities, and where the constraints on eliminating them are powerful, private firms may have a distinct advantage, especially if they employ unorganized labour. (This advantage may diminish if employees of private firms organize, however.)

Do profit-seeking firms provide poorer services?

A frequent argument is that the principal incentives operating in profit-seeking private firms work to keep costs at a minimum, which is most readily accomplished by diminishing services or the quality of those services (American Bar Association 1986: 4). However, at least in the early stages of contracting, there appear to be certain disincentives to diminish services: if performance falls below agreed-upon standards in those 'showcase' facilities, firms risk losing contracts and clients. Some managers also argue that cutting services creates morale problems among both inmates and staffs and makes facilities more difficult to manage (Rees 1987). For whatever reason, studies of facilities operated by private firms in recent years have generally reported finding good conditions and services, relative to the public facilities (Logan 1991; Urban Institute 1989; Green undated).

Are prisoners' rights diminished or jeopardized?

One obvious worry is that prisoners' rights and welfare will be sacrificed if they conflict with the pursuit of private profit. Even if private firms agree to respect established rights, it is feared the exercise of these rights will be curtailed. Because prisons are so hidden from public view, the likelihood of detecting such violations is low, and prisoners are relatively powerless to bring attention to their grievances. (This is not unique to private prisons, however, for the actions of public officials managing prisons are kept from public view with nearly equal ease.)

Although these concerns are real, private imprisonment is not likely to be a reprise of the nineteenth century private prisons and jails, at least in the United States. The principle is well established that what matters with respect to supporting prisoners' various rights are the actions of the prison officials, and whether they conform to the existing law and standards, and not the name on the officials' shoulder patch. Moreover, the courts have stepped in and established prisoners' rights, have set standards for prisons and prison officials to meet, and in some instances have hired private individuals ('special masters') to monitor the prison administration's compliance with court orders. To increase further the monitoring of conditions and the operators' compliance with law and standards, several institutional arrangements recommend themselves. These include establishing independent ombudsmen in the private prisons, grievance procedures—including independent grievance and disciplinary boards, and putting full-time government monitors in the private facilities. Procedures for protecting prisoners' rights can also be written into the contract, so that failure to uphold them can be termed a violation of the contract.

PUBLIC IMPRISONMENT BY PRIVATE MEANS

Has a 'penal-industrial complex' captured policy making?

Some observers have argued that the emergence of private imprisonment firms is hastening the development of an unhealthy alliance of private/public interests resembling the military-industrial complex. Schoen (1985) warns that private operators, whose business opportunities derive from the shortfall of cell space relative to demand, may provide influential support for 'get tough' sentencing policies that heighten the demand for prisons and jails. Lilly and Knepper (1992) note further that the real money in the corrections industry is being made not by private prison operators but by firms that supply goods and services to corrections agencies, and conclude that 'the corrections-commercial complex operates without public scrutiny and exercises enormous influence over corrections policy'. Moreover, observing that these firms are increasingly marketing their wares outside the United States, they see a 'correctional-policy imperialism' at work, whereby 'First World nations' are finding 'another means to increase their control over the future of punishment in Third World nations'.

Using the terms 'imperialism', 'subgovernments', and 'military-industrial complexes', Lilly and Knepper paint a picture in which public correctional and penal policy making is distorted—and even captured—by private interests. However, this is a misreading of public–private dynamics in the United States, at least—the only country I know well. There is no evidence that private firms have had any influence over the key decisions that have created the booming prisoner populations. Sentencing laws began to get tougher in the early 1970s for a number of reasons, including a turn away from civil commitment of drug abusers toward one that relied on tough criminal sanctions, growing public fears of crime, and the discovery by political leaders that being tough on crime was an effective strategy for getting elected. Moreover, a key strategy among Republican Party leaders seeking to attract conservative Democratic voters into the Republican tent was to focus attention on social and cultural issues rather than economic ones. Coming on the heels of widespread turmoil in the United States—with the civil rights and black power movements, student unrest, and a popular uprising against the Government's war in Vietnam—calls for 'law and order' became very effective political tools. Contemporary penal policy in the United States was thus forged in the course of a political and policy battle, in which self-interested private correctional interests have played no significant role.

To be sure, businesses have made money from this growing industry, as they have from all large-scale, capital-intensive government programmes. Governments themselves do not manufacture goods, and many businesses have emerged to provide needed services. There has also been a movement of personnel between private firms and public correctional policy making positions (e.g., Sir Edward Gardiner left Parliament to join a private imprisonment firm), but this does not in and of itself indicate that *sentencing* policy is being distorted by private interests. Where private firms are more likely to affect government decision making is in the choice of public or private provision of correctional services. Private firms have been aggressive in lobbying governments to convert at least some of their public operations to privately contracted ones. Where governments have to be careful is to avoid becoming too dependent upon private provision. Strategies to minimize the risks of this include government retaining ownership of existing correctional facilities, and contracting only for management of new ones—because firms that establish themselves with physical assets in a particular

43

jurisdiction may develop an unbeatable edge over potential competitors in future contract competitions.

The Challenges to Public Administration

The likely outcome of current developments is that correctional systems will probably not be wholly public or wholly private, and that public imprisonment responsibilities will be delivered by differing mixes of private firms and public agencies. At least in the United Kingdom and the United States, interest in introducing market mechanisms such as contracting into more command-oriented public administration will probably survive changes in governing parties. The issue of whether imprisonment operations should be delegated to private contractors will certainly remain controversial, however, because the intersection between state power and individual liberty is felt most sharply in prisons, jails, and other detention centres. Not surprisingly, views about private imprisonment services are most closely linked to deeper political values, which makes it difficult to resolve the public policy debate about contracting. However, knowing more about the actual experiences and consequences of contracting will go a long way toward identifying the most desirable combinations of public and private responsibilities and interests.

There are, I think, three principal challenges to public policy that are posed by private imprisonment firms, all of which deserve the attention of the research community. The first is to devise procedures to assure that prisoners' rights and welfare are protected (which is, of course, a challenge in publicly-operated prisons and jails as well). This is not a difficult task, and there are well-developed models to follow. Learning about the effectiveness of these models in privately operated prisons should be a high priority for research.

The second challenge is to prevent governments' dependence upon private firms, and especially upon entrenched suppliers. Ideally, one might accomplish this by governments creating conditions that engender competition among firms rather than monopolistic dominance by a few giants. (Privatization does not necessarily create a competitive environment.) Precisely how this can be done is difficult to prescribe, as the future shape of a mature private imprisonment industry is not yet known. Current experience offers a relatively wide array of cases to learn from, which are characterized by varying combinations of large and small jurisdictions, centralized and decentralized (or fragmented) correctional systems, differences in scope of contracts (including whether facilities are owned or only operated by contractors), and different contracting arrangements.

The third challenge is to protect the integrity of government procurement processes—one that is faced in nearly all areas of public administration. To the extent that new knowledge needs to be developed here, looking beyond corrections to those other areas of administration is likely to be profitable.

REFERENCES

ADAM SMITH INSTITUTE (1984), *The Omega Justice Report*. London: Adam Smith Institute.
AMERICAN BAR ASSOCIATION (1986), *Report to the House of Delegates*, unpublished document. Chicago: American Bar Association.

—— (1989), *Report to the House of Delegates*, unpublished document dated February 13. Chicago: American Bar Association.

AMERICAN CORRECTIONAL ASSOCIATION (1991), *Directory*. Laurel, MD: American Correctional Association.

AMERICAN FEDERATION OF STATE, COUNTY, AND MUNICIPAL EMPLOYEES (AFSME) AFL-CIO (1984), *Passing the Bucks: The Contracting Out of Public Services*. American Federation of State, County and Municipal Employees, AFL-CIO.

BERNAT, B. (1991), American Civil Liberties Union, National Prison Project. Personal communication with author, 27 September.

BIVENS, T. (1986), 'Can Prisons for Profit Work?', *Philadelphia Inquirer Magazine*, 3 August.

BOWMAN, G. W., HAKIM S., and SEIDENSTAT, P., eds (1992), *Privatizing the United States Justice System: Police, Adjudication, and Corrections Services from the Private Sector*. Jefferson, NC: McFarland and Company.

BRONICK, M. J. (1989), 'The Federal Bureau of Prisons' Experience with Privatization', unpublished paper. Washington, DC: US Bureau of Prisons.

BROWN A., GERARD, R., HOWARD, R., KENNEDY, W., LEVINSON, R., SELL, C., SKELTON, P., and QUAY, H. (1985), *Private Sector Operation of a Correctional Institution: A Study of the Jack and Ruth Eckerd Youth Development Center, Okeechobee, Florida*. Washington, DC: National Institute of Corrections.

BUREAU OF JUSTICE STATISTICS (1991), *Prisoners in 1990*. Washington, DC: US Department of Justice, Bureau of Justice Statistics.

Carter v. Carter Coal Company (1936), 298 US 238.

CHAIKEN, J., and MENNEMEYER, S. (1987), *Lease-Purchase Financing of Prison and Jail Construction*. Washington, DC: National Institute of Justice.

CLARKE, K. (1992), 'Prisoners with Private Means', *The Independent*, 22 December.

CLEAR, T., HARRIS, P., and RECORD, A. (1982), 'Managing the Cost of Corrections', *The Prison Journal*, 62.

COATES, R. B., MILLER, A. D., and OHLIN, L. E. (1978), *Diversity in a Youth Correctional System: Handling Delinquents in Massachusetts*. Cambridge, MA: Ballinger Publishing Company.

Corpus Juris Secundum (undated), vol. 8, section 87. St Paul, MN: West Publishing Company.

CORRECTIONS CORPORATION OF AMERICA (1985), *Proposal for State of Tennessee*. Nashville, TN: Corrections Corporation of America.

—— (1992), 'CCA Wins First British Prison Contract,' press release, 8 December. Nashville, TN: Corrections Corporation of America.

CORRECTIONS CORPORATION OF AUSTRALIA (1992), *Borallon Correctional Centre*. Ipswich, Queensland: Corrections Corporation of Australia.

CREW, A. (1933), *London Prisons of Today and Yesterday*. London: I. Nicholson and Waston.

DELOITTE, HASKINS and SELLS (1989), 'A Report to the Home Office on the Practicality of Private Sector Involvement in the Remand System', unpublished document.

DiIULIO, J. J. (1990), 'The Duty to Govern: A Critical Perspective on the Private Management of Prisons and Jails', in D. C. McDonald, ed., *Private Prisons and the Public Interest*. New Brunswick, NJ: Rutgers University Press.

DONAHUE, J. D. (1990), *The Privatization Decision*. New York: Basic Books.

FEELEY, M. M. (1991), 'Privatization of Prisons in Historical Perspective'. In W. Gormley, ed., *Privatization and its Alternatives*. Madison, WI: University of Wisconsin Press.

FORD, R. (1992), 'Private Prison Firms Start Brain Drain from Public Sector', *The Times*, 24 December.

GILL, L. F. (1992), 'Private Sector Involvement in the Prison System of England and Wales', unpublished paper delivered at Australian Institute of Criminology Conference, Wellington, New Zealand, 30 Nov.–2 Dec. 1992.

—— (1993), Home Office Remand Contracts Units. Private communication with author on 4 January.

GREEN, P. (undated), *Private Sector Involvement in the Immigrant Detention Centres*. London: The Howard League for Penal Reform.

HARDING, R. (1992), 'Private Prisons in Australia', *Trends and Issues in Crime and Criminology*. Canberra: Australian Institute of Criminology.

HM PRISON SERVICE (1992), *Briefing* 54, 10 November.

—— (1993*a*), 'In House Team to Run Manchester Prison', News release, 15 July.

—— (1993*b*), 'Michael Howard Unveils Plan for More Private Sector Involvement in the Prison Service', News release, 2 September.

HMSO (1988) *Private Sector Involvement in the Remand System*, Cm. 434.

HOLDSWORTH, W. S. (1992–4), *A History of English Law*, vol. 4, 3rd edn. London: Cambridge University Press.

HOME AFFAIRS COMMITTEE (1987), *Contract Provision of Prisons, Fourth Report of the Home Affairs Committee*. HC 291.

HOME OFFICE (1990) 'Court Escorts, Custody and Security: A Discussion Paper'. London: Home Office.

—— (1992), 'Tender Documents for the Operating Contract of HM Prison Manchester', Schedule 2: Outline Brief. London: Home Office.

HOWARD LEAGUE FOR PENAL REFORM (1990), 'Private Sector Involvement in the Remand System: The Howard League Response to the Discussion Paper "Court Escorts, Custody and Security" '. London: The Howard League for Penal Reform.

HUGHES, R. (1987). *The Fatal Shore*. New York: Alfred A. Knopf.

IMMARIGEON, R. (1987), 'Privatizing Adult Imprisonment in the US: A Bibliography', *Criminal Justice Abstracts*, vol. 19, pp. 136–9.

JOINT COUNCIL FOR THE WELFARE OF IMMIGRANTS (1988), *Annual Report 1988*.

JOINT STATE GOVERNMENT COMMISSION (1987), 'Report of the Private Prison Task Force'. Harrisburg, PA: General Assembly of the Commonwealth of Pennsylvania.

KEATING, M. J. (undated), *Seeking Profit in Punishment: The Private Management of Correctional Institutions*. Washington, DC: American Federation of State, County and Municipal Employees.

KENNEDY, J. J. (1988), *Final Report of the Commission of Review into Corrective Services in Queensland*. Brisbane: State Government Printer.

LAWRENCE, D. (1986), 'Private Exercise of Governmental Power', *Indiana Law Journal*, 61: 649.

LEGISLATIVE RESEARCH COUNCIL, COMMONWEALTH OF MASSACHUSETTS (1986), *Prisons for Profit*. Boston: Legislative Research Council, Commonwealth of Massachusetts.

LEONARD, H. B. (1986), *Checks Unbalanced: The Quiet Side of Public Spending*. New York: Basic Books.

—— (1990), 'Private Time: The Political Economy of Private Prison Finance', in D. McDonald, ed., *Private Prisons and the Public Interest*. New Brunswick, NJ: Rutgers University Press.

LERMAN, P. (1982), *Deinstitutionalization and the Welfare State*. New Brunswick, NJ: Rutgers University Press.

LILLY, J. R., and KNEPPER, P. (1992), 'An International Perspective on the Privatisation of Corrections', *The Howard Journal*, 31/3: 174–91.

Logan, C. H. (1990), *Private Prisons: Cons and Pros*. New York: Oxford University Press.

—— (1991), *Well Kept: Comparing Quality of Confinement in a Public and a Private Prison*. Washington, DC: Report to the National Institute of Justice.

Logan, C. H., and McGriff, B. W. (1989), 'Comparing Costs of Public and Private Prisons: A Case Study', *NIJ Reports*, 216: 2–8.

Logan, C. H. and Rausch, S. (1985), 'Punish and Profit: The Emergence of Private Enterprise Prisons', *Justice Quarterly* 2: 303–18.

Macionis, S. (1992), 'Contract Management in Corrections: The Queensland Experience', unpublished paper written for a conference, 'The Private Sector and Community Involvement in the Criminal Justice System', in Wellington, New Zealand, 30 Nov.–2 Dec. 1992.

McConville, S., and Williams, J. E. H. (1985), *Crime and Punishment: A Radical Rethink*. London: Tawney Society.

McDonald, D. C. (1980), *The Price of Punishment: Public Spending for Corrections in New York*. Boulder, CO: Westview Press.

—— (1989), *The Cost of Corrections: In Search of the Bottom Line*. Washington, DC: US Department of Justice, National Institute of Corrections.

—— (1990a), 'The Costs of Operating Public and Private Correctional Facilities', in D. C. McDonald, ed., *Private Prisons and the Public Interest*. New Brunswick, NJ: Rutgers University Press.

—— (1990b), ed., *Private Prisons and the Public Interest*. New Brunswick, NJ: Rutgers University Press.

—— (1990c), 'When Government Fails: Going Private as a Last Resort', in D. C. McDonald, ed., *Private Prisons and the Public Interest*. New Brunswick, NJ: Rutgers University Press.

—— (1992), 'Private Penal Institutions: Moving the Boundary of Government Authority in Corrections', in M. Tonry, ed., *Crime and Justice: An Annual Review of Research*. Chicago: University of Chicago Press.

McKelvey, B. (1977), *American Prisons: A History of Good Intentions*. Montclair, NJ: Patterson Smith.

Miller, A. D., Ohlin, L. E., and Coates, R. B. (1977), *A Theory of Social Reform: Correctional Change Processes in Two States*. Cambridge: Ballinger Publishing Company.

Mullen, J. (1985), 'Correction and the Private Sector', *Privatization Review* 1: 12.

Mullen, J., Chabotar, K., and Carrow, D. (1984), *The Privatization of Corrections*. Washington, DC: National Institute of Justice.

National Institute of Justice (1987), *Contracting for the Operation of Prisons and Jails*. Washington DC: US Department of Justice.

National Criminal Justice Statistics Association (1987), *Private Sector Involvement in Financing and Managing Correctional Facilities*. Washington, DC: National Criminal Justice Statistics Association.

O'Hare, M., Leone, R., and Zeagans, M. (1990), 'The Privatization of Imprisonment: A Managerial Perspective', in D. C. McDonald, ed., *Private Prisons and the Public Interest*. New Brunswick, NJ: Rutgers University Press.

Peterson, J. (1988), *Corrections and the Private Sector: A National Forum*, proceedings of a conference. Washington, DC: National Institute of Justice.

President's Commission on Privatization (1988), *Privatization: Toward More Effective Government*. Washington, DC: The White House.

Press, A. (1990), 'The Good, the Bad, and the Ugly: Private Prisons in the 1980s'. in D. C.

McDonald, ed., *Private Prisons and the Public Interest*. New Brunswick, NJ: Rutgers University Press.

REES, J. (1987), private communication with author. (Mr Rees was the chief manager of the Correctional Corporation of America's staff at the Santa Fe County jail.)

ROBBINS, I. P. (1988), *The Legal Dimensions of Private Incarceration*. Washington, DC: American Bar Association.

RUTHERFORD, A. (1990), 'British Penal Policy and the Idea of Prison Privatization'. in D. C. McDonald, ed., *Private Prisons and the Public Interest*. New Brunswick, NJ: Rutgers University Press.

SCHEARING, C. D., and STENNING, P. C. (1981), 'Modern Private Security: Its Growth and Implications'. *Crime and Justice: An Annual Review*. Chicago: University of Chicago Press.

SCHOEN, K. (1985), 'Private Prison Operators', *The New York Times*, 28 March.

STEWART, J. K. (1986), 'Costly Prisons: Should the Public Monopoly Be Ended?', in P. B. McGuigan and J. S. Pascale, eds, *Crime and Punishment in Modern America*. Washington, DC: The Institute for Government and Politics of the Free Congress Research and Education Foundation, pp. 365–88.

TAYLOR, M., and PEASE, K. (1987) Unpublished document, later published in R. Matthews, *Privatizing Criminal Justice*. London: Sage.

TOLCHIN, M. (1985*a*), 'Prisons for Profit: Nashville's CCA Claims Operations Aid Government'. *The Tennessean*, 24 Feb.

—— (1985*b*), 'Private Concern Makes Offer to Run Tennessee's Prisons', *New York Times*, 13 Sept.

—— (1985*c*), 'Experts Foresee Adverse Effects from Private Control of Prisons', *New York Times*, 17 Sept.

US HOUSE OF REPRESENTATIVES (1986), *Privatization of Corrections: Hearings Before the Subcommittee on Courts, Civil Liberties, and the Administration of Justice of the Committee of the Judiciary, House of Representatives, Ninety-Ninth Congress, First and Second Sessions on Privatization of Corrections, November 13, 1985 and March 18, 1986*. Washington, DC: US Government Printing Office.

URBAN INSTITUTE (1989), *Comparison of Privately and Publicly Operated Corrections Facility in Kentucky and Massachusetts*. Washington, DC: Report to the National Institute of Justice.

WAYSON, B. L., and FUNKE, G. S. (1989), *What Price Justice? A Handbook for the Analysis of Criminal Justice Costs*. Washington, DC: US Department of Justice, National Institute of Justice.

YOUNG, P. (1987), *The Prison Cell*. London: The Adam Smith Institute.

THE NEW PENOLOGY AND POLITICS IN CRISIS

The Italian Case

Massimo Pavarini*

An Overview of Comparative Statistics: The Italian Penitentiary 'Paradise'

Italy of the four mafia organizations ('Cosa Nostra' in Sicily, 'Ndrangheta' in Calabria, 'Camorra' in Campania, and 'Nuova Corona Unita' in Puglie—roughly a quarter of the nation in the hands of organized crime); Italy of administrative corruption and political scandals on an endemic scale; Italy with the largest number of heroin addicts after the USA; Italy of bloodshed by Fascists and left-wing terrorists; Italy in which the Codes dating back to Mussolini's era are still in force, providing the possibility of draconian prison sentences for the most minor offence. This is the criminal and penal Italy which has had one of the lowest prison populations in Europe over the last 20 years. This state of affairs changed radically in the early nineties.

On 1 September 1988 the imprisonment rate per 100,000 inhabitants was 60.4 in Italy, 75.8 in Spain, 81.1 in France, 84.9 in Germany, and 96.7 in the United Kingdom (Council of Europe 1990: 6). The only European nations with lower imprisonment rates were Cyprus, Iceland, Holland, Norway, and Sweden—countries which for a number of reasons are difficult to compare with Italy. The year chosen, 1988, was certainly not one of the best in terms of prison population in Italy. There were already over 34,000 prisoners that year, whereas the seventies average was below 30,000, with nadirs which even fell to 20,000 (ISTAT 1991). An even more remarkable insight into the Italian prison situation emerges for minors. For the same year, 1988, there were only 1.4 juveniles imprisoned per 100,000—the lowest in Europe (Council of Europe 1990: 7); around 17 times lower than the United Kingdom (23.8 per 100,000).

As these relatively low rates of imprisonment are not related to the positive effects of typical decarceration strategies (such as de-penalisation policy, and/or diversion, and/or alternatives to imprisonment), the atypical status of the Italian prison situation must be seen to be even more singular. From this standpoint the Italian penal system of justice lags far behind its European neighbours (Dolcini and Paliero 1988). There is still no significant process of diversion for adult deviancy. The last 20 years have seen a growing increase in the number of new penal regulations enacted and in the severity of punishment. Alternative measures have been constantly under-implemented (Di Lazzaro 1988: 27–40).

These few figures give a good idea of how atypical has been the state of penal affairs in Italy. I shall attempt to root out the underlying causes for this, but shall first outline

* Professor of Penology, Faculty of Law, University of Bologna.

This essay is a reflection on some of the aspects which have emerged from an ongoing research project on 'Sentencing in the Executive Stage', co-ordinated by Giuseppe Mosconi and Massimo Pavarini, and 60 per cent funded by the Ministry of Justice for the years 1991 and 1992. Anne Collins translated the text.

how that historical stage appears to have come to an end. Whether it is over for good I do not know, but one thing is certain; from 1990 onwards the growth rate in the prison population had pushed the total over the threshold of 50,000 prisoners by the end of January 1993. If this trend continues, with an increase of roughly 1,500 prisoners a month,[1] Italy will reach the current imprisonment rates of the United Kingdom in little over a year. This sudden turnabout in events warrants some explanation.

A Prince Paying Lip-service to Severity, an Indulgent Judge, and a Populace 'Distracted' by Politics

The Italian criminal justice system is characterized by unusually severe sanctions. This reflects both the authoritarian legal system of the thirties, which is still in force, and subsequent democratic legislation (offering ad hoc solutions to numerous emergencies), which has further raised the threshold of punishment. However, the adoption of a particularly severe criminal policy at the level of primary criminalization has always been contradicted—even, in part, during the Fascist era (Neppi Modona and Violante 1978)—by particularly lenient, if not openly indulgent, judicial and administrative strategies; that is, in the area of secondary criminalization (Dolcini 1991: 47–92).

To some extent, the very existence of a severe legislation lacking political legitimacy (since it was the offspring of fascism), has fostered the process of leniency in sentencing and enforcing legal punishment in the democratic era. The penal system has thus been constantly attacked for not being in tune with the new liberal-democratic culture, and there have been frequent calls for reform. For one reason or another, the reform has never come about (Marinucci 1981: 297–318), and only partial adjustments have been made to the penal, procedural, and penitentiary laws.

The lack of penal reform, which some have now deemed 'impossible' (Stortoni 1981: 273–80; Marra et al. 1981: 249–72), after nearly half a century of failures, has rendered virtually legitimate widespread practices of 'softening' the implementation of penal sanctions. With very few exceptions, the judicial authorities have constantly applied only the minimum sentences provided by the law, with an almost automatic use of suspended sentences and conditional discharge (Dolcini 1991: 47–91). Moreover the post-war legislator, unable to reform criminal law and often under pressure to exacerbate its severity, has resorted to generous provision for amnesty and indulgence (every three years on average), further curbing the levels of penal repression (Mazza-cuva 1983).

I do not, however, think that the explanation lies simply in the antinomy between the severe law and a lenient repressive application, since it is well known that 'law in fact' has little in common with 'law in books'. I am rather inclined to see it as a situation offering the structural conditions for an excessive severity merely in words and a paternalistic indulgence in practice. The exaggerated recourse to criminal law must be construed in the light of the qualitative changes made to the legal system (also) as a result of the welfare state, particularly the ensuing development of state intervention in the interests (and aim) of penal action (Delmas-Marty 1985: 165).

This mistake has long pervaded critical appraisals of the legal transformations in the changeover from a state of law to the social state, and the literature is well known (Uger

[1] This information was officially confirmed by the office responsible for the Institutions of Prevention and Punishment of the Ministry of Justice in several press conferences recently reported in the daily newspapers.

1976; Groll 1985; Mussgnug 1984). I shall be brief on this point. From being an instrument protecting a natural order, criminal law becomes an instrument to bolster an artificial order in the social state's process of monopolizing the penal resource. The monopoly was achieved in the artificial creation of what is penally protected—when what is penally protected belongs to the state insofar as it was artificially created by the same. But often lacking any social and cultural counterpart, such monopoly is proffered only as 'organization', merely 'regulations' governing a given social action (Sgubbi 1990). Being formulated as 'technical rules', penal regulations, in Lascoumes's words, bring about 'technological public orders' (Lascoumes 1986: 301).

From a structural standpoint a significant evolution has taken place. Insofar as what is protected by criminal law is turned into a public aim, the law becomes a 'public resource', which as such cannot be the 'object of political exchange'. Penal law falls into the category of so-called goods of authority—those being goods which, according to the procedures of the neo-corporative model, are the object of bargaining between the public authorities, on the one hand, and organized social groups, on the other (Rose 1984). This collective bargaining of penality, aimed at a social distribution of punishment, is carried out in a neo-contractualist context, where the strongest tries to grab the largest possible share of this public resource. In so doing, the strongest penalizes the conduct of others, and tries to make its own actions immune, thus producing an unequal distribution of punishment.

Penal law has thus become an element within social conflict, constituting rules which support and confirm the contractual-institutional power of collective social individuals and organized interest groups (Savelsberg 1987: 529). This 'artificial distribution' of penal immunity and liability is therefore one aspect of the 'political distribution' of social wealth in the broad sense, the contingent outcome of social conflict, which will thus allocate penalty in society in relation to such outcome.

Just as this process explains why the sphere of criminal offence has widened, it also accounts for the relative lack of influence this expansion has had on effective levels of repression. In other words, the effective levels of repression have proved to bear little relation to the unequal allocation of an artificial punishment in society. Rather, they depend on social demands for repression, that is, social demands for greater or lesser punishment. Here lies the peculiarity of the Italian situation; in actual fact the demand for punishment at the social level has long been weak. Social conflict and crisis—key features of recent Italian history—have not been turned into equally strong social demands for punishment. Recurrent 'law and order' campaigns promoted by conservative political forces, and often a source of fear, have always yielded poor results in terms of spreading social panic.

The reasons which have long hampered the socio-economic cycle from producing social changes in the punitive lexicon, aimed at raising the threshold of eligibility for punishment, are complex and have seldom been addressed (Melossi 1988). Why, in other words, until recently did people not fall easy prey to widespread manifestations of insecurity from crime, despite being no materially better off than others who have experienced this fear elsewhere at different times? What for so long stopped people adopting the view that the criminal question was one of the most serious and urgent problems to be solved by means of repression? Briefly, I will summarize some of these 'strong reasons', but with no claim to being exhaustive, or to having grasped the full complexity of the issue.

In the first place, there is a strong and widely held social perception of crime as a political question. This has been bolstered not only by a Marxist cultural tradition, but above all by its politics—in no way comparable to the situation of other western countries—of left-wing parties often ambiguously oscillating between reform and revolution. The Italian left has never taken a benevolent attitude to crime. On the contrary, the left was often the first to pinpoint the need to fight criminals as the worst 'enemies of the state and the working class' (Ingrao 1975: 508–14). Yet they seldom invoked the strategy of penal repression, opting for policies of integration of the socially deprived, hence including criminals, in the struggle for political renewal and social change. It can be argued that this invitation to collective protest to change an unequal society, instead of struggling individually, and unlawfully, against an unjust society, is rhetorical to say the least. But it did foster a widespread social culture able to think of the crime question as an issue to be solved by politics rather than by penal repression.

This is further confirmed by the fact that in Italy the question of crime has long been aligned with the 'southern question', a political issue par excellence. Southerners in Italian prisons are like blacks in American penitentiaries: they constitute the over-whelming majority and suffer the worst conditions. The as yet unresolved problem of a backward south, economically and socially ever further divided from its centre-north counterpart means that there are, in fact, 'two Italys'. Indeed the problem may well have become a selection criterion in penal repression in which class variables have ended up coinciding with cultural and geographical factors, further dividing civil society between a 'legal Italy' in the north, and a 'criminal Italy' in the south. Beyond a doubt, this has collectively been construed as placing the legitimacy of the political system as a whole, and the penal system in particular, at risk.

This is a good reason to opt for an unemotional approach to the question of crime, in which the historical-political extent of the issue has always held sway, even in social manifestations. Another underlying reason is the widespread social perception, especi-ally among the lower classes, of the penal justice system as a violent means of preserving an unequal society. I doubt whether what Young calls the 'easy-going ideology of the working class' (Young 1981; 141–73) has ever produced such a deep-rooted demorali-zation in other contemporary societies as it has in Italy. This is underscored by a conflictual concept of law, which has long been taken as a paradigmatic model which also serves to interpret crime.

In the Italian national context, the very concept of social control has never been fully assimilated, as it has in England and Wales and the USA. In Italian culture a conflictual political paradigm persists which construes problems of social order in terms of domination, hegemony—in a word, power (Pitch 1989: 14). The dichotomy of this perception is that it embodies a twofold vision of the social system which it resists and counteracts; the criminal is put on a par with the resistance fighter against those in power. In this sense, the very concept of control is tantamount to coercion, in which the criminal justice system constitutes a paradigm of social order. In extreme terms, a conception of political crime is more in keeping with Italian culture than one of social crime, unlike the situation in other national contexts. Finally, the events of political terrorism and the long struggle of repression played a key role in the seventies and the early eighties. Both these processes further reinforced the political perception of crime and the criminal justice system in the mind of Italian civil society.

Quite different from the turn of events in Germany, for example, 'red terrorism' in

Italy was socially construed as an all too understandable phenomenon in its politico-cultural roots, and by no means irrational. In short, it was something that was rooted in the history and culture of the left, so much so that the feats, proclamations, and actions of the proselytes of armed politics were reminiscent of the 'family album' of a recent national past. The response to terrorism was vigorous, forceful, and in the end, victorious for both state and civil society. But it was a political reaction even when it made use of the criminal justice system. The level of widespread social conscience seldom absorbed the image of the terrorist as a blood-thirsty criminal (Grossi 1985: 309–34; Mosconi 1985: 335–44), despite the fact that the struggle against terrorism led to marked social cohesion.

For all these reasons antibodies of resistance to the system of penal repression have long been present in Italy. A diffident culture, prone to suspicion, has been more concerned about the perils of repressive agencies than the perils of criminality. From the university law faculties, where criminal law has long been taught as the 'magna carta of the criminal' rather than the 'honest citizen', to the emergence in the late seventies of a minority, but politically radical, left-wing magistracy; from cultural movements in support of a 'minimum criminal law' (Baratta 1985; Ferrajoli 1989) to prompt reports by the mass media of the constant risk of criminal repression of political dissent; and of course the protest over the infernal prison conditions by political and social movements—all this contrived to keep the legitimacy level of the penal system at a very low ebb, if not at crisis point, and consequently to curb the repressive system's productivity. A low imprisonment rate was one of the numerous effects of this process.

As a whole these complex reasons reveal the singular political and cultural status of Italian history. For many years, collective feelings of insecurity in Italy, unlike other nations, were vented in a political demand for change and enhanced democratic participation. In other words, via the lexicon of politics, social communication fostered in itself an attitude of conflict and unrest well beyond the moral categories of guilt and punishment. The reason behind this attitude is partly borne out by the current situation. Given the crisis of the politico-cultural model of the past, we are faced with an unrestrained flood of moral indignation, inclined to delegate the solution to every problem to the 'sword of justice'. As if any battle could be won by identifying an enemy and a legal punishment, ever increasing levels of punishment are invoked socially and sanctioned institutionally.

More punishment, like more morality, is the magic misunderstanding of every moral crusade against crime. The moral question has thus escaped the sphere of politics—socially discredited as immoral—to be sublimated in the symbolic exercise of allotting liability by increasing the punishment. Since the late 1980s the situation has changed, and I shall return to that later. Now, I shall pinpoint the changes inflicted in the interim on what Garland (1985) calls punishment in welfare: Italian prisons.

Decarceration and Social Control Strategies in the Seventies and Eighties

The Italian 'decarceration' process reflects the general Western trend of social control policies to reduce the amount of time spent in gaol (Cohen 1985a: 5–48, 1985b). The most widely shared traditional interpretation of this process ascribes a major role to the crisis of legitimacy of imprisonment in response to crime (Pavarini 1983: 1–45). I am inclined to think that the obsolescence of the practice of imprisonment lies in the global change in conditions heralding the various social control policies. It is in these that institutional survival has gradually changed within the disciplinary strategy favourable to social integration rather than exclusion (Lea 1979: 217–35).

Of course, detention in Italy as elsewhere retains an unsuppressible but different function within this disciplinary system. Prison loses its—albeit justificatory—rehabilitative function to become increasingly radical as an extreme response; a deterrent or means of incapacitating those deviants for whom the 'soft' social control system has proved inadequate, if not abortive (Pavarini 1985: 31–42). In institutional practice, this process is seen in the diverging tendencies of an enhanced 'flight' from imprisonment. This is accompanied by a persistent resistance to prison increasingly attracted to maximum security options for all those defined as 'dangerous', for the very reason of having been abandoned by the network of welfare and rehabilitation services (Pavarini 1978: 39–61; Pitch 1989).

The two phenomena, crisis of the segregation paradigm and non-segregational social control, are implicitly related. What is not implicit is that there exists a causal mechanism between the two. The crisis of the custody model therefore reflects the fact that prisons no longer occupied a central role in criminal policies. Faced with this step backwards by the threshold of carceration in terms of quality rather than quantity (Ruggiero 1991: 127–41; Matthews 1987: 15), systems of social discipline 'outside the walls' of prison started to emerge (Pavarini 1986: 251–87).

Otherwise defined, the process I have described came into play in a period of de-institutionalization, and one in which conflict and problem situations were being subjected to social control policies involving new solutions and different strategies of settlement. In the Italian context, this process interfered with the administrative decentralization of social policies from central government to local authorities (regions, provinces, municipal councils, and city districts) (Nascetti 1983). This process also brought another series of problems to the forefront, and I shall mention these briefly albeit summarily.

One problem can be summed up as follows. The more detention alone proved inadequate (and hence the more this option lost weight compared to other strategies of control), the more imprisonment tended to develop a radically different function with respect to its original purpose. In other words, the survival of the original hard control strategies became attenuated in relation to new soft control alternatives (Pavarini 1978: 39–61; Ruggiero 1991: 127–41). This further process has been repeatedly defined as a 'scissor-like opening' or the game of Chinese boxes (Cohen 1978: 44–62). Together, these metaphors illustrate the formal implementation of social control strategies between minimum and maximum coercion in which hard control (usually segregation) is justified by the need for 'differentiated security'.

Heuristically, these metaphors are confined to one key feature; differentiation constitutes a function in the move from institutional control to control in the community. In fact, those categories of criminal actually exposed to soft social discipline are those whose behaviour suggests they are appropriate for 'being taken into care' and 'helped', rather than being in need of simple control. By contrast, the 'dangerous' category serves to select the deviant in relation to an array of more severe disciplinary measures (De Leonardis 1985: 323–50).

54

Some leitmotifs emerge. In Italy too, social control tends to expand as a direct result of the growth in the welfare state, in which welfare policies will be the first to multiply. Yet as soft discipline worries tend to accrue, there will be a parallel increase in the situations not considered 'deserving', i.e., not eligible for this solution. If the mouth of the disciplinary funnel widens, more problem situations will end up passing through its neck. Hence, segregation not only survives, but totally absorbs the control function of social control as the extremity of the disciplinary spectrum.

Moreover, the ideology which originally legitimized the practice of detention (therapy, rehabilitation, correction) has abandoned the institution to become a vector legitimizing the 'exit' from prison process. The institution is robbed of justification; prison thus loses any ideological veil which could socially justify its existence in technocratic terms for what it really is: an instrument of incapacitation for those who cannot be otherwise controlled (Baratta 1984: 5–30). All these points confirm the close links existing between taking responsibility for the problem situation and then incapacitating and neutralizing the situation perceived as dangerous.

At a more profound theoretical level, it may be more useful to resort to another interpretation which would highlight a different variable not considered so far and resulting from the relations between formal social control and informal social control. This interpretation could be summarized thus: 'soft' modalities of formal social control multiply, curbing not so much the room for segregation, but the field controlled by informal social control. The outcome is that 'soft' means of social control are not alternatives to 'hard' measures, but to informal strategies of social discipline. This explanation accounts for some of the phenomena inherent in social control policies in Italy which would otherwise appear contradictory.

In Italy the expansion of 'soft' means of formal control has not been accompanied by an appreciable fall in the numbers of those subjected to hard control tactics. Very often the opposite has been true (Pease 1984). Statistically, there is a tendency for the policy of shifting more problem situations outside prison to be accompanied by a rise in the number of people 'restrained' in prison (Ruggiero 1991: 27–41). The label 'alternative' which is usually attributed to soft, as opposed to hard, control systems, is a reductionist tag, in that soft systems structurally end up leaning on hard ones, be it by threat or actual enforcement (Feely and Simon 1992: 449–74). In practice, soft and hard forms of social control are interlocked in what can be called a 'disciplinary exchange'.

This 'disciplinary exchange' is based on various degrees of soft social control in relation to the controlled subject's willingness to adhere to the control action. The degree of his willingness results from a conflictual acceptance, or even participation, in the treatment programme (De Leonardis 1985: 323–50; Pitch 1989). It matters little whether this willingness to co-operate is sincere or not, pretence is quite sufficient.

This complex picture of the tensions which have marked social control has had serious repercussions on the prison subsystem. I shall provide a snapshot of the current prison context in Italy though I cannot do full justice to the many dynamic processes underway. One of these processes is prison 'differentiation' (Pavarini 1978: 36–61). By this I mean that prison is increasingly structured as an indiscriminate 'bin' of crime, a compound resembling an artichoke with a relatively compact uniform heart, covered by layer upon layer of leaves. The outermost leaves coincide with various degrees of 'attenuated' enforcement measures, such as alternatives to prison or partial segregation strategies (Pavarini 1988: 49–53).

55

Hand in hand with the above process, what we could call 'prison monocentrism' is falling apart, pulverized into a sort of fragmentary institutional 'polycentrism' (Pavarini 1986: 264–87). The dynamics of prison differentiation and pulverization are linked to the basic mechanisms of 'entry' and 'exit' from prison, i.e., 'carceration' and 'decarceration'. As we know, decarceration is one of the most controversial topics and not only in Italy. If 'alternatives' to prison are activated to 'take on board' 'released' prisoners, they end up as prison substitutes or parallel facilities, albeit partial ones (Melossi 1988a: 13–17).

In turn, this process is structurally linked with a larger scale movement; placing problems and social conflicts 'inside' and 'outside' the criminal justice system. The quality of this phenomenon differs from that mentioned above. Here I perceive a twofold contradictory trend in the opposite direction. On the one hand, certain situations no longer involve the criminal justice system (through its stages of de-criminalization, de-penalization, de-legalization and diversion), and are thus entrusted to other systems of social control, from community-based social and welfare services to the health and psychiatric services. Other situations do involve the penal system via the different pathways of the new criminalization.

Globally speaking, this now accelerated tendency to move problem situations inside/outside the penal justice system appears to respond to some need, further emphasizing the merely symbolic dimension of the penal system (Baratta 1984: 5–30). This is also evident in the decision to free the criminal justice system from those situations of unrest and conflict, which were originally criminalized and have gradually lost their social stigma to be perceived as 'needy' or 'deserving' situations eligible for help. All this was accompanied by the elephantine growth of penal protection measures against new situations, to increase the risks attached to certain activities rather than effectively to punish them (Sgubbi 1990).

The complexity of these mechanisms stretches the imagination in trying to grasp their mutual independence. One level of understanding is, however, possible. At this level, a centrifugal force is struggling to pull all forms of correction and indirectly all rehabilitative justificationary rhetoric away from the gravitational centre of prison. In this sense, the obsession with correction has been confined to the fringes of the penal justice system, with an overflow 'outside' it. A scenario appears in which the correctional urgency has already escaped the prison walls, marginally pervading the criminal justice system, but basically taking root in new or well-worn practices of non-penal discipline.

Since the mid-seventies, Italian criminology has denied the rehabilitative function, embracing hints of deterrence (Stella and Romano 1980; Ferrajoli 1989), or 'desert' (Mathieu 1978), or ended up reappraising the aim of rehabilitation from a standpoint which has nothing to do with treatment compromise (Bricola 1973; Dolcini 1979; Eusebi 1991; Cattaneo 1990). What little timid correctional resistance persists is 'outside' prison, basically in the application of alternative strategies.

But where correctional faith and practice thrive is 'outside', not only the prison circuit, but also outside the very system of criminal justice. Clearly, I am referring to correctional measures used with some types of offenders who have temporarily or permanently been taken outside the criminal justice system; the chief example that springs to mind in the Italian context is the experience of therapeutic communities for drug abusers who have not committed other crimes.

56

Socio-political Crisis and New Re-carceration Process in the Early Nineties: 'Paradise Lost' and the New Penology

In the two-year period 1991–2 the Italian prison population doubled. Such increases—on the scale of 50 per cent a year—have been unheard of throughout Italian prison history (Melossi 1988a; 13–17; Ministero di Grazia e Giustizia 1990). The exceptional status of this phenomenon is not confined to figures, alarming as they are. What changed radically was the make-up of the prison population as a result of new selection procedures in the imprisonment process.

In two short years, the number of drug abusers rose from under 20 per cent to over 60 per cent of the entire prison population (Castellani and Di Lazzaro 1990; Pavarini 1991: 113–38). In the same period the percentage of prisoners originating from outside the EEC rose from 5 per cent to over 20 per cent (Piroch *et al.* 1992). The repressive selectivity basically directed at these two ostracized social groups highlights a significant change in what society takes to be a new danger. In the new collective perception the paradigm of 'political danger' gives way to 'social danger'. In the first place, this inversion is due to the deep political crisis currently underway in Italy: a crisis on a scale which threatens to wipe out the very parties which embodied this policy, and held the institutional stage for half a century.

The crisis affects every one of the political parties, but has been felt most keenly and most radically by the left, where the collapse of any prospects for social change has been taken to imply that the present reality is the only one possible. The fear and unrest aroused by the present crisis have failed to find an outlet in a social demand for a better future. What is being asked for is a better present—straight away—which is a politically absurd claim, in that it is impossible. Because this social demand cannot be met, it is pervertedly turned into moral intransigence, manifesting itself in obsessive crusades in search of scapegoats responsible for present ills.

Two recent national surveys on the social representation of the problems most afflicting public opinion (Doxa 1992; Eurisko 1993) concur in placing street crime, particularly crimes committed by young drug abusers, top of the list. This is then followed by political corruption, youth unemployment, the recession, and pollution. In the list of factors responsible for crime, over 25 per cent of the sample interviewed made explicit reference to wide scale drug abuse.

One example which can explain the significant change of paradigm in what society perceives as the enemy within, is what the Italian press have dubbed the ongoing 'clean hands' campaign of judicial repression for political corruption. Political corruption has always been endemic in Italy, as it probably is elsewhere. The way in which this unlawful activity is carried on in Italy can be described as a sort of 'protection agreement' between private enterprise and the political representatives in charge of the area in which the companies have their businesses (Della Porta 1993: Pavarini 1993; 9–11). The protection agreement only benefits certain enterprises, turning them into a business listing which can profitably carry on its affairs, irrespective of market laws. For this service, enterprises pay into the coffers of the political parties involved, what can be deemed a protection fee, i.e., the price of political action (favouring one business and debarring another). This money which serves to fund the costs of politics, is nothing more than a production cost, which the protected undertakings offset by the present political price charged for the business services supplied.

One could object that this mechanism operates in other nations where a business listing has been created by political corruption. In my view, what makes the situation different in Italy is the singular status of the Italian political system, in which the total lack of political turnover fosters the long-term stabilization of those involved in protection agreements. Where there is a healthy political turnover, enterprises are forced to deal with different representatives; there is renewal, or at any rate the risk of a changeover, even between those guilty of unlawful dealings. In Italy, the relative absence of political mobility, in national and local government, has promoted a sort of mutual arrangement in the agreement between the party system as a whole and big business.

It is not one party or another which from time to time unlawfully procures funds by offering protection to this or that business. It is the party system as a whole (often with no distinction between those in office and those in opposition, majority or minority), which is privy to the protection agreement. This revived feudal system of relations between politics and business is intrinsically harmful for politics and the economy alike. When political corruption turns into a system involving the entire apparatus of political parties in a context already dominated by public over private enterprise, the business listing, on the one hand, and the system of unprotected enterprises on the other, for opposite reasons, escape any tests by market laws, and risk lowering the overall competition threshold of the economy.

There is also a more fearsome risk. Insofar as this protection agreement exists unlawfully, the party system and the enterprises involved must appropriate criminal know-how to spawn efficient strategies able to operate in the illegal market, allowing underhand circulation of economic resources (Pizzorno 1992; 13–74). Although there is room for speculation, I am of the opinion that the illegal market is itself an oligopoly under the sway of criminal organizations. Some of the transactions on which protection agreements between parties and enterprises were based may well have made use of the same facilities offered by organized crime. I suspect that these same criminal organizations are interested in becoming go-betweens for enterprises and parties alike.

Such a complex ramified phenomenon has long been socially tolerated as the inevitable cost of relations forged in Italy's past between political parties and business. It is only with the hoped-for future change in these relations that we can hope to defeat such illegal practices. Socially, the practice was perceived as being 'in formal conflict with the law', but certainly not inclined to arouse a movement of moral indignation. The current economic crisis (more and more sacrifices for the population), is accompanied by the party system's loss of legitimacy in the absence of any prospect of change. These two factors have determined opposite ways of how society construes political corruption; dishonest politicians in league with the mafia to rob the nation of its wealth have suddenly become the only culprits of the recession.

The political paradigm of how society views corruption gives way to moralism. The magistrates conducting investigations into political corruption have become the latest public idols, great 'moralisers' because they are great 'judges'. A television programme announcing a long interview with some of the magistrates engaged in investigations into corrupt dealings had audience ratings which exceeded the number of viewers who watched the Madonna concert. The names of these magistrates have been daubed on the walls of cities all over Italy, covering those of rock stars and football heroes.

Another example of how social panic is perceived by Italian society is the new social consensus accorded the fight against the mafia in Italy today. Here too, we are not facing a new criminal setting—the mafia existed before the nation came into being; nor are we witnessing a more threatening change in the way the mafia operates. Nowadays, the mafia is seen to be more awesome even though it is objectively no more of a threat than it was in the past (Gambetta 1992). Society now perceives the mafia as far more dangerous a threat because the mafia question has also been constructed outside a political paradigm unable to justify it, but certainly able to understand it as a social, cultural, and anthropological phenomenon. Outside this paradigm the mafia is seen as exclusively evil. For the first time in Italy the mafia has become socially 'only' a criminal issue.

The extent to which the system of criminal justice and the judicial and police apparatus have achieved legitimacy is unequalled in the history of the Italian Republic. A recent opinion poll (Eurisko 1993) shows that the police forces (traditionally as highly feared as they were little respected in Italy) have the support of 88 per cent of the population in their action against organized crime; magistrates were accorded 75 per cent. But this widespread support for repressing the activities of the mafia and corrupt politicians has rendered legitimate a much wider repression. The consensus gained in the struggle against two great emergencies—political corruption and organized crime—has justified an indiscriminate rise in the levels of punishment. For every mafia criminal sent to gaol, a hundred criminal drug addicts are imprisoned; for every corrupt politician lawfully detained, a hundred black immigrants are interned.

REFERENCES

BARATTA, A. (1984), 'La teoria della prevenzione–integrazione: Una "nuova" fondazione della pena all'interno della teoria sistemica', *Dei Delitti e delle Pene*, 1: 5–30.

—— (1985), 'Principi del diritto penale minimo. Per una teoria dei diritti umani come oggetti e limiti della legge penale', *Dei Delitti e delle Pene*, 3: 443–73.

BRICOLA, F. (1973), 'La teoria generale del reato', *Muovissimo Digesto Italiano*, 19: 47–137.

CATTANEO, M. A. (1990), *Pena, diritto e dignità umana*. Turin: Giappichelli.

CASTELLANI, R., and DI LAZZARO, A. (1990), *Indagine nazionale sui soggetti tossicodipendenti e affetti da virus HIV detenuti negli istituti penitenziari*. Rome: Direzione Generale degli Istituti di Prevenzione e Pena.

COHEN, S. (1978), 'Uno scenario per il sistema carcerario futuro', in F. Basaglia and F. Basaglia Ongaro, eds., *Crimini di Pace*, 44–62. Turin: Einaudi.

—— (1985a), 'Lo sviluppo del modello correzionale: chiacchere e realtà del controllo sociale', *Dei Delitti e delle Pene*, 1: 5–48.

—— (1985b), *Visions of Social Control: Crime, Punishment and Classification*. Cambridge: Polity Press.

COUNCIL OF EUROPE (1990), *Bulletin d'Information Pénitentiaire*, 15.

DE LEONARDIS, O. (1985), 'Statuto e figure della pericolisità sociale tra psichiatria riformata e sistema penale: note sociologiche', *Dei Delitti e delle Pene*, 2: 323–50.

DELMAS-MARTY, M. (1986), 'L'enjeu d'un code penal, reflexions à propos de l'inflation des lois penales in France', in *Mélanges Legros*. Brussels.

DI LAZZARO, A. (1988), 'Le misure alternative alla detenzione prima e dopo la Gozzini', *Inchiesta*, 79–80: 27–39.

DOLCINI, E. (1979), *La Commisurazione della pena. La pena detentiva*. Padua: CEDAM.

—— (1991), 'La commisurazione della pena tra teoria e prassi', in A. M. Stile, ed., *Le discrasie tra dottrina e giurisprudenza in diritto penale*: 147–72. Naples: Jovine.

DOLCINI, E., and PALIERO, C. E. (1980), *Il Carcere ha alternative ? Le sanzioni sostitutitive alla detenzione breve nella esperienza europea*. Milan: Giuffrè.

DELLA PORTA, D. (1992), *Lo Scambio occulto. Casi di corruzione politica in Italia*. Bologna: Il Mulino.

DOXA (1992), 'La percezione della delinquenza', *Bollettino della Doxa*: 19–20: 216–47.

EURISKO (1993), *Ciò che fa più paura agli Italiani*. Indagine condotta per conto dell' osservatorio permanente sulla comunicazione, Ministero dell' Interno.

EUSEBI, L. (1991), *La Pena 'in crisi'. Il recente dibattito sulla funzione della pena*. Brescia: Morcelliana.

FEELEY, M. M., and SIMON, J. (1992), 'The New Penology: Notes on the Emerging Strategy of Corrections and its Applications', *Criminology*, 4: 449–74.

FERRAJOLI, L. (1989), *Diritto e ragione. Teoria del garantismo penale*. Naples: Laterza.

GAMBETTA, D. (1992), *La Mafia siciliana. Un'industria della protezione privata*. Turin: Einaudi.

GARLAND, D. (1985), *Punishment and Welfare. A History of Penal Strategies*. Aldershot: Gower.

GROLL, K. M. (1985), *In der Flut der Gesteze*. Dusseldorf.

GROSSI, G. (1985), 'Informazione e terrorismo: un modello interpretativo del "caso italiano" ', in R. Grandi, M. Pavarini, and M. Simondi, eds., *I Segni di Caino. L'immagine della devianza nelle comunicazioni di massa*, 309–34. Naples: ESI.

INGRAO, P. (1975), 'Per una politica criminale del movimento operaio', *La Questione Criminale*, 3: 508–14.

ISTAT (1991), *Statistche Giudiziarie, 1989*, vol. 33, Rome.

LASCOUMES, P. (1986), *Des erreurs pas de fautes. La gestion disrète du droit des affaires*. Paris: Médicine et Hygiène.

LEA, J. (1979), 'Disciplina e sviluppo capitalista', *La Questione Criminale*, 2: 217–35.

MARINUCCI, G. (1981), 'L'abbandono del Codice Rocco: tra rassegnazione e utopia', in *La Questione Criminale*, 2: 297–318.

MARRA, R., PAVARINI, M., and VILLA, E. (1981), 'La codificazione impedita. Alcune ossevazioni in tema di "nuovo" diritto penale e funzione della pena', *La Questione Criminale*, 2: 249–72.

MATHIEU, V. (1978), *Perchè punire? Il collasso della giustizia penale*, Milano: Rusconi.

MATTHEWS, R. (1987), 'Decarceration and Social Control: Fantasies and Realities', *International Journal of Sociology of Law*, 15.

MAZZACUVA, N. (1983), *Il principio di difesa sociale e i provvedimenti di clemenza. Profili di una politica criminale e analisi per una ricerca storica*. Bologna: Litografia Lorenzini.

MELOSSI, D. (1980), 'Oltre il Panopticon. Per uno studio delle strategie di controllo sociale nel capitalismo del ventesimo secolo', *La Questione Criminale*, 2–3: 277–363.

—— (1988*a*), 'Incarcerazione, vocabili punitivi e ciclo politico-economico in Italia (1896–1965): rapporto su di una ricerca in corso', *Inchiesta*, 79–80: 13–18.

—— (1988*b*), *The State of Social Control*. Cambridge: Polity Press.

MINISTERO DI GRAZIA E GIUSTIZIA, DIREZIONE GENERALE DEGLI ISTITUTI DI PREVENZIONE E PENA (1990), *La Prigione in Italia: storia, evoluzione e prospettive*, Rome.

MOSCONI, G. (1985), 'Semplificazioni comunicative e sistema giuridico in una situazione di emergenza', in R. Grandi, M. Pavarini, and M. Simodi, eds., *I Segni di Caino. L'immagine della devianza nelle comunicazioni di massa*: 335–49. Naples: ESI.

—— (1988), 'La trasformazione della pena nello spazio della cultura diffusa', *Inchiesta*, 79–80: 1–12.

MUSSGNUG, R. (1984), 'Die Durchsetzung des Rechts im Spannungsverhaeltnis zwischen Legalitat und Opportunitat', *Die Durchsetzung des Rechts*. Mannheim.

NASCETTI, G. P. (1983), *Decentramento amministrativo, governo locale e controllo sociale della devianza*. Bologna: Lorenzini.

NEPPI MODONA, G., and VIOLANTE, L. (1978), *Poteri dello stato e sistema penale*. Turin: Tirrenia Stampatori.

PADOVANI, T. (1981), *L'utopia punitiva. Il problema delle alternative alla detenzione nella sua dimensione storica*. Milan: Giuffrè.

PAVARINI, M. (1978), ' "Concentrazione" e "diffisione" del penitenziario. Le tesi di Rusche e Kirchheimer e la nuova strategia del controllo sociale in Italia', *La Questione Criminale*, 3: 39–61.

—— (1983), 'La pena "utile", la sua crisi e il disincanto: verso una pena senza scopo', in *Rassegna penitenziaria e criminologica*, 1: 1–45.

—— (1985), 'Al di là della pena, al di là del carcere . . . appunti e note teoriche in tema di decentramento e amministrativizzazione del controllo sociale', in G. Zappa, ed., *Carcere, ente locale e opinione pubblica*: 31–42. Bologna: GLUEB.

—— (1986), 'Fuori dalle mura del carcere: la dislocazione dell'ossessione correzionale', *Dei Delitti e delle Pene*, 2: 251–87.

—— (1988), 'Misure alternative al carcere e decarcerizzazione: un rapporto problematico', *Inchiesta*, 79–80: 49–53.

—— (1991), 'La pena tossica. Carcere e misure alternative della libertà per il condannato e l'imputato tossicodipendente', in F. Bricola and G. Insolera, eds, *La riforma della legislazione penale in materia di stupefacienti*: 113–38. Padu: CEDAM.

—— (1992), 'Sistema dei partiti e corruzione politica', *Sicurezza e territorio. Per una politica della prevenzione della criminalità*, 3: 9–11.

PEASE, K. (1984), 'Community Service and Prison: Are they Alternatives?' in *Community Service by Order*. Edinburgh: Scottish Academic Press.

PIROCH, W., MIEKLE, M. R., D'OTTAVI, A. M., and LUCHINI, D. (1992), *Detenuti stranieri in Italia. La loro condizione*. Milan: Franco Angeli Editore.

PITCH, T. (1989), *Responsabilità limitate. Attori, conflitti, giustizia penale*. Milan: Feltrinelli.

PIZZORNO, A. (1992), 'La corruzione nel sistema politico', Introduction to D. della Porta, *Lo scambio occulto: casi di corruzione in Italia*. 13–76, Bologna: Il Mulino.

ROSE, L. (1984), *Understanding Big Government*, London: Sage.

RUGGIERO, V. (1991), 'Carcerizzazione e decarcerizzazione', in *Dei Delitti e delle Pene*, 1: 127–41.

SAVELSBERG, J. J. (1987), 'The Making of Criminal Law Norms in Welfare States', *Law and Society Review*.

SCULL, F. A. (1977), *Decarceration: Community Treatment and the Deviant. A Radical View*. New Jersey: Prentice Hall.

SGUBBI, F. (1990), *Il reato come rischio sociale. Ricerche sulle scelte di allocazione dell'illegalità penale*. Bologna: Il Mulino.

STELLA, F., and ROMANO, M., eds., (1980), *Teoria e prassi della prevenzione dei reati*, Bologna: Il Mulino.

STORTONI, L. (1981), 'Fallimento di una riforma penale e impossibilità di un nuovo codice penale nel presente momento storico', *La Questione Criminale*, 2: 273–80.

UGER, R. M. (1976), *Law in Modern Society*, New York.

YOUNG, J. (1981), 'Oltre il paradigma consensuale: una critica del funzionalismo di sinistra nella teoria delle comunicazioni di massa, Il fallimento della criminologia: per un realismo radicale', in R. Grandi, M. Pavarini, and M. Simondi, eds., *I segni di Caino. L'Immagine della devianza nelle comunicazioni di massa*, 141–73, Naples: ESI.

RUSSIAN PRISONS AFTER PERESTROIKA

End of the Gulag?

ROY D. KING*

Introduction: A Moscow Conference

At the opening of the International Conference on Penal Reform in Former Totalitarian Societies held in Moscow in November 1992, Boris Zolotukhin, Deputy Chairman of the Legislative Commission of the Russian Supreme Soviet and a member of the Moscow Helsinki Group claimed that 'reform of the penal system is going on better than other reforms in Russia . . . and that any unprejudiced observer would appreciate that the legislative body has started the process of self-limitation within the constitution'.

There can be little doubt that some progress has been made towards what academician Vladimir Kudryatsev (1989) called the Socialist Rule-of-Law State: but in the three years since he wrote, progress has been less fast and more patchy than the optimists had hoped. While Moscow officials confidently claimed they had introduced changes which were irreversible, representatives from Belarus, the Ukraine, Azerbaijan, Moldova, Uzbekistan, Kazakhstan—occasionally themselves former 'dissidents'—painted a picture of more precarious reforms, speaking of their struggles to reduce their prison populations, improve the diet of prisoners, and to humanize the system against a background of political chaos and near total collapse of the old Soviet economy. From the same platform, and from the floor, human rights activists criticized the reforms for coming too late, for not going far enough even on paper, and for not being fully implemented in practice. In their conference literature they claimed that death rates from tuberculosis are 17 times higher in Russian prisons than in Russian society generally, that 'torture is widespread' and that human rights violations are a 'constant, systematic and scandalous' feature of the Gulag[1] today. Not surprisingly, attention was given to the application of international standards—although at one stage Al Bronstein of the American Civil Liberties Union felt constrained to remind his Russian hosts that Western prisons too were often dirty, dangerous, insanitary, overcrowded, and were by no means immune from breaches of international norms regarding human rights.

* Professor of Social Theory and Institutions, University of Wales, Bangor.

I am indebted to Alexander S. Mikhlin, Professor of Law at the Research Institute of the Ministry of the Interior for making this research possible, and for his many kindnesses throughout my stay. Ministry officials in Moscow, St Petersburg, Vladimir, Perm and Ryazan greatly facilitated my work and I am grateful to them and to the governors, staff and prisoners in the 14 prisons and corrective labour colonies which I visited for their co-operation often in the most difficult of circumstances. Special thanks are due to Leonid Shinkarev of *Izvestia*; Valery Abramkin, Director of the Moscow Centre for Prison Reform; and to Gerald Brooke and Valentin Arkatov who kindly shared their specialized knowledge with me. None of this would have happened were it not for my interpreter and translator, Kathy Judelson. I am grateful for her diplomatic skills, her quickly acquired capacity to cope with prison argot, as well as her support networks in Moscow and St Petersburg. Finally I am grateful to Mike Maguire, Rod Morgan, and especially Marjorie Farquharson for their helpful comments on an earlier draft. Needless to say, however, the responsibility for what is written here is mine alone.

[1] GULag is an acronym for *Glavnoye Upravlenie Lagerei*, the Central Administration of Camps.

The conference ended without significant agreement on any resolutions, other than one aimed at the gradual abolition of capital punishment. Although officials and reformers alike were careful to call for co-operation, it was perhaps inevitable that discussion often degenerated into mutual recrimination between representatives of the Ministry of the Interior—virtually all of whom had survived the transition from the Soviet system—and their detractors.

Two or three years earlier, as the meaning of 'glasnost' and 'perestroika' filtered down to the prisons context, officials had begun to open up the system. For the first time it became possible for journalists, human rights campaigners, and penal reformers to enter the Gulag, to ask questions, even to make video films. But the relationship between officials and reformers could never be easy. After criticism of the Ministry's 1988 and 1990 drafts of a new corrective labour code, and the development of a more radical alternative version drawn up by lawyers and criminologists from the University of Tomsk, a new Commission, chaired by Supreme Soviet Deputy A. F. Bir, and with a wide-ranging membership including the leading prisoners' rights activist, Valery Abramkin, Director of the Moscow Centre for Prison Reform, was charged with agreeing a third version.

A compromise was reached, but when that stalled in its progress through Supreme Soviet committees, expectations had already been raised and the situation in the prisons and colonies then deteriorated. In September 1991 riots broke out in a number of colonies and special troops were sent to the regions ready to restore order. On 21 October 1991 the Ministry of the Interior introduced several reforms, anticipating that part of the new code which was eventually to become law on 12 June 1992. But in the autumn of 1991 the Supreme Soviet still had no plans to review the new draft corrective labour code, which had dropped back in the list of political priorities, until the end of 1993. Abramkin called upon prisoners to take peaceful strike action which was set for 13 November 1991.

The extent and effectiveness of the strikes remain hotly disputed—just as did those instigated by PROP (Fitzgerald 1977) in England during the 1970s—and the legacy is an atmosphere of suspicion and mistrust. One of the most contentious issues concerns the causes, nature, and duration of the riots at the strict regime colony in Krasnoyarsk, and the circumstances under which it was ended in November 1991 by the intervention of armed troops. Ministry officials first accused Abramkin of fanning the flames of the riot and then sought to undermine his position by alleging that he colluded with the procurator in calling in the troops to put it down. By the end of the conference officials were poised to sue for libel over allegations that prisoners had been deliberately infected with tuberculosis.

At the time of writing (June 1993) Russia is in the queue to join the Council of Europe and to ratify the European Convention for the Prevention of Torture. In the nature of things it is difficult for academic researchers to do much more than record the allegations and denials in relation to the grosser incidents of what ordinarily constitutes 'torture' in the public imagination. But as Morgan and Evans (1994) show elsewhere in this volume the activities of the Council of Europe Committee for the Prevention of Torture have as much to do with the daily inhumanities of custodial conditions—witness its recent report on the United Kingdom which found that the combination of overcrowding, lack of integral sanitation, and paucity of out of cell activities in Brixton, Wandsworth, and Leeds constituted 'inhuman and degrading treatment' (Council of

Europe 1991)—as it does with torture properly so-called. In the circumstances it is important to try to get some understanding of the size, shape, and structures of the Russian system of corrective labour and of the conditions which currently obtain in its prisons and colonies. It is perhaps no less important to try to place them in the context of contemporary Russian society. This paper aims to provide at least the beginning of such an exposition.

Methodology

Although members of Helsinki Watch groups first gained access to Soviet institutions in the 1980s, and Amnesty International has conducted investigations since 1991, the research on which this paper is based is probably the first by any independent academic researcher to be conducted inside Russian prisons and corrective labour colonies. It was carried out during just six weeks in November and December 1992 and it is important at the outset to say something about the methodology, thereby noting the limitations of the project.

Access was arranged through the good offices of the scientific staff at the Research Institute of the Ministry of the Interior. Some time was spent interviewing officials at the two main administrative offices in Moscow concerned with persons sentenced to deprivation of liberty—namely the Office for Forest Zone Corrective Labour Establishments and the Office for Non-Forest Zone Colonies and Prisons—as well as their counterparts at regional level in three regions: St Petersburg, Vladimir, and Perm. A representative of one or other of these offices, or from the Research Institute, was involved in all of the visits to institutions.

A programme of research visits to 14 'representative' institutions was negotiated. The term representative is placed in quotation marks because there was no basis for knowing in advance either the nature or the number of institutions which make up the system. Indeed there appears to be no published list of the institutions in use, their population characteristics, or their functions from which a sample could have been drawn. In any event, the size of the former Soviet Union (as it still was when the initial overtures for the research were made) and the present Russian Federation, would have precluded a geographically representative sample. Officials were asked to organize a programme that would give a reasonable picture of the system for adult men and women, 'warts and all'. They were asked to bear in mind the author's interests in custodial conditions for remand prisoners (King and Morgan 1976); procedures for dealing with 'difficult and dangerous offenders' (King and Elliot 1978; King and McDermott 1990; King 1991), and the conditions in prison systems generally (King and McDermott 1989; King and Morgan 1980).

It is a remarkable testament to the new spirit of openness that the eventual programme included the massive and much troubled remand prisons—Butyrki in Moscow and Kresty in St Petersburg—as well as the notorious Byely Lebed in Solikamsk, in spite of a hostage-taking incident there just two days before the visit, in which the procurator and one of the hostage-takers were killed. Byely Lebed, or the White Swan, some 36 hours from Moscow by train and jeep, was the prototype for a number of institutions intended to break the influence of the so-called 'thieves in law'—

leaders of the inmate community who are defined as the most troublesome within the colonies: it is the institution on which human rights agencies claimed their files were thickest. The programme also included what the Russians consider to be one of their most secure, end-of-the-line establishments, the maximum security prison at Vladimir, 175 kilometres east of Moscow. Vladimir is one of the institutions best known to Amnesty International because it held a significant group of prisoners of conscience until 1978 when they were transferred to Chistopol, another 700 kilometres further east. The remaining institutions comprised two further remand prisons, three corrective labour colonies for men and three for women, and a colony for prisoners suffering from open tuberculosis. These 13 establishments for adults did not quite cover the full range. No general regime colony for male first offenders was included. Nor was it possible to visit a colony settlement where offenders live in remote and largely unguarded open communities. Although a study of institutions for young offenders was not specifically requested, the fourteenth establishment visited was an educational labour colony for female minors.

Visits to prisons and colonies varied considerably, both in duration—from one to four days—and in the degree of freedom of movement permitted to the researcher. The whole idea of anyone wanting to do sociological research in prison, let alone being allowed to do so, was novel. In the more remote regions officials were sometimes so pleased, even honoured, to be visited by the first foreign scholar that they wished to provide the best possible hospitality and were surprised, but hopefully not offended, by a determination to ask questions first and eat and drink later. Most people were wholly unprepared for the battery of questions, especially the supplementary questions, with which they were beseiged. One governor, presumably so used to lying in response to questions under the old regime, lied openly and outrageously on matters that were immediately contradicted by the first six prisoners interviewed both in private and in the governor's presence. Another had to be reminded that it was now perfectly all right to give out the production figures to a foreigner.

In some establishments, mostly those where it had been possible to negotiate repeated visits over several days (Butyrki, Kresty, Vladimir, Reinforced Regime Colony No. 5) it was reasonably easy to view the premises with a single guide, and then to interview staff and prisoners alone. In these institutions staff enjoyed the analogy that a researcher getting to know a prison was like unpeeling the layers of an onion. In others it was difficult to avoid a Cook's Tour in the company of several officials (on one occasion the entourage numbered as many as ten people and must have resembled a royal procession) and in these circumstances considerable firmness had to be exercised to create any situation in which it was possible to talk to individuals tête à tête. Four visits (Zagorsk Remand Prison, the TB Colony at Moshchevo, Women's General Regime Colony No. 32, and the Colony for Female Minors at Ryazan) were either so brief, or so encumbered by officialdom, that there was little or no opportunity to delve beneath the surface—though even here sometimes the opportunities which did present themselves were very revealing indeed. The remaining institutions fell somewhere in between. The outcome of a particular visit often depended upon whether it was a member of the Research Institute, an official from the local region, or an official from headquarters in Moscow who accompanied the researcher, and how they defined their role.

In each institution the aim was to visit, and wherever possible photograph, the

65

housing units, the places of work, the kitchens, dining rooms, recreation and exercise facilities, bath houses, medical facilities, and punishment cells. Interviews were conducted with the governor and/or one or more of his or her deputies, as well as with front line staff and with prisoners.

All told, some 27 interviews were conducted with prisoners in conditions of complete privacy, and every effort was made to minimize the possibility that the authorities presented specially selected individuals for interview. Many further interviews were held within earshot, and sometimes the full frontal presence, of staff. Surprisingly, some of the latter turned out to be very fruitful since they sometimes set up an intriguing discussion or debate and, on at least one occasion, a fierce dispute. It was as difficult to interview staff in private as it was prisoners. Whilst every effort was made to interview someone from all the key positions in the staff hierarchy across the study as a whole, in any individual institution there was only time to interview a few staff in any depth. Finally it must be stressed that all interviews were conducted through a female British interpreter.

One of the most important differences between Russia and the United Kingdom, in respect of prisons at least, is that, with some estimates of the numbers who have passed through the Gulag reaching 50 millions, a far higher proportion of the Russian population has direct personal or family experience of these matters. Whereas in Britain a prison researcher is unlikely, in the normal course of events, to come across many of his or her research subjects socially, in Russia it is quite impossible to avoid them. The legacy of the Gulag touches almost every family, including the intelligentsia. As a result almost every waking hour formed a part of the research process.

A short period of research in a country where the researcher does not speak the language and cannot directly access the literature, cannot pretend to have done more than scratch the surface. All too often the full complexity of the answers to a huge battery of questions has probably remained elusive. In many situations interviewees needed to verify their own sources and it was rarely possible to check what was said against documentary evidence. Nevertheless, an extraordinary amount of information was absorbed and a great deal of data accumulated, much of which remains to be translated. Only a fraction of this material can be reported here. It is hoped that the grosser errors have been avoided or eliminated and that, if not, enough will have been said to whet the appetite of those better qualified to pursue such matters at greater depth. Meanwhile, the present study probably has sufficient breadth and depth to offer some independent basis for a preliminary delineation of the system and an appreciation of its problems.

The Use of Custody

The statistics relating to imprisonment in Russia are still not routinely published, but they are now made available on request. The Soviet tradition of presenting statistics in percentages without making clear the absolute numbers on which they are based continues. Piecing them together and collating them with criminal and court statistics, which were published for the first time in 1990 (see Butler 1992; Dashkov 1992 for recent analyses), therefore, remains a major research undertaking beyond the scope of this paper, but at least for the future the extraordinary and ingenious lengths to which researchers (Van Den Berg 1985, for example) have had to go to make even quite partial estimates should no longer be necessary.

According to official statistics supplied by the Ministry of the Interior there were, in November 1992, almost 760,000 persons in prisons and corrective labour colonies within the Russian Federation, out of a population approaching 150 million. About 600,000 of them had been sentenced to deprivation of liberty and about 160,000 were remanded in custody before trial or were awaiting sentence. Like many another matter, however, these figures were disputed. The documentation prepared for the Moscow Conference by the Centre for Prison Reform claimed that there were one million people in prison. It seems likely that the difference between the two figures is accounted for by persons who had been sentenced to correctional tasks (and thus according to some definitions would be considered as part of the Gulag) but who are not actually deprived of their liberty although they may be sent to work sites far from home. Such persons are technically subject to a non-custodial penalty of penal work which can take one of two forms: either the offender is required to continue at his or her existing workplace but has 20 per cent of salary deducted; or the offender is obliged to work wherever (s)he is sent (often alongside ordinary civilian workers), whilst the threat of a custodial sentence is suspended. Even on the lower figure, however, this suggests a crude rate of imprisonment of over 500 per 100,000 population. Although it has to be acknowledged that rates expressed in this way leave out too much to be very meaningful it is nevertheless some five times greater than for England and Wales, and somewhat higher than for the United States.

It is hazardous to go into much greater detail on the statistics, not least because of the dramatic changes of jurisdiction arising out of the break-up of the Soviet Union. The figures which follow might thus be best viewed as indicating approximate orders of magnitude rather than precise measures. On this basis the three-fifths of a million people who are unambiguously currently serving sentences in custody are the product of a sentencing system which now sends about 35 per cent of all those convicted by the courts to prison. That this proportion has declined from 66 per cent in the 1950s gives some indication of the relative diminution in the proportionate use of custody since Khrushchev's reforms. But compared to the current figures of about 17 per cent for adult males and 6 per cent for adult females for England and Wales, the relative use of custody as a court disposal in Russia remains very high.

Moreover, this has to be set against the official level of recorded crime before something approaching meaningful comparisons can be made. Although both ordinary Russians as well as Russian politicians and opinion formers are presently obsessed by what they perceive to be a 'crime wave', officially recorded crime remains low, if rapidly rising (Dashkov 1992). One amongst many problems here, however, is that although it is known that the police historically have recorded only those crimes which they have already solved, know they can solve, or which would otherwise suit their political masters, there is no obvious formula by which such under-recording can be taken into account. No one supposes that the official figures of about 2.7 million crimes in the Russian Federation (population almost 150 million) during 1992 could be taken at their face value. But if they could, then the crime rate in Russia would be about six times less than it is in England and Wales. With a proportionate use of custody for those found guilty running at some five times the rate for England and Wales, the cumulative effect would be a worst case scenario of up to 30 times greater use of imprisonment in Russia than in England and Wales.

When faced with such rough and ready statistical calculations the official response tends to be that very serious offences, particularly homicides and rapes, form a much higher proportion of the total of Russian crimes than is the case for other jurisdictions. From the limited data cited in Butler (1992) for the USSR in 1989 it would appear that there is indeed a higher proportionate rate of both homicides and rapes (including attempts in both cases) than in England and Wales. But since it is not clear how threats and conspiracy to murder, and unlawful sexual intercourse (both separately categorized in England and Wales) are handled in the former USSR it would be premature to draw conclusions. However, it seems most unlikely that such a huge difference in imprisonment could be explained in this way, and there would certainly remain considerable scope for further reductions in the Russian use of imprisonment.[2]

Under present legislation the maximum length of sentence which can be imposed by the courts for a single very grave offence, or cumulated (*slozhonniye*) grave offences, is a fixed term of 15 years. For prisoners serving less than 15 years who commit further offences whilst in custody the courts may impose additional sentences, so long as the total does not exceed 15 years. The death penalty, in spite of the resolution of the Moscow conference, is likely to remain in force for the forseeable future since public opinion surveys have apparently favoured its retention and there seems to be no mood amongst politicians or officials for its abolition, at least in the short term. There is no life sentence available directly to the courts. In July 1993 the Supreme Soviet rejected a proposal to substitute an alternative fixed sentence of 25 years for premeditated murder but decided that where the death sentence is commuted a life term may be imposed instead of the previous period of between 15 and 20 years. The Supreme Soviet also approved an increase in the maximum sentence allowed on a cumulative basis to 25 years in order to provide a more effective sanction for offences committed whilst in custody.

The average length of sentence imposed by the courts, according to Ministry officials, is 66 months, although the length of time actually served after allowance for amnesties and early release is 37 months. Since the average length of sentence imposed by magistrates' courts in England and Wales is less than three months and by Crown Courts less than 21 months, it is apparent that one reason for the larger prison population in Russia is the existence of a much heavier tariff. Comprehensive sentencing data are not to hand at the time of writing, but on the basis of information provided about the population in the institutions visited in this study, as well as the more fragmentary and impressionistic biographic materials gathered in interviews with prisoners, it would seem that many offenders are swept into the prison system for much more trivial offences, for much longer periods, and at much earlier points in their criminal careers than would be the case in Britain. One young man, interviewed with his defence counsel who expected him to go down for at least four years in a strict regime colony, was charged with his first offence of housebreaking (which had netted property at the then exchange rate worth £45). He had three prior convictions for pickpocketing and shoplifting (for amounts at the then exchange rates of less than £10)

---

[2] Translation of tables relating to crimes and the use of corrective labour is currently in progress and it is hoped to report on these in more detail in due course.

since the age of 16, all of which had attracted custodial sentences. No violence had been involved.

The Russian System of Prisons and Corrective Labour Colonies

Perhaps the best known account of conditions under the Soviet system of corrective labour is Amnesty International's (1980) report, *Prisoners of Conscience in the USSR*. There are also at least two formal expositions of the system by Soviet academics which have been published in English. The first is by Natashev (1985) from the Academy of the USSR Ministry of the Interior, in the form of a response to 'bourgeois propaganda' which was delivered to the Seventh United Nations Congress on the Prevention of Crime and the Treatment of Offenders in Milan. He argued that in the 'present day ideological struggle . . . [there was] an organised campaign of slander and misinformation about the alleged infringement of human rights in the USSR . . . particularly . . . [concerning] . . . the procedure and conditions under which sentences involving deprivation of liberty are served' (Natashev 1985: preface). The second is by Alexandr Uss (1991), from the Department of Law and Criminology at the University of Krasnoyarsk. This was prepared for the seminar on international perspectives on prisoners' rights and prison conditions at the Max Planck Institute in Freiburg in 1989 at a time when the first drafting of the new codes on the use of corrective labour had been completed. While the two documents are rather different in tone, they present a broadly similar picture with regard to the basic structure of the custodial system and the rules which then governed it. Since the reforms of 21 October 1991 and 12 June 1992, referred to in the introduction to this paper, there have been a number of changes to the rules to which attention will be drawn below.

The structure of the present system of prisons and colonies is quite simple, and reflects elements of the old tsarist system as well as the obvious legacy of the Soviet use of forced labour in camps that formed an integral part of the huge industrial and agro-forestry complex.

Persons awaiting trial or sentence, men, women and minors, are held in cellular *remand (or isolation) prisons*, which may also hold a small number of sentenced prisoners, either on a temporary basis whilst awaiting transfer to a colony, or more permanently as cleaners, food service workers, or in some other capacity. The vast majority of sentenced adult male prisoners are held in *corrective labour colonies*. These are of five types with, for the most part, allocation to them prescribed by the courts according to rigid criteria:

1. *General regime colonies* are for first offenders who have committed minor crimes, or more serious crimes carrying penalties up to three years' deprivation of liberty;
2. *Reinforced regime colonies* are also for first offenders, but those who have committed more serious crimes carrying sentences of longer than three years;
3. *Strict regime colonies* are for recidivists, whatever the nature of their crime, and for persons convicted of particularly serious crimes against the state;
4. *Special regime colonies* are for particularly dangerous recidivists and for those prisoners whose death sentences have been commuted into sentences of imprisonment;
5. *Colony settlements* are effectively open prisons, that is with no fence at all, to which

69

some prisoners may be transferred after having served at least one third of their sentence in a colony of general, reinforced, or strict regime. There are also some colony settlements which receive prisoners convicted of crimes of negligence, and others for prisoners convicted of some commercial and similar crimes, directly upon sentence.

There are also a number of hospital colonies, although the psychiatric hospitals which once came under the Ministry of the Interior have been transferred to the Ministry of Health; and there are also two colonies for prisoners who were former state employees or staff of law enforcement agencies.

Only just over 1 per cent of prisoners are contained in *cellular prisons*, which are regarded as the most severe sanction that the system has to offer. The court may specify that deprivation of liberty should be in a prison for either the whole or part of the sentence in respect of certain particularly dangerous recidivists, or those who have committed particularly dangerous crimes carrying long custodial sentences. Prisoners can also be transferred to prison as a punishment for misbehaviour in the colonies.

For women there are only two types of colony: those with a general regime for first offenders, and those with a strict regime for particularly dangerous recidivists. A small number of women are housed in cellular prisons.

Minors between the ages of 14 and 18 years may not be sentenced to more than ten years' imprisonment. They are held in *educational labour colonies* with a general regime which is available (separately) for both males and females; or, for male recidivists only, with a reinforced regime.

Table 1 gives data on the numbers of institutions of different types and the numbers of prisoners contained in them at the end of 1992.

Remand Prison Conditions

Remand prisons are usually in urban centres of population, and, to judge from the four included in this study, the physical conditions are generally exceedingly poor.

Butyrki is one of two main remand prisons in Moscow which come under the jurisdiction of the Ministry of the Interior (the other is Mariners' Rest which now accommodates the plotters of the August 1991 putsch). Lefortovo, the former KGB establishment, remains under the Ministry of State Security. Butyrskaya prison was built in 1771. It was to here that Pugachev, the leader of the peasant rebellion, was brought back in a cage under orders from Catherine the Great. Here, too, Tolstoy researched his novel *Resurrection*. There was some restoration carried out in 1878, but, apart from alterations to the women's wing, there has been no refurbishment for over 100 years.

Butyrki contains some 434 cells of which 101 are large rooms, perhaps (which is to say measured by eye not a ruler) 6 metres by 12 metres. If the built-in coat hooks are a guide they were originally intended to house 20–25 prisoners in each. A further 301 cells are smaller, probably comparable in area to those in the new model prison at Pentonville, and originally intended to house no more than four prisoners each. The remaining 32 cells were for punishment. That would have given an original capacity of approximately 3,500 prisoners with about 2.5 square metres of space per person— which is the present agreed norm to which the system aspires for remand prisoners. But

TABLE 1   *Population of the Prison System of the Russian Federation in 1992*

Type of Establishment	Non-forest zones		Forest zones	
	Establishments	Prisoners	Establishments	Prisoners
Remand prisons	160	199,923*	–	–
Hospitals	30	16,417	12	5,970
Men's colonies				
General regime	54	56,733	2	657
Reinforced regime	103	00,580	13	8,972
Strict regime	232	194,492	59	46,025
Special regime	23	17,192	30	18,310
Former staff	2	1,765	–	–
Settlements	34	12,110	145	34,890
Men's prisons	13	4,894	–	–
Women's colonies				
General regime	24	15,243	2	657
Strict regime	2	1,700	–	–
Settlements	–	–	1	22
Women's prisons	1	45	–	–
Male minors				
General regime	52	17,886	–	–
Reinforced regime	4	664	–	–
Female minors				
General regime	3	876	–	–

Source: Data supplied by Ministry of Internal Affairs.
* This total includes 6,967 women and 143 minors. It also includes an unspecified number of prisoners who are convicted and sentenced, but for one reason or another remain in the remand prisons.

in November 1992, the prison housed over 5,100 prisoners, with an average space of 0.9 square metres per prisoner.

Some 19 of the 300 or so Russian prisoners currently on death row were accommodated in Butyrki in conditions which were kept as sheltered as possible. Some effort was also made to keep the smaller cells to six prisoners or fewer. But the larger cells were grossly overcrowded, with 50 or more prisoners apiece, and one containing 67 prisoners at the time of the research. In such circumstances prisoners not yet found guilty live for 23 hours a day. They eat in batches at the kind of combined table and benches to be found in the picnic areas of parks and which could accommodate perhaps 12–16 prisoners at a squeeze. They take turns to sleep on the floor when the continuous two tier bunks—sleeping platforms is perhaps a better description—on either side of the cell are full. There was insufficient floor space even to pace out the cell.

Each cell has one toilet and a small sink in the corner, sometimes with a curtain for privacy, but sometimes not. In some cells there is a television set, provided by the families of prisoners, but this is permitted only on condition that it becomes the property of the prison on release or transfer. This being a remand prison there is no work. Prisoners leave their cells, as a group, for daily exercise which takes place in the company of the same cell mates, in a cage on the roof which is approximately the same size as the cell. They get a weekly shower, again as a group, in a bathhouse whose permanently wet stone and cement walls and benches are irridescent with excrescent mineral salts.

71

The main thing that remand prisoners might have to look forward to is a morning appointment with the magistrate investigating their case, and perhaps an afternoon meeting with their defence lawyer. But the process of justice, which appears to allow little or no room for bail, and to have no effective legal aid, is fraught with delay: investigation of cases which supposedly should be completed within two months is frequently extended, especially where there are multiple defendants, and, even when completed, there may be a long wait before cases come to trial. During this time visits are at the discretion of the investigating magistrate, but are almost never permitted until the investigation is complete, and may be withheld right up until the trial. Statistics on the length of time spent on remand were not readily available, but prisoners claimed they had been held virtually incommunicado often for many months, sometimes for years. There may be further delays after the trial before a sentence is brought into effect, but by then a prisoner's visits will be determined by reference to his status under the prison rules.

In Kresty, the main remand prison for St Petersburg, the conditions are not dissimilar. Indeed, apart from the fact that it has nothing comparable to Butyrki's large cells, its reputation is, if anything, worse. Kresty is approaching its centenary, though it looks and feels older. It was built according to a familiar pattern with cells on each of four storeys, on each of four wings, in two cruciform cell blocks. What is less familiar is the presence of guard dogs inside the 'centre'. The first thing one sees on entering the prison is an imposing chapel and it can only be a matter of time—given the extraordinary resurgence of the church in Russian prisons as in Russian society—before it is restored to its original use. Meanwhile, Kresty, like most other establishments, has a makeshift chapel converted from existing cells for the use of prisoners.

Kresty was built by Nicholas II, it is said, to house 1,000 prisoners. Today with no improvements to its fabric, and certainly no changes to increase its capacity, it is reputed to be the largest European prison with, in mid-November 1992, over 7,200 prisoners. A typical cell, approximately 3 metres long by 2.5 metres wide, with the usual toilet and sink in the corner by the door, might accommodate ten prisoners—six would sleep in the three-tiered bunks on either side of the cell; two more would sleep in the shallow spaces *underneath* the two sets of bunks; a ninth prisoner would sleep across the width of the cell on a narrow ledge under the cell window; the tenth would sleep on the floor between the two bunks. By no means all cells were so cramped. Some housed only six prisoners, a few only four. But it was also said that sometimes the same size cell accommodated 14 prisoners, although without having seen this occupation rate at first hand, it is not possible to describe where the additional prisoners could have slept.

Feeding over 7,000 prisoners three times a day on a budget of 88 roubles (at the then rate of exchange 15 pence) per prisoner per day must have been as daunting to staff as it was unsatisfactory for prisoners. The menu, on the day we visited the kitchens, described as 'soup with vestiges of meat', will be familiar to readers of Solzhenitsyn. It was not especially appetising, but nor was it very far removed from what was on offer in the staff canteen. Although one prisoner said he had lost weight since being in Kresty, another said the food was no different from other prisons, and still another thought that it was adequate.

In such conditions of overcrowding there are inevitable anxieties about vermin and disease. It is not uncommon to see prisoners proceeding in a crocodile, with bedding bundles over their shoulders, for delousing once their cell had been shown to be

72

infested. The hospital was short of dressings and drugs but it was claimed that all prisoners were tested for TB and for HIV and Hepatitis B. Some 200 prisoners are regarded as active TB cases in Kresty with a further 100 under observation, but it was said that only two cases of HIV have been discovered in the last two years.

At the Moscow conference it was alleged that on occasions Kresty cells had accommodated as many as 16 prisoners and that with poor ventilation it was so difficult to breathe that prisoners lost consciousness. In February 1992 it was alleged that there had been mass beatings of prisoners following protests about the conditions where up to 16 prisoners were given as little as five minutes for their weekly shower; and in May 1992 some Kresty prisoners went on a hunger strike which lasted for seven days.

The realities of life in the large cells at Butyrki, where staff, with some trepidation, only open the doors for exercise, bathing, and to escort prisoners to an interrogation or to the courts, can scarcely be imagined. At the top of the prisoner hierarchy there might be a thief in law (*vor v zakone*) who regards himself, and is so regarded by others, as having an effective licence to do what he likes. Below him might be self-appointed leaders (*pakhans*), likely to have considerable criminal records and able to command the loyalties of several henchmen (*shestyorki*) who exert pressure on their behalf. Below them are peasants or drones (*muzhiki*). One prisoner, now in a colony but who had been on remand in a small cell at Butyrki, told of how he had been beaten up by prisoners and how his situation had been ignored by the guards. He dressed and bandaged his wounds with the stuffing and ticking torn from his mattress.

On the other hand, it also has to be said that one of the overriding impressions when smaller cells were opened up—in both the men's and the women's sections of remand prisons—was the extraordinary resilience and good humour with which up to ten prisoners faced the circumstances of their confinement. It is said that the Russian character has been so moulded by adversity that there is almost nothing with which it cannot cope.

Officials made no attempt to hide the facts, or to conceal their sense of humiliation that such conditions exist in the name of the state: on more than one occasion they could jokingly parody what once they might even have been taught to recite: 'Of course, Soviet prisons are the best in the world.' But they feel powerless to do anything about it. In the present economic climate it is a struggle to find funds to feed and clothe prisoners—but officials are all too aware that it is a struggle for ordinary Russian citizens to feed and clothe their families outside. There is a massive shortage of staff, no money to recruit them and no money for building or refurbishment. And in a situation where the crime rate is rising rapidly, reinforcing traditionally highly punitive Soviet attitudes towards criminals, the relief offered to Kresty by the opening of Remand Prison No. 5 for the Leningrad Region in early 1993 seems likely to be temporary. Elsewhere things seem likely to get worse before they get better: as at June 1993 the prison population was said to be rising by 4,000 a month.

Conditions in the Colonies and the Prisons

Corrective labour colonies are much more widely dispersed than remand prisons and many of them are far from centres of population. It is thought that between a third and

73

a half of sentenced prisoners still 'sit out' their sentences, as the Russian phrase has it, in Siberia. Although four of the colonies included in this study were forest zone colonies in the Perm province in the northern Urals it was obviously not possible to include the most remote institutions.

Natashev (1985), in his defence against bourgeois criticism, goes to some lengths to distinguish corrective labour *colonies* both from the former corrective labour *camps* (which were 'abolished' under Kruschev's reforms in 1958) on the one hand, and from *prisons* on the other. Whilst there is something here of the internationally familiar penal practice of dressing up old institutions in new terminological garb, there is no doubt that significant reforms were then introduced—including the abolition of night time interrogation and the powers to sentence persons deemed to have committed 'analagous crimes' to those actually included in the criminal code. Most importantly, the codification of the procedures for the execution of sentences, including deprivation of liberty, dates from that time. Nevertheless, old hands in the colonies acknowledged the historic change of name but were inclined to date actual attempts to implement the reform procedures as being much more recent.

In theory, at least, the Soviet system of corrective labour was legitimated by reference back to Lenin's insistence on the replacement of prisons by educational institutions and, somewhat less convincingly, to his principle that deprivation of liberty should be commuted to a penalty not involving isolation from society (Natashev 1985: 29). The prison, as that concept evolved in the late eighteenth and early nineteenth centuries in Western Europe and in Pennsylvania, with a separate system based on cellular confinement, is better suited to penitential contemplation than to productive work. In New York, and elsewhere in the United States, the prison was developed in alternative ways to accommodate to the work ethic of a growing capitalist economy.

In Soviet practice, the cellular prison, whilst not formally relieved of its role in 'labour re-education', offered only restricted opportunities for work, and its threatened use served instead as an effective deterrent against potential misbehaviours in the colonies. The camps/colonies, by contrast, were systematically linked to the process of organized industrial production through the centralized command economy, to which they contributed substantially both in the form of fulfilled production targets and the return of profit to Moscow. The system provided cheap communal accommodation for prisoner work teams often close to the supply of raw materials or some other industrial resource. Although prisoners were paid, the level of deductions was such that they constituted effectively a slave labour force. They were forced to work regardless of the state of their health or the safety of the conditions; 'encouraged' to meet their quotas through the prospect of relieving hunger; and threatened with punishments for falling short of their targets. In the mid 1980s the Ministry of the Interior was the fourth most profitable in the Soviet Union.

The problem for the Russian authorities is to re-legitimate a system which has, more than most, been discredited by its past usage. On the face of it, the legacy of a few cellular prisons and a large number of colonies, systematically differentiated according to the levels of criminal involvement of their inmates, and given over largely to industrial production, offers a convenient marriage between the incentives and punishments, beloved by the advocates of 'progressive stage' prison systems on the one hand, and the rhetoric of reform and re-education on the other. But the authorities face enormous problems. Unlike Poland, where some 7,500 staff chose to leave the prison

74

service rather than work with the new reforms,[3] the Russians seek to distance themselves from the past with virtually all their former staff still in the same posts. Moreover, while they have formally abandoned punitively reduced diets they now find they can barely afford ordinary diets for their prisoners as the profits from prison industries disappear with the old command economy, and prices outside escalate alarmingly.

This is not to say, however, that anyone who has visited institutions such as Ford or Ashwell, or even Featherstone, say, would have any difficulty at all in recognizing any of the Russian corrective labour colonies for males included in this study as rather run-down and under-resourced low to medium security prisons. What sometimes seems rather antiquated or makeshift in the provision of physical security is compensated for by the armed troops who man the watchtowers. Although they are not allowed to shoot women and minors who attempt escape, they may do so in the case of men after firing a warning shot. In many cases the harsh climatic conditions in situations of extreme geographical isolation provide a sufficient deterrent to would-be escapers.

The most striking thing about the corrective labour colonies is that in spite of the rigid determination to distinguish between minor first offenders, more serious first offenders, recidivists, and particularly dangerous recidivists, and to send them to quite separate colonies where they wear distinctively different uniforms, the similarities between the regimes far outweigh the differences. Only in the case of special regime colonies are there important differences in the daily living conditions.[4] The system is thus predicated on the same contamination theories which led to the development of separate cellular confinement, except that here it is applied to categories of prisoners rather than to individuals. Indeed, it is ironic that the Russian system—which is viewed in the West as one where executive and administrative convenience prevail over judicial authority—should cling so firmly to the arbitrary legal statuses of offenders in determining the shape and structure of its correctional system when Western systems have moved towards greater administrative discretion in the location and treatment of prisoners. Thus, although it has apparently been held as a penological principle since about 1970 that prisoners should 'sit out' their sentences close to home, officials could not apparently conceive of overturning the legal principle, enshrined in the Fundamentals of the Corrective Labour Legislation and rigorously applied by the courts, that different classes of prisoner should be housed separately. The resolution of the conflict between these principles, still produces—especially for women and girls—a situation where prisoners may end up in the nearest camp of the appropriate type but which takes their families many days in travel time to visit.

What most of the colonies have in common is a pattern of domestic living in dormitories or barracks within a residential compound, and a commitment to industrial production within an adjacent industrial complex. There is a comparatively rigid physical separation between these two spheres—often as complete as between the colony and the outside world—but for the most part movement is now comparatively

[3] Personal communication from Rod Morgan based on NACRO seminar on Changes in the Polish Prison System, 6 July 1992.

[4] Under the new Corrective Labour Code it is expected that the remaining differences of regime between general, reinforced, and strict colonies will be abolished. All will be designated as general regime, although the separation of prisoners by legal category will remain. As a first step, in July 1993, the distinction between general and reinforced regimes was abandoned.

unrestricted within the residential area. Neither the outer nor the inner doors of the dormitories are locked, and although there are often residual fenced compounds which mark off one dormitory's territorial area from another, these have largely fallen into disuse, except perhaps in special regime colonies. Staff have found such compounds inconvenient barriers to the use of communal facilities and they no longer seek to prevent the persistent breaches of these boundaries by prisoners. In special regime colonies there is a mixture of cellular and dormitory accommodation with prisoners spending the first half of their sentence in cells (unless the court has ruled otherwise in respect of a minor current offence committed by one who is technically a 'particularly dangerous recidivist') before 'progressing' to dormitories.

All colonies have limited, and not especially secure, cellular accommodation which can be used for long term disciplinary segregation of prisoners for periods up to six months (a year for special regime prisoners); and a number of punishment cells, the use of which is limited to a maximum of 15 days, for disciplinary offences. Until recently it was the case that prisoners might be briefly released from one period of punishment or segregation only to be returned immediately for another. Measures to limit the use of segregation to a maximum of six months in any year (there seems to be no similar protection for special regime prisoners) and the use of punishment cells to a maximum of 60 days in the course of a year, have recently been introduced. In theory prisoners may not be returned to punishment cells without the commission of a further offence. It is not clear how effective these protections are because allegations of breaches still occur. The old disciplinary punishment of feeding prisoners a 'normal', but reduced, diet one day and bread and water the next, which when combined with being required to strip down and sleep in cold cells with very little bedding, had sapped the health of generations of prisoners, was abolished in 1988. Punishment cells were now said to be properly heated, and prisoners were now said to be allowed both normal clothing and bedding. Though they are denied other privileges whilst on punishment they now receive daily exercise and weekly baths. For serious offences or persistent indiscipline prisoners may be transferred to prisons for periods of up to three years. Cellular confinement is not the same as solitary confinement: it is normally the case, both in the colonies and in prisons, that prisoners share cells with several others. Even prisoners serving short periods in punishment cells may well find they have cell mates, although punishment facilities for solitary confinement in very small cells certainly still exist. The ones in Vladimir, for example, measured no more than 2.5×1 metre, had rough cement rendering (known as 'fur') on the walls, and poor lighting—but on the occasion of our visit were well heated (see Amnesty International 1980: 160 for another account).

The White Swan was developed in 1981 as a facility with special cellular accommodation (*pomeshcheniya kamernovo tipa* or PKT) to which prisoners who had been defined as particularly difficult could be transferred from general, reinforced, and strict regime colonies for periods of up to six months, and from special regime colonies for periods up to 12 months. The officially stated intention—reminiscent of the arguments deployed by Radzinowicz (ACPS 1968) for the development of special segregation units or subsequently for the development of CI 10/74 procedures in Britain (see King and McDermott 1990)—was to deal with such prisoners in circumstances where they could no longer be an influence on the general population. It was also argued that the creation of special institutions would enable staff to develop particular expertise in dealing with the so-called 'thieves in law'. Not surprisingly the White Swan has attracted a great deal of controversy, although space precludes further discussion of that here. The White Swan and the several other institutions which have been opened on the same lines have somewhat reduced the role that prisons such as Vladimir used to play in this regard.

The other side of these disciplinary measures is that the system permits the transfer from prison, or from special regime colonies, to colonies with less severe regimes, and from those colonies to settlement colonies after prescribed periods of good behaviour. Conditions in the colonies probably vary most notably according to their location, with a general rule being that the more isolated they are the more spartan are likely to be the conditions. Officials made no secret of the fact that conditions for both staff and prisoners in the more distant colonies in the forest zones, which could not be reached by road for much of the year, were extremely primitive. The colonies visited in this study had domestic facilities which in many respects were only rather marginally more crowded and impoverished than would have been the case for the several hutted military camps which were taken over as open prisons in Britain after the Second World War.

The other main differences between the colonies derive essentially from the legal status of the prisoners who are sent to them and relate to correspondence, visits, food parcels, the use of telephones, and eligibility for parole. Two further matters—the spending of money at the prison shop and eligibility for home leave—are best dealt with when considering the whole question of prison work. Changes in the rules in relation to some of these were at the heart of the reforms announced in September 1991 which became law on 12 June 1992, following their introduction on a pilot basis in a number of women's colonies.

All prisoners have limited, but now considerably enhanced, rights to visits and food parcels: typically the entitlement during the first third of the sentence is between four and six food parcels a year, and between four and six short visits (normally two hours) a year depending on the severity of the regime. Subject to good behaviour during that time, the entitlements are thereafter increased effectively to one visit a month and one food parcel a month for prisoners in general, reinforced, and strict regime colonies. It is important to note that Russia has long permitted conjugal visits—known as long visits—which are restricted to family members and which may last for up to three days. Under the new rules, after the first third of the sentence has been served, half the visits each year may be on this basis, effectively alternating each month with a short visit. In the course of the research long visits' accommodation was seen in several establishments where it was possible to interview prisoners and their visitors (as often as not their mothers, who came and provided home cooking) in situ. The entitlements for persons in special regime colonies and in prisons, however, are less generous. Since July 1992 it has been theoretically permissible for some prisoners to use the telephone: in practice this has become a contentious matter because in many colonies, especially the more remote ones where visiting is in any case difficult, there were no telephone lines available.

Some prisoners may become eligible for parole after they have served one-third, a half, two-thirds or three-quarters of their sentence, depending upon legal category, work record, and other criteria. Particularly dangerous recidivists are excluded from parole consideration, as are reprieved murderers, and the eligibility criteria are interpreted strictly so that only about 8 per cent of prisoners actually receive substantial parole.

What has been routinely most controversial about the colonies in the past—apart from specific allegations of torture or abuses of power—has been their role as forced labour camps. Today Russian prisoners are still compulsorily required to work, normally on the basis of an eight-hour day, a six-day week with Sundays off, just as, of course, according to Rule 28(1) of the Prison Rules (1964) prisoners in England and Wales are 'required to do useful work for not more than ten hours a day'. In Britain, as in Russia, refusal to work is technically a disciplinary offence. Indeed, it is a striking comment on the two societies that at the Moscow Conference concern was still being expressed that in effect prisoners were 'slaves of the state' (a phrase many prisoners have tattooed on their hands) whereas Plotnikoff (1986), in her commentary on the British Prison Rules, echoing much concerned British opinion, argues that the most significant omission in the Rules is that they specify a maximum 'but not a minimum' working day. Clearly the status of the Russian system of corrective labour colonies as forced labour camps depends not so much on whether work is compulsory—for that is 'normal' in prison systems—but much more crucially upon how that is enforced and whether those subject to such a system are legitimately and lawfully imprisoned for a criminal offence.

Leaving those rather large questions on one side, for the moment, there are important similarities and differences between the Russian system and the British one. Just as in Britain, whatever the rules actually say, there is now not enough work to go round. In spite of one's knowledge of the history and of the squalid and unhealthy working conditions, it was sometimes hard not to be moved by prison staff whose pride in their past production records had been sadly dashed as their empty or underused workshops faced closure in the absence of raw materials, the inability to get contracts, or because bad debts had not been paid by their customers in the southern republics. Just as in Britain, quality control is a problem. But unlike in Britain, many of the jobs are real jobs, and although conditions may be poor, they are, at least in theory, governed by the same system of (inadequate) rules and inspections as apply to outside industry. Russian prisoners, moreover, are paid wages which come close to the rate for the job in outside industry, rather than the 5 per cent or less of the average wage which prevails in Britain. In some cases they got paid the same as, or more than, some categories of prison staff. Unlike their British counterparts, Russian prisoners are now eligible for 15 days of paid annual leave. These holidays may mean no more than not going to work, but in some circumstances can be taken at home. Since September 1992 monthly cohorts of prisoners have left their respective colonies to spend 15 days at home—as in the outside world travel time is extra.

In the past one of the main criticisms of the Gulag has been the level of deductions from prisoners' earnings to defray the costs of maintaining corrective labour institutions. Since the recent reforms limits have been imposed on the amounts deducted for food and uniform; providing they have work prisoners appear to have sufficient earnings to send some money home, to make some savings towards release and to buy additional items from the prison shop, even after they have paid any compensation which may have been ordered by the courts. Unfortunately, prisoners are not always in work, although in these circumstances they are fed and clothed without going into debt to the institution, and when they do have money to spend they face even more

78

problems than their fellow citizens face outside. Inflation has enormously eroded the value of money, and the prison shop has hardly anything on the shelves.

One of the most important differences between Russian corrective labour colonies and British prisons concerns the social organization of the domestic and work spheres. Readers of Solzhenitsyn (1963) will be familiar with the role of work team leaders who stand as a kind of buffer between the ordinary prisoners and the industrial staff in the allocation of tasks, the determination of quotas, and ensuring they are met. Work teams may not only work together but effectively live together, sharing a dormitory with other work teams to make up a larger section or detachment of perhaps 100 or 120 prisoners. Typically the detachment will be under the supervision of a detachment head, a senior member of prison staff, usually a graduate in education from one of the ministry academies who reports to the deputy governor in charge of education. The detachment head, who is usually the *only* member of staff in the dormitory, plays a role somewhere between a social worker and an assistant governor, perhaps most like housemasters once did in borstals. Under the old Soviet system his or her educational task involved giving many uplifting lectures on Marxism–Leninism and the importance of meeting production targets to the assembled detachment (see Amnesty International 1988: 145 for testimony on the intellectual quality of these sessions). Such occasions are still a feature, but having passed through a transitional stage which stressed that 'hard work is the guarantee of success for perestroika' these talks are now more likely to become explanations of the new humanitarian rules, and why it is important for prisoners not to strike or to abscond from the new privilege of home leave. As principal compilers of the prisoners' records—a task for which they are sometimes called 'fairytale tellers'—detachment heads play a key part in most of the discretionary decision making.

A final word. It became apparent that many staff felt that the new reforms, welcome though they were as humanizing measures, nevertheless undermined their position by removing levers over the behaviour of inmates. Nowhere was this more strongly expressed than in institutions for women where new privileges have been added to those already allowed for pregnant women and mothers with young children, which staff believe have gone too far. Thus, from the fourth month of pregnancy women are free of the obligation to work and remain so until their child is three years old. During that time the only sanction available in the event of disciplinary offences is for the governor to place a written reprimand into the prisoner's file. It is said that many women prisoners now seek to become pregnant for the immunity it gives them—a tactic employed by women prisoners of conscience in the past.

Conclusion

It would clearly be premature to attempt to draw definitive conclusions from a preliminary piece of research such as this. Rather like the house surveyor who warns that although every effort has been made to lift the carpets he cannot guarantee there is no dry rot in the places he could not see, it is incumbent upon the researcher to remind readers of the dangers that lurk beneath the surface. The dangers are surely all too obvious. Nevertheless, it is important to say something of how far the Russian system appears to have come and where it seems to be going even if that does render up some hostages to fortune.

In considering the future direction that any prison system should take it is always tempting to paraphrase the man who, having been asked the way from A to B, replied, 'If it was me I wouldn't start from here'. But no system can avoid its history, and the history of the Russian system, under Stalin and to lesser degrees his successors, though it has yet to be fully told, is evidently more gruesome than most. The testimony of Sakharov (1975), Solzhenitsyn (1978), and many other dissidents past and present, is eloquent. Too many prisoners have died. Too many others contracted tuberculosis or had their health broken. Millions have passed through the system, frequently without having committed anything that would normally be considered a criminal offence, and with scant regard for due process of law. Ministry officials confirm, albeit unofficially, that sentences were often delivered by judges at the telephone direction of local party officials.

Do such things happen today? Allegations are made with vehemence but are no less vehemently denied. What seems obvious is that in a system seeking to re-legitimate itself, where the same judges, the same procurators, the same ministry officials, and the same prison staff remain in post, the onus is upon them to *demonstrate* that such things are not now possible rather than simply to *assert* it. As one prison governor put it: 'It has been hard for some of the staff to change their stripes.' It may be even harder to convince outsiders that they have done so. It is not sufficient to point to changes in the corrective labour code, however important they may be. In the West the questions of how to develop proper structures for inspection, review, and redress of grievances have dominated penological thinking in recent years. Given the history it is vitally important that credible structures are erected to ensure that well-intentioned reforms are carried through and not subverted by political or private corruption. As a leading *Izvestia* journalist Leonid Shinkarev—one of the first to be allowed into the colonies— observes: 'It is very difficult to check on stories of abuse and torture, but you must remember that in the more remote regions a prison governor is God and the tsar rolled into one.' Nevertheless, a start has been made and it is possible to see things of merit in the nature and structure of the Russian system of corrective labour when compared to much that is on offer in the West. The level of integration of prison industry with the wider economy—both in terms of its output and its being subject to the same rules of health and safety at work, however inadequate they may be; the relative levels of wages; and the ability to support families and compensate victims, for example, were all once part of the long forsaken agenda of the Advisory Council on the Treatment of Offenders (see Cooper and King 1965). It is ironic that both prison industry and the economy into which it is integrated should both be collapsing just as the system becomes opened up to public view. The real questions concerning forced labour in Russia are not about whether or not prison work is compulsory but about the circumstances of its enforcement and whether or not those who experience it should be in prison at all. Certainly there is a growing public view that once Yeltsin emptied Perm Colony 35 of its remaining political prisoners, the force of the old arguments about the Gulag were weakened. Nevertheless, there is impressionistic evidence from this study that there are still many people in custody—and some of them have been inside for very long periods—for offences that in Britain would not normally attract a custodial sentence.

In terms of prison conditions it is impossible to view the remand prisons without raising important questions about bail, legal aid, and the rights of persons not yet found guilty not just to a speedy trial but to much more generous contact with their families. Elsewhere, though, it is equally impossible to view prison conditions in terms of international standards for space, crowding, food, and general facilities without at least some understanding of those matters for ordinary Russian citizens. Arguably the contextual gap between prison and the society of which it is a part is smaller in Russia than in Britain. Certainly Shinkarev now argues that by the time he has got to work, having watched crowds of Russians shuffling past the kiosks at the metro stations selling goods which Russians cannot afford and no Westerner would wish to buy, to discover that the crime figures have soared again, he finds it harder to write about the need for prison reform. That, of course, is not to say that meaningful standards should not be struck and diligently observed. But given the dilapidated conditions in most institutions, and the abandonment of the command economy which has drastically hit prison industries, it is difficult to see how the system can survive in anything like its present form. If international standards are to be realistically approached imprisonment will become a much more expensive commodity than it has been in the past, and on current trends in the economy, Russia is unlikely to be able to afford a system on its present scale. How a society which, in spite of its undoubted sympathy for the political victims of the Gulag, sustains a fundamentally punitive attitude towards crime will cope with the surge in crime that will surely accompany the growth of the market economy, is anybody's guess.

Inevitably, a study such as this, more than is usually the case for any piece of research, raises many more questions than it answers. Perhaps the most hopeful thing is that even a few years ago such a study would have been unthinkable. Now the lines of communication have been generously opened.

References

ACPS (1968), *The Regime for Long Term Prisoners in Conditions of Maximum Security*. Report of the Advisory Council on the Penal System (The Radzinowicz Report). London: HMSO.

Amnesty International (1988), *Prisoners of Conscience in the USSR: Their Treatment and Conditions*. Sunbury: Quartermaine House.

Butler, W. E. (1992), 'Crime in the Soviet Union: Early Glimpses of the True Story', *British Journal of Criminology*, 32/2:144–59.

Cooper, M. H. and King, R. D. (1965), 'Social and Economic Problems of Prisoners' Work', *Sociological Review Monograph*, 9: 145–73.

Council of Europe (1991), Committee for Prevention of Torture CPT/Inf(91)11: *Report to the United Kingdom Government on the Visit to the United Kingdom from 29 July to 10 August 1990*. Strasbourg: Council of Europe.

Dashkov, G. V. (1992), 'Quantitative and Qualitative Changes in Crime in the USSR', *British Journal of Criminology*, 32/2, 160–6.

Fitzgerald, M. (1977), *Prisoners in Revolt*. Harmondsworth: Penguin Books.

King, R. D. (1991), 'Maximum-security Custody in Britain and the USA: a Study of Gartree and Oak Park Heights', *British Journal of Criminology*, 31/2: 126–52.

King, R. D., and Elliott, K. W. (1978), *Albany: Birth of a Prison—End of an Era*. London: Routledge and Kegan Paul.

King, R. D., and McDermott, K. (1989), 'British Prisons 1970–87: The Ever-deepening Crisis', *British Journal of Criminology*, 29/2:107–28.

—— (1990), 'My Geranium is Subversive: Notes on the Management of Trouble in Prisons', *British Journal of Sociology*, 41/4:445–71.

KING, R. D., and MORGAN, R. (1976), *A Taste of Prison: Custodial Conditions for Trial and Remand Prisoners*. London: Routledge and Kegan Paul.

—— (1980), *The Future of the Prison System*. Farnborough: Gower.

KUDRYATSEV, V. N. (1989), 'Towards a Socialist Rule-of-Law State', in A. Aganbegyan, ed., *Perestroika Annual*. Futura Publications.

MORGAN, R. and EVANS, M. (1994), 'Inspecting Prisons: The View from Strasbourg', in this issue.

NATASHEV, A. E. (1985), *Soviet Corrective-Labour Policy and its Implementation by the Ministry of the Interior Agencies*, edited by A. I. Zubkov. Presented to Seventh UN Congress on the Prevention of Crime and the Treatment of Offenders, Milan.

PLOTNIKOFF, J. (1986), *Prison Rules: A Working Guide*. London: Prison Reform Trust.

SAKHAROV, A. (1975), *My Country and the World*, edited by H. Salisbury. New York.

SOLZHENITSYN, A. (1963), *One Day in the Life of Ivan Denisovich*. Harmondsworth: Penguin.

—— (1978), *The Gulag Archipelago*. London: Collins.

USS, A. (1991), 'The Union of Soviet Socialist Republics', in Van Zyl Smit and Dunkel, eds, *Imprisonment Today and Tomorrow: International Perspectives on Prisoners' Rights and Prison Conditions*. Deventer and Boston: Kluwer.

VAN DEN BERG, G. P. (1985), *The Soviet System of Justice: Figures and Policy*. Dordrecht: Martinus Nijhoff.

THE GROWTH OF IMPRISONMENT IN CALIFORNIA

Franklin E. Zimring and Gordon Hawkins*

This article reports on a study of trends in imprisonment in the state of California over the period 1980–91. Documenting and analysing imprisonment in California is important to an international audience for two reasons. First, the pattern in California since 1980 is representative of a widespread trend in the United States of expansion in the scale of the prison enterprise. At least 90 per cent of American states are currently imprisoning offenders at a higher rate than at any other time in the twentieth century. The unprecedented expansion in California prison population is part of this pattern; and studying events in California is one approach to comprehending developments and conditions in most American states.

The second reason why California's situation demands attention is that the growth in imprisonment in that state has been singular in both its pace and its magnitude. The number of prisoners in California increased more than fourfold in 11 years. The current 104,000 prisoners in California is by far the largest prison population in the Western world, more than twice the national prison populations of West Germany and Great Britain. Never has a prison system grown by so much in so short a time during a period of political and social stability. Figure 1 compares the 1990 prison population in California and three other large American states with national prison populations in major European countries.

At the beginning of the 1980s, each of the European systems profiled was larger than all of the state systems. By 1990, three of the American state systems had grown to surpass each of the three European systems; and Florida was larger than Germany and Italy. The average major state system doubled in the decade while the average European system declined modestly.

The second visually striking conclusion from Figure 1 is that California was in a category by itself in prison growth during the 1980s. The other three major American systems averaged growth levels about half that experienced in California. The fourfold increase in this major state to a prison population twice as large as any Western European country in 1990 seems a singular event in American correctional history.

Our presentation of data from the California study proceeds in two parts. The first part (The California Story) uses statistics from California and sister states to document: the pace and extent of prison population growth in California; the extent to which the California pattern reflects the experience of other American states; the correlation between variation in potentially explanatory variables like crime and arrest rates and changes in imprisonment rates; and the way in which recent California experience has been used for projecting further growth in the prison system.

The second part of the analysis (Policy Perspectives) will discuss three of our findings which are of importance to students of imprisonment policy in Western democracies. We seek to draw particular attention to the open-ended potential for prison population growth in periods of stable criminality; the enormous margin of error generated from

* Earl Warren Legal Institute, University of California at Berkeley.

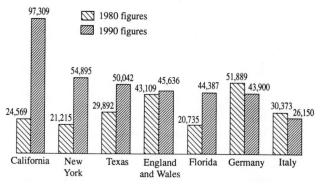

FIG. 1   1980 and 1990 Prison Populations in Major Systems (US Bureau of Justice Statistics, *Prisoners in 1990* (United States); Home Office Statistical Service, *Prison Statistics, England and Wales* 1981, 1991 (England and Wales); Istituto Nazionale di Statistica, *Annuario Statistico Italiano*, 1981, 1991 (Italy); Statistiches Bundesamt, *Statistiches Jahrbuch*, 1991 (Germany))

estimates of future prison populations that are derived from straight-line projections that use high-growth periods as a base; and the opportunities presented by rapid and extensive growth in imprisonment in California to study the nature and extent of the incapacitation effect generated by changes in correctional policy.

The California Story

The pace and extent of California growth

Figure 2 shows the variation in the number of prisoners and the rate of imprisonment in California from 1950 to 1990.

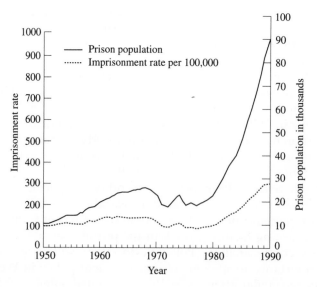

FIG. 2   Trends in Prison Population and Rate of Imprisonment per 100,000 in California, 1950–90 (California Department of Corrections, Prisoners and Parolees Series, 1988, 1989, and 1990)

The number of prisoners climbed steadily under the pressure of expanding population from 1950 to 1968, while the rate of imprisonment held steady. Both numbers of prisoners and rates of imprisonment per 100,000 population dropped in the early 1970s with the drop in the rate of imprisonment more than balancing increases in state population, so that prison numbers do not exceed their mid-1960s levels for 14 years.

In January 1980, while the number of prisoners was at an average level of 23,000 for the 1970s, the rate of imprisonment reflected in that figure had fallen by more than 25 per cent since 1968. From 1981 onward, both numbers and rate increase without interruption. Even as the base rate of imprisonment increased throughout the 1980s, the rate of increase from that base does not diminish. By the end of 1985, the prison population had more than doubled from its 1980 population base. By the end of 1990, the population had doubled once more.

Figure 3 shows the growth for both prison and jail population in California by year during the 1980s. The prison population consists of convicted felons sentenced to terms of more than one year in state custody (though less time may be served). The jail population consists of persons convicted of felonies and misdemeanours who are sentenced to less than one-year terms and those awaiting trial who are held in custody. Jails are under local county management in California.

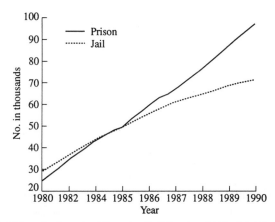

FIG. 3   Prison and Jail Populations by Year in California, 1980–90 (California Department of Corrections, California Board of Corrections)

Both jail and prison populations increased substantially through the decade, but the pattern for jails was slightly different. Jail population expanded from 28,946 to 70,845 over the 1980s, but three-quarters of that growth occurred prior to 1987. The annual growth in jail population had slowed to about 5 per cent by the decade's end.

Prisons passed jails in total population in 1985 and continued to grow in the late 1980s at a rate twice that of jails. After 1985, the California system added more prisoners each *year* than the system added in the average *decade* between 1950 and 1980. Between 1980 and 1991, California experienced seven times as much total growth in prison population as in the previous three decades combined.

The figure most comparable to English and European prison statistics is the combination of prison and jail numbers. During the 1980s, the total number in prisons

85

FRANKLIN E. ZIMRING AND GORDON HAWKINS

and jails more than tripled from 52,000 to 170,000, while state population increased 30 per cent. In one decade, one American state added more than 100,000 extra prison and jail inmates to its correctional population.

Parallels to the experience of other states in the United States

The correctional growth experience in California in the 1980s was simultaneously a singular event in American correctional history and not untypical of the performance of most other states during this most unusual decade. What was distinctive about the California experience was the sheer size of the expansion: no state had ever added 75,000 prisoners or increased prison and jail populations by 115,000 in one decade. Yet the trend in California was not that far removed from the pattern in most other American states. Figure 4 compares changes in California's rate of imprisonment with parallel data for the rest of the United States in the aggregate.

FIG. 4   Rates of Imprisonment per 100,000 of Population: California and the United States, 1950–90 (California Department of Corrections, Prisoners and Parolees Series)

The two trend lines are quite similar during the 1980s. Rates of imprisonment start to rise in the mid-1970s in the other states, so that by 1980 there was a significant gap between California and non-California rates of imprisonment. But during the 1980s, California imprisonment rates first closed the gap and then moved into a slight lead.

Three statistical elements combined to produce the unprecedented build-up in prisons. First, California followed the national trend toward higher rates of imprisonment and this feature alone would account for about half of California's prison population growth. The 1980s were a decade in which the average jurisdiction's prison population more than doubled. A second factor contributing to the explosive growth in prison population was the interaction of these higher imprisonment rates with a 30 per cent increase in the state's population.

The third development in California that helps to explain the expansion in prison

86

population is that California also changed its standing in imprisonment levels relative to other states. In 1980 California's rate of imprisonment per 100,000 was in the middle of the state distribution, ranking twenty-fourth in relation to the 50 states and the District of Columbia (Zimring and Hawkins 1991*b*: 149). By 1991 California's rank had climbed to fifteenth (US Department of Justice 1992: 1).

Each element of this experience interacted with the other elements in a multiplicative way. A 30 per cent increase in state population would produce a 30 per cent increase in prison population if imprisonment rates were stable. But a 30 per cent increase in state population would be causally associated with an additional 90 per cent increase in prison population due to the higher population at risk if the imprisonment rate tripled at the same time that state population expanded. With this kind of interaction the extent of change that can be attributed to a particular contributing factor is debatable; the order in which changes are placed into the equation could influence the amount of leverage attributable to a particular change.

Causes and non-causes

What forces are associated with this unprecedented growth in imprisonment? The historical evidence we examined clearly excludes a number of explanations for the increase in imprisonment and suggests two trends that between them account for a major share of that increase.

Whatever may have caused the explosive growth in prison population, crime trends in California, and the level of arrests for non-drug felonies are not significantly related to the imprisonment boom. Crime rates decreased during the first half of the 1980s in California and that pattern holds whether the subject is total reported crime, index felony offences, or violent offences. The decline in crime while prison population was soaring might tempt many observers to conclude that the increase in imprisonment was a major cause of the decline in crime. The plausibility of that hypothesis suffered a setback in the latter part of the decade as rates of serious crime edged back toward 1980 levels while the additional imprisonment imposed each year in California increased in the late 1980s by unprecedented amounts. For the decade as a whole, there is no apparent relationship between trends in crime and trends in imprisonment, as is shown in Figure 5.

If the crime trends in California do not explain the changes in imprisonment, what about changes in criminal justice policy? Here the pattern is less clear. No major change in sentencing structure or legislatively announced punishments is associated with the expansion of prison population that began in 1980. The switch from indeterminate to determinate prison sentences in California was effective in 1977 and produced a substantial decline in prison numbers at first, because a large number of offenders with greater-than-average prison sentence lengths under the old regime were given sentence reductions under this new system (Zimring and Frase 1980: 864). These major structural changes did not for the most part constrain the discretion of the courts to select or avoid imprisonment as a sanction. There were some legislative changes that may have influenced the rate of imprisonment, such as a law disapproving lesser charges and non-prison sanctions that came into effect in the early 1980s. And the same spirit that inspired the sentencing reforms of the mid-1970s may have led to a general toughening in public attitudes toward offenders and in judicial sentencing policy. But

87

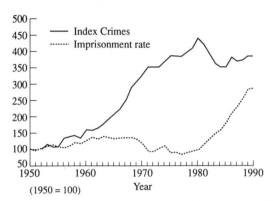

FIG. 5 Trends in Index Crimes and Imprisonment Rates in California, 1950–90 (FBI Uniform Crime Reports; California Department of Corrections, Prisoners and Parolees Series, 1988, 1989, and 1990)

no piece of legislation appears to have been directly responsible for most of the increase in imprisonment.

The two statistical trends most clearly responsible for the increase in imprisonment are increases throughout the decade in the proportion of felony convictions that produced sentences of imprisonment and the explosive growth in the number of individuals arrested for, convicted of, and imprisoned for drug offences. Figure 6 shows the proportion of felony convictions leading to prison commitment in California for each year from 1980 to 1990.

Figure 6 shows the principal cause of the imprisonment boom in California and if anything understates the nature of the shift toward more severe sanctions as the explanation of that boom. The increases in rates of imprisonment during the 1980s were much greater for crimes of lesser seriousness, such as larceny and automobile theft that have low rates of imprisonment at the beginning of the decade, than for more serious crimes, such as robbery, which have higher base rates of imprisonment. The number of robbers in California prisons increased by 104 per cent between 1980 and 1990, as compared with a 338 per cent increase in the total number of prisoners and a 565 per cent increase in the number of persons imprisoned for the less serious residual categories of theft.

The influences that led to this 'get tough' sentencing policy were more a matter of sentiment than legislation. Without any central direction, the large increases in the percentage of offenders imprisoned represent aggregate measures of the discretion of individual prosecutors and judges all over the state of California. This progressive toughening was not evenly spread over all California counties. Los Angeles county experienced a larger increase in the percentage of felons sent to prison than non-Los Angeles counties. Nevertheless, the extent of the general shift toward more severe discretionary decision making was not merely remarkable in California, but reflected a pattern throughout the United States.

Substantial increases in arrest, conviction, and imprisonment for drug offences are the other major influence on the general rate of imprisonment that our study identifies. Between 1980 and 1990 the annual total of males in prison for drug offences in California grew fifteenfold from approximately 1,500 to 22,600. Another way of stating

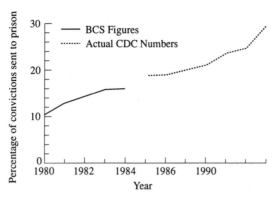

FIG. 6 Proportion of Non-drug Felony Convictions Resulting in Imprisonment in California, 1980–90 (California Department of Corrections (imprisonment numbers); Bureau of Criminal Statistics (conviction numbers))

the magnitude of the change is to point out that more persons were in prison in California for drug offences in 1991 than were in prison for *all* offences in California at the end of 1979 (Zimring and Hawkins 1992*b*: 32).

Is the large increase in drug cases evidence of a drug crime wave or merely of changing policy in relation to drug offences? Unlike non-drug felony crime, the number of felony arrests for drug offences increased rapidly throughout the 1980s, so that a comparison of arrest trends and imprisonment trends is not decisive on the question of causation in the same way that holds for burglary and robbery. There are, however, strong indications that changes in drug law enforcement rather than increases in drug taking have fuelled both arrest and imprisonment totals. National household surveys that have become the official governmental benchmark for illicit drug use indicate a persistent decline in the prevalence of the use of most illicit drugs during the 1980s (Zimring and Hawkins 1992*a*: 199). Yet imprisonment rates for drug crime rose sharply on a national basis after a high-intensity 'War on Drugs' was launched in the mid-1980s.

It is probably correct that the new policy emphasis on drugs was the principal reason for shifts in drug arrests as well as the increased severity in the sentencing of drug offenders. Yet an increase in drug arrests is far from a sufficient cause of the increase in prison population in California. From 1966 to 1976 the volume of drug arrests in the state of California increased almost twentyfold while the number of persons in prison fluctuated almost without trend (Zimring 1990: 23). What happened in the 1980s to produce the explosion in drug imprisonment was an interreaction between a shift toward 'get tough' attitudes and an increasing volume of drug arrests.

Identifying a movement in public and official sentiment as the major cause of California's imprisonment boom raises as many questions as it resolves. Criminal offenders never rate highly in public favour; but why the changes noted in the 1980s? Furthermore, once this sort of trend takes hold in a criminal justice system, what forces limit the influence of punitive sentiments? And how are new equilibrial conditions found and maintained? These are among the significant questions that careful studies of the California scene might profitably address.

89

Growth and the projection of future prison population

Rapid growth in the population under confinement puts pressure on those who maintain the system to make projections of future needs and to formulate and implement plans to meet those needs. In California, as the expanding prison population consumed the space added in the 1990s, the capacity of the system to accurately project future population and construction needs became a central element of criminal justice planning.

In 1991 the California Department of Corrections issued an official projection that by mid-year 2000, or nine years and three months after the projection, California prisons would confine 224,641 prisoners. The State Department of Finance estimated that $10.2 billion in additional construction would be necessary over the next ten-year period to hold that number of prisoners under conditions of tolerable crowding (California State Department of Finance 1991: 24).

That level of prison population for a single American state would be unprecedented, but at the same time would represent continuity in trend. The 224,641 estimate projected a smaller proportional growth than California had experienced in the previous nine years (see Figure 1). Yet the total projected growth was phenomenal. 224,000 prisoners would represent a prison population ten times as large in the California of the year 2000 as had existed 20 years before. Indeed, the projected total would exceed the total number of prisoners in all federal and state facilities in the United States in 1973.

The method used to obtain these estimates was a 'straight-line' projection that gave special weight to trends in prison admission closest to the time the projection was made and continued those trends forward for however many years the policy analyst had requested. Because heavy emphasis was placed on short-term trends, relatively small fluctuations in prison admissions created large changes in the projected prison populations.

A dramatic example of this occurred in California between the autumn of 1990 and the autumn of 1991. During that year, the prison population grew by 3,903 fewer prisoners than had been projected because the number of new admissions to prison did not grow as expected. This 3,900 prisoner shortfall resulted in a reduction of estimated prison population for the year 1996 that was ten times as great. In the autumn of 1991, it was anticipated that 132,972 prisoners would be in the system in 1996; 40,000 fewer than had been projected 12 months previously. Figure 7 shows the contrast.

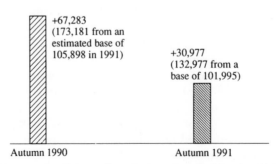

+67,283
(173,181 from an
estimated base of
105,898 in 1991)

+30,977
(132,977 from a
base of 101,995)

Autumn 1990   Autumn 1991

FIG. 7 Projected Change in Prison Population for California 1991–6: Two Estimates (California State Department of Corrections, 1990 and 1991)

Analysis of the California projections suggests two reasons why long-range predictions are particularly prone to error during periods when correctional populations are undergoing either sharp expansion or contraction. First, so-called 'straight-line' projections assume that short-term trends will continue for longer periods. When periods of extraordinary change precede the projection, this is rather like seeing a coin flip turn up heads three times in succession and predicting heads for the next 27 trials.

A second problem generated by the California projections was that they inadvertently assume that penalties for felonies would grow harsher during the 1990s. The Department of Corrections projections tended to assume that the level of sentence severity in California would stay constant over the 1990s. Thus, it was assumed that the prison terms meted out over the 1990s would be as long but no longer than the terms being imposed currently (California State Department of Corrections 1990). But the projection also assumed that the number of prison admissions would continue to increase at the rate that had been recently experienced in California. This assumed continued increase in the severity of punishment because one of the major reasons why prison admissions had been increasing in the late 1980s was that the proportion of convicted offenders receiving prison sentences had increased.

We can illustrate the problem and show the inconsistency involved in the California projection methodology with a hypothetical example. Assume that the proportion of all convicted burglars sent to prison increased from 20 per cent to 40 per cent between Year 1 and Year 2 and that the average term of imprisonment each burglar received moved up from 12 months to 18 months. In that case, the California method would assume that the average prison sentence for burglary remained at 18 months when estimating Year 3 results because it assumes constancy in the level of punishment. But because it continues the trend in levels of prison admissions, the California method would estimate that the number of prison admissions in Year 3 would double again and grow to a level equal to 80 per cent of convicted burglars. We are aware of no basis on which this inconsistency can be resolved.

Of the two assumptions, consistency of level of severity and continuity in trend of severity, the assumption of consistency of level of severity seems much the more prudent. Thus, when changes in the proportion of offenders committed to prison are a significant part of the changes experienced in the level of prison admissions, this must be brought to the attention of those who undertake to make projections. We are not aware of a prior illustration of these problems that was as sudden in its impact or as large in its statistical effect as the California experience.

Policy Perspectives

An increase in prison population of the magnitude and suddenness of that in California is worthy of international attention whenever and wherever it occurs. But there are three dimensions beyond the scale of change in California that should be of special concern to those persons and offices involved in the analysis of correctional policy in democratic governments. The three policy lessons already available for international consumption concern: (a) the open-ended potential for prison population increase; (b) the error generated by straight-line correctional growth projections; and (c) the existence of volatile prison growth as a natural laboratory for assessing the impact of imprisonment on crime rates.

91

The open-ended potential for prison population increase

Both the quality and quantity of change documented in California speak to the open-ended capacity for change in correctional systems. Most of the increased imprisonment in California was not directly related to either increases in crime or changes in population. Most crime levels in 1990 were close to their 1980 rates. While the state population had increased by 30 per cent, this element alone would have accounted for less than 10 per cent of the growth experienced by California prisons if rates of imprisonment per 100,000 had remained at 1980 levels. And the kinds of crime associated with the largest share in California's prison expansion—drug offences, housebreaking, and theft—are precisely the offences that flood the criminal justice systems of every major Western democracy. We think that the sorts of policy shifts observed in California could double the prison population of any country in Western Europe experiencing no net population growth or change in the volume or character of crime.

There is also a second respect in which prison growth in California was open-ended that is worthy of special attention. In the 1970s, Alfred Blumstein and his associates put forward a 'theory of the stability of punishment': a 'homeostatic hypothesis' according to which when a nation's prison population begins to fluctuate, pressure is generated to restore the prison population to a stable rate (Blumstein and Cohen 1973; Blumstein *et al.* 1976; Blumstein and Moitra 1979). This process of restoration

would typically be through some form of 'adaptation' by the various agencies within the nation's criminal justice system. One form of adaptation could result in changes in the manner in which discretion is exercised by the various functionaries within the criminal justice system. If prison populations get too large, police can choose not to arrest, prosecutors can choose not to press charges, judges can choose not to imprison, or parole boards can choose not to deny requests. (Blumstein and Moitra 1979: 376)

Under the 'homeostatic hypothesis' one would expect an increase in population or arrests that might exert upward pressure on prison population to be counteracted by forces that would push in the opposite direction. But what is remarkable in California is that every significant policy change during the 1980s pushed in the same direction. Compensatory or equilibrating forces were invisible in California prior to 1991. The absence of any apparent compensatory forces to bring about the 'homeostatic shifting' (Blumstein and Moitra 1979: 376) hypothesized by Blumstein and his associates was notable even as both total prison population and rate of imprisonment extended many standard deviations from previous average levels. It is further remarkable that not only did prison population movement run counter to the predictions of the theory of the stability of punishment, but that sentencing changes that continued through the middle and late 1980s also ran in precisely the opposite direction to that which the homeostatic hypothesis would predict.

There is one final way in which the prison growth in California was open-ended. There was no change in the formal penal law in the state of California that appears responsible for the changes in penal policy that occurred after 1980. The growth of imprisonment in California was thus a textbook illustration of the legal realist maxim that there is only a loose association between the law on the statute books and the law in action. The number of persons in confinement can double and triple with no change in the legal framework for criminal justice. The absence of any major statutory change to explain the California prison growth also means that changes in penal law will not necessarily serve as early warning signals of change in penal policy.

The paradox of prison population projections

Our earlier discussion of prison population projection exercises in California touched on errors in these exercises that were designed to estimate prison population in the late 1990s and the year 2000. But the particular errors noted in those exercises should not divert attention from the more general problem—such exercises cannot provide useful long-range planning estimates when correctional populations have been fluctuating significantly.

We do not here suggest that all long-range correctional forecasts are inaccurate. No one has rigorously evaluated a set of such projections. We suspect that long-range projections made during periods of stability in correctional populations will project stable trends far into the future; not infrequently these will be correct. Figure 8a shows a straight-line projection of future prison population (dotted line) derived from a stable recent history (straight line). Figure 8b, by contrast, displays recent growth in prison population (straight line) and two alternative future projections (dotted lines).

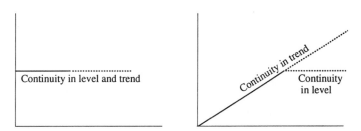

FIG. 8.   Projections from Contrasting Hypothetical Recent Trends in Prison Population: (a) From Rate Stability. (b) From Recent Growth

The dotted line representing the higher projection in Figure 8b reflects the assumption of continuity in trend from the historical data. The lower estimate reflected in the other dotted line was derived from the same historical data but assumes that prison population will remain stable at the level last noted in those data. Both are 'straight-line' projections; neither has a superior position a priori. One reason why the projection illustrated in Figure 8a might lead to fewer errors is that there is no disagreement in such circumstances between estimates based on continuity in trend and estimates based on continuity in level: they are represented in the same dotted line.

The problem we wish to emphasize here is that long-range correctional projections are most unreliable when they are most needed—in the midst of changing circumstances. Indeed, there is no single projection with a superior claim to validity under such circumstances. Forecasts are least error-prone in those circumstances when they are less needed, during periods of exceptional stability. Their real function in such circumstances is to predict the obvious. Of course, even when populations have been stable, straight-line projections will frequently prove inaccurate. But when prison populations are already fluctuating significantly, the problem is intractable: either continuity-of-trend or continuity-of-level projections must be wrong and there is no way of choosing the most likely error.

The California data we have been discussing illustrate this point all too well. Throughout the 1980s, growth in the California prison population would best have been described by a continuity of trend projection, a trend which turned out to extend for a decade; much longer than historical patterns in California would have suggested. At the end of 1990, however, the rate of increase in prison admissions flattened to a pattern more closely approximating continuity in level from mid-1990. As Figure 7 demonstrates, this difference in short-term trend generated a discrepancy of 40,000 prisoners in two 1996 projections made one year apart. It is all but inevitable that this type of flattening out will eventuate. But when such changes will happen is beyond the competence of projection technology. And this renders prison population forecasting all but useless in volatile periods.

The California experiment

A final respect in which the California experience merits international attention is as a natural experiment on the impact of large changes in rates of imprisonment on rates of crime. A major intended effect of imprisonment is the reduction of the number of crimes committed in the community as the result of the incapacitation of persons who would re-offend if at liberty. This incapacitation potential is the clearest comparative advantage of imprisonment over non-incarcerative penal sanctions such as probation, fines, and community service orders. In the discussion of imprisonment policy, much is assumed and estimated about the volume of crime prevented as a result of particular levels of incarceration. Few of the estimates that have been put forward have been rigorously tested (*see* Shinnar and Shinnar 1975; Blumstein *et al.* 1978; Zedlewski 1987; Cohen and Canela-Cacho 1992).

The experience of California since 1980 provides an important opportunity for studying the effect of changes in imprisonment on crime rates. The California increases in imprisonment occurred over a relatively short time period without any contemporaneous major social dislocation or changes in the nature of government or criminal justice. The statistics on crime, population, and punishment in California are not without defects, but they are among the highest quality data which are available on these topics. While the 'natural experiment' we have in mind is not the equivalent of controlled experimentation, the opportunity presented in California to assess the impact of additional imprisonment on crime rates is the best we have yet observed.

Conclusion

The explosive growth in California's prisons was a revolution of practice rather than theory. The celebrated shift to 'just deserts' sentencing was not the mechanical cause of the huge increase in prison population that began four years later. These population shifts were not associated with long prison terms, and principally involved larger numbers of property and drug offenders being sentenced to prison (see Zimring and Hawkins 1992*a*: chapters 1, 3). While the shifting public mood that resulted in the reform in California sentencing may have also contributed to the discretionary decisions of prosecutors and judges to imprison that fed the prison population increase, this indirect connection is hardly the model of legislative influence that is usually put forward.

The California experience has shown that long-term projections of future correctional needs cannot be made during periods of volatile change in rates of imprisonment over the short term. Yet the state's Department of Finance was ready to ground a multi-billion-dollar building programme on nine-year prison population projections of 224,000.

The radical change in penal policy that California has experienced may also be an unprecedented opportunity to assess the impact of so much extra imprisonment on crime rates. To have performed such a radical experiment without assessing its consequences would be unforgivable.

REFERENCES

BLUMSTEIN, A., and COHEN, J. (1973), 'A Theory of the Stability of Punishment', *Journal of Criminal Law and Criminology*, 64: 198–207.

BLUMSTEIN, A., COHEN, J., and NAGIN, D. (1976), 'The Dynamics of a Homeostatic Punishment Process', *Journal of Criminal Law and Criminology*, 67: 317–34.

——, eds. (1978), *Deterrence and Incapacitation: Estimating the Effects of Criminal Sanctions on Crime Rates*. Washington, DC: National Academy of Sciences.

BLUMSTEIN, A., and MOITRA, S. (1979), 'An Analysis of Time Series of the Imprisonment Rate in the States of the United States: A Further Test of the Stability of Punishment Hypothesis', *Journal of Criminal Law and Criminology*, 70: 376–90.

CALIFORNIA STATE DEPARTMENT OF CORRECTIONS (1990), *Prison Population Projections, 1990–1996*. Sacramento, CA: California State Department of Corrections.

—— (1991), *Prison Population Projections, 1990–1997*. Sacramento, CA: California State Department of Corrections.

CALIFORNIA STATE DEPARTMENT OF FINANCE (1991), *1991 Capital Outlay and Infrastructure Report*. Sacramento, CA: State Department of Finance.

COHEN, J., and CANELA-CACHO J. (1992), 'Patterns in Incarceration for Violent Crime'. Paper prepared for the National Academy of Science's Panel on the Understanding and Control of Violent Behavior.

SHINNAR, R., and SHINNAR, S. (1975), 'The Effects of the Criminal Justice System on the Control of Crime. A Quantitative Approach', *Law and Society Review*, 9: 581–611.

US DEPARTMENT OF JUSTICE, BUREAU OF JUSTICE STATISTICS (1992), *Prisons and Prisoners in the United States*. Washington, DC: US Department of Justice.

ZEDLEWSKI, E. (1987), 'Making Confinement Decisions', *National Institute of Justice Research in Brief*. Washington, DC: National Institute of Justice.

ZIMRING, F. E. (1990), 'Correctional Growth in Context', in *Growth and Its Influence in Correctional Policy*. Proceedings of a conference, 10–11 May 1990, Berkeley, CA. Berkeley, CA: University of California, Center for Study of Law and Society.

ZIMRING, F. E., and FRASE, R. (1980), *The Criminal Justice System: Materials on the Administration and Reform of the Criminal Law*. Boston: Little, Brown and Company.

ZIMRING, F. E., and HAWKINS, G. (1991), *The Scale of Imprisonment*. Chicago: University of Chicago Press.

—— (1992a), *The Search for Rational Drug Control*. Cambridge, MA: Cambridge University Press.

—— (1992b), *Prison Population and Criminal Justice Policy in California*. Berkeley, CA: University of California, Institute of Governmental Studies.

RACIAL DISPROPORTION IN US PRISONS

Michael Tonry*

Outside the United States, probably the best known characteristics of America's correctional system are that capital punishment continues in use and that American incarceration rates are four to 15 times higher than those in other developed countries. Within the United States, the most notable characteristics are the absolute numbers in confinement and that they are disproportionately black. Blacks in 1991 made up 12 per cent of America's population but 48 per cent of both prison and jail inmates.[1] Forty per cent of the occupants of 'death row' on 31 December 1991 were black. In public juvenile facilities in 1989, 48 per cent were black. Americans of Hispanic origin, by contrast, America's second largest minority group, in 1991 constituted 9 per cent of the general population, 13 per cent of the prison population, 14 per cent of the jail population, and 8 per cent of the death row population.

America's incarceration rates[2] are seen by many as evidence of draconian criminal justice policies. The overrepresentation of black offenders is seen by many as evidence of racial bias. Both critiques have merit; the latter rests, however, in part on a misconception that racial disproportion in prisons is markedly worse in the United States than elsewhere. This appears not to be the case.

Four findings stand out when incarceration rates are disaggregated by race in Australia, Canada, England and Wales, and the United States. First, the white American incarceration rate, compared with those in other English-speaking countries, is not as much higher as is generally believed. Secondly, patterns of differential incarceration by race in England and Wales (white and black), Australia (non Aboriginal and Aboriginal), and Canada (white and native) resemble American patterns. In all these countries, members of disadvantaged visible minority groups are seven to 16 times likelier than whites to be confined in correctional institutions.

Thirdly, when the different racial compositions of national prison populations are taken into account, apparent differences in national rates of incarceration diminish. Table 1, shown later in this essay, presents disaggregated incarceration rates for blacks, whites, and others for America and for England and Wales. It invites intriguing comparisons. If, for example, America's 1990 general population were, like England and Wales's in 1991, 94.1 per cent white and 1.8 per cent black, America's jails and prisons in 1990 would have housed 759,632 black and white inmates (the actual black and white total was 1,133,820). This assumes that incarceration rates by race would be the same as in 1990 (see Table 1). The national incarceration rate (assuming the 1990 rate of 241 per 100,000 for the residual 4.1 per cent 'other') would fall from 474 per 100,000 to 315.

When the opposite exercise is carried out, if England and Wales's black/white

---

* Sonosky Professor of Law and Public Policy at the University of Minnesota.
[1] With some exceptions, prisons hold convicted offenders serving terms of one year or longer; jails hold pre-trial detainees and convicted offenders serving terms up to one year.
[2] 'Incarceration rate', as used in this essay, refers to the numbers confined on a census date, or the average daily confined population, per 100,000 residents.

97

general population percentages were America's, the results would be more striking. In 1990, combining remand and sentenced prisoners, England and Wales incarcerated 77 whites per 100,000 whites and 547 blacks per 100,000 blacks. If the general population were 80 per cent white, 12 per cent black, there would be 30,732 white and 32,748 black prisoners and an overall incarceration rate (attributing the current 164 per 100,000 rate to the remaining 8 per cent of prisoners) of 140 per 100,000. England and Wales would have more black than white prisoners and its national incarceration rate would be more than 50 per cent higher (140 versus 89). This assumes that a sixfold increase in the black population would not be accompanied by heightened racial tensions that would exacerbate existing racial disproportions in confinement decisions and patterns (e.g., Hood 1992).

Fourth, racial disproportion in prisons within countries is distributed in ways not commonly recognized. In 1988, for example, black–white incarceration rate differentials in some southern American states were relatively low (4 to 1 in Mississippi, South Carolina, and Tennessee). In some states traditionally considered politically liberal and governmentally progressive, like Wisconsin (12 to 1), Iowa (16 to 1), Connecticut (17 to 1), and Minnesota (19 to 1), the differentials were much higher. Similar patterns exist in Australia where Aboriginal–non-Aboriginal differentials ranged from 3.4 to 1 in Tasmania to 19.7 to 1 in Western Australia in January 1993.

This essay examines racial differences in incarceration, mostly in the United States but with occasional mention of other English-speaking countries. To anticipate the conclusion, a large part (but by no means all) of the long-term incarceration rate differential by race in the United States results from racial differences in participation in the kinds of crime, like homicide, robbery, and aggravated assault, that typically result in prison sentences; a recent short-term worsening of racial incarceration differences results from foreseeable discriminatory effects of conscious policy decisions of the Reagan and Bush administrations in launching and conducting the federal 'War on Drugs'. More generally, rough comparability in majority and minority group incarceration patterns in Australia, Canada, England and Wales, and the United States exposes the failure of social policies aimed at assuring full participation by members of minority groups in the rewards and satisfactions of life in industrialized democratic countries.

One caveat concerning data reliability needs mention. Analyses such as this one that depend on unadjusted general population census data share the limits of the data. In the United States, for example, the decennial population survey conducted by the US Bureau of the Census undercounts members of minority groups. With a complete general population census, the black population count would be higher, which would make black denominators in incarceration rates larger and the resulting black rates lower. Similarly, after blacks, whites, Native-Americans, and Asians are counted, the 1990 census reports nearly 10,000,000 respondents as 'others', which distorts denominators, and rates, in unknown ways. Likewise, the prison and jail censuses report residual 'other, not known, or not reported' categories which necessarily lend imprecision to these data. In this essay, I rely on official black and white counts and generally do not adjust for estimates of the racial composition of 'other' groups, except in Figure 1 showing long-term trends where Hispanics are included within black and white counts.

Here is how this essay is organized. Part 1 (Long-term Trends) describes long-term patterns of racial differences in incarceration rates in the United States. Part 2 (Cross-national Comparisons) examines American and other countries' comparative reliance on incarceration. Part 3 (Sub-national Comparisons) shows American state-by-state comparisons. Part 4 (Explanation of Minority Over-representation) examines the underlying causes of both long-term patterns and recent worsening of racial differentials in incarceration rates. Part 5 (Redressing Racial Imbalance) suggests lessons for criminal justice and social welfare policies that derive from those differences.

Long-term Trends

That members of ethnic and racial minority groups are disproportionately involved in common law crimes and disproportionately ensnared in the American criminal justice system, by itself, is neither unprecedented nor especially worrisome. These patterns typically characterize low-income immigrant groups and typically abate as subsequent generations are assimilated into American economic and social life.

America's first national crime commission, the US National Commission on Law Observance and Enforcement (1931), concentrated on two subjects—prohibition and 'crime among the foreign-born'. The commission's final report examined patterns of criminality among the foreign-born in general and Mexican immigrants in particular. The fundamental findings were that crime was less common among the foreign-born than among either non-immigrants or the immigrants' children and grandchildren. The relatively low involvement by immigrants in crime should come as no surprise. Most chose the uncertainties and dislocations of immigration and were determined to work hard and succeed. For many, material conditions of life in America as immigrants compared favourably with conditions in the natal homeland.

The problem of immigrant crime was preponderantly among the second and third generations to whom English was a native tongue, to whom worse conditions in the old country were mere words, and on whom relative deprivation could have a corrosive effect. Victims too often of ethnic stereotyping and discrimination, enjoying fewer legitimate opportunities than did assimilated middle-class and working-class youth, second and third generation immigrants were especially susceptible to the allure of juvenile gangs and especially likely to exploit illicit opportunities when legitimate opportunities were few, unattractive, or blocked (Glazer and Moynihan 1963).

Mass immigration declined after the 1930s. From 1900 to 1930, the United States received nearly 19 million people, thereafter falling to 1.5 million from 1930 to 1950 and 2.5 million during the 1950s (Bureau of the Census 1992, table 5). By the 1950s, the phrase 'crime and the foreign-born' had an archaic if not xenophobic ring, and had disappeared as a major symbol of crime problems.

In retrospect, 'crime and the foreign-born' as a prominent public policy problem in the 1920s and 1930s was a foreseeable, and foreseeably temporary, product of the transition of newly arrived immigrants into what was once called a 'melting pot'. Similar patterns appeared among southern black farm labourers and tenant farmers, made technologically obsolete by the mechanization of agriculture, who migrated to northern cities in the 1950s and 1960s. Employment rates were higher, and welfare dependency was lower among southern-born black migrants in the 1960s and 1970s than among northern-born blacks (despite the higher average education among the northern-born) (Wilson 1987: 55–6; Katz 1989: 203). Participation in crime by adult

99

migrants was less extensive than was that of their children. Recent reports of developing Asian youth gangs look like a variation on a familiar story, as the children of Asian immigrants of the 1970s and 1980s face the problems confronted by children of eastern and southern European immigrants early in the twentieth century.

Unfortunately, the migration-is-comparable-to-immigration hypothesis is at best a partial explanation of modern patterns of crimes and punishments of American blacks. If the immigration analogy were apt, crime among Northern American blacks should be little more salient today, 45 years after the beginning and 25 years after the end of the major South-to-North migration, than was crime among Southern and Eastern Europeans in the 1950s.

The American pattern of social and economic progress by blacks is much more complicated. Something akin to Disreali's two nations is appearing within the American black community. A large portion of the black population is becoming much more fully assimilated into American economic and social life; black/white gaps in education, household income, residence patterns, and various public health measures are closing. By some measures—e.g., personal and household incomes of college-educated younger blacks, especially females—some groups of blacks are doing as well or better than their white peers (Jaynes and Williams 1989; Hacker 1992; Jencks 1992).

However, a minority of blacks, disproportionately located in 'Rust belt' and 'Snow belt' cities, are not making progress and by many measures—welfare dependence, labour force participation, illegitimacy, single-parent households, crime victimization, criminality—are doing worse. It is from this group, sometimes (and sometimes controversially) called the black urban underclass, that black offenders and prisoners grossly disproportionately come.

For the urban black underclass, at least, the immigration hypothesis does not appear to explain social conditions or criminality. Explanations abound and range from conservative 'culture of poverty' and 'welfare dependence' (Murray 1984) arguments to centrist social and structural accounts that emphasize the flight of unskilled jobs and the black middle class from the inner city and general economic conditions (Wilson 1987) to liberal 'legacy of racism' (Lemann 1991) and radical 'contemporary racial discrimination' explanations. Whatever the ultimate reasons, and those mentioned here are but a few among many that have been offered, American blacks' involvement in crime and their presence in jails and prisons remain high.

Figure 1 shows demographic trends in selected American correctional populations. Because of variation in statistical and reporting systems, data for different populations cover different periods. Recent changes and inconsistencies in reporting of data on Hispanics complicate some trend reports. Until 1980, Hispanics generally were included in black and white counts, sometimes with separate supplementary counts of Hispanics alone. More recently, some reports count non-hispanic whites, non-hispanic blacks, Hispanics, and others (sometimes reporting data on Asians and Native Americans). When possible, I have included Hispanics within racial groupings.

Figure 1a shows admissions to state and federal prisons by race from 1960 to 1989, the most recent date for which national admissions data on race have been published. White percentages declined and black percentages increased continuously. Between 1986 and 1989, the racial mix reversed, from 53 per cent white, 46 per cent black to 53 per cent black, 46.5 per cent white. The black proportion has probably continued to

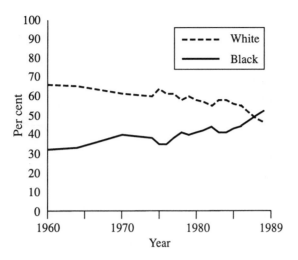

Hispanics are included in black and white populations

FIG. 1*a* Admissions to Federal and State Prisons by Race, 1960–89 (Langan 1991; Gilliard 1992; Perkins 1992; Perkins and Gilliard 1992)

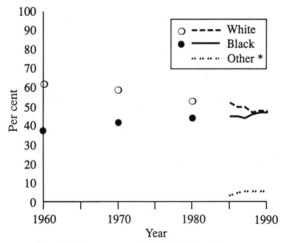

* Hispanics in many states, Asians, Native Americans

FIG. 1*b* Prisoners in State and Federal Prisons on Census Date, by Race, 1960–90 (for 1960, 1970, 1980: Calahan 1986, table 3.31; for 1985–90: Bureau of Justice Statistics 1987, 1989*a*, 1989*b*, 1991*a*, 1991*b*)

grow (as is shown for selected states in part 4 (Explanation of Minority Over-representation)).

Figure 1b shows the racial composition of state and federal prison populations on census dates for selected years from 1960 to 1980 and successively from 1985 to 1990. The continuous trend is one of decreasing white and increasing black percentages. By

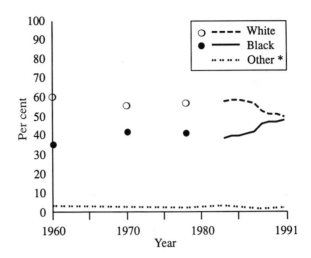

* White and black figures for 1988 and 1991 are estimated: white
non-Hispanic, black non-Hispanic, and Hispanic reported; Hispanic
racial breakdown assumed to be the same as in 1990 for which racial data
were reported.

FIG. 1c   Jail Inmates at Mid-year, by Race, 1960–91 (for 1960–83: Calahan 1986, tables 4.15, 4.21; for 1984–91: Bureau of Justice Statistics 1984, 1985, 1991c, 1992)

1990, American prisons housed as many blacks as whites. Reported black numbers in recent years are an understatement because many Hispanics, some of whom are black, are reported as 'race unknown' by some states, including Florida and Texas, which have sizeable Hispanic populations.

Figure 1c shows the composition on census dates of jail populations for selected years from 1960 to 1978 and for successive years from 1983 to 1991. The trend again is one of continuing white decrease and black increase in population composition, reaching near parity in 1991 when 50 per cent were white and 48 per cent black.

The patterns shown in Figure 1 for adult offenders also characterize juveniles. The proportion of whites in custody in public juvenile facilities fell from 70 per cent in the 1950s to 60 per cent in the late 1970s. By 1980, 42 per cent of confined juveniles were black, 40 per cent were white, and 15 per cent were Hispanic (if adult patterns hold, roughly two-thirds are white and one-third are black). Between 1987 and 1989, the number of confined white juveniles fell by 5 per cent, while the number of confined black juveniles grew by 14 per cent (Calahan 1986, tables 5–30, 5–31; Allen-Hagen 1991; Krisberg and DeComo 1992).

Most people are instinctively uneasy about black rates of incarceration that appear to be three to four times higher than white rates. The uneasiness is warranted but the disproportion is far greater than three or four to one. The initial tendency to compare American blacks' proportion of the general population, 12 per cent, to their presence in the prison and jail populations, 48 per cent, is understandable, but wrong, and it greatly underestimates the scale of the problem. The better comparison is between racially disaggregated incarceration rates measured as the number of confined persons of a racial group per 100,000 population of that group. By that measure, black incarceration rates are six to seven times higher than white incarceration rates. Table 1

102

shows racially disaggregated jail and prison incarceration rates for the United States and for England and Wales for 1990.

Hereafter, in this article, racially disaggregated incarceration rates, and their ratios, as illustrated in Table 2, are regularly used as indicators of racial patterns in the criminal justice system.

TABLE 1   *Black, White, and Other Incarceration Rates, 1990*

		General population	Prison population	Jail population	Prison+Jail population	Rate per 100,000
United	White	199,686,000	369,485	206,713	576,198	289
States	Black	29,986,000	367,122	190,500	557,622	1,860
	Other	19,038,000	37,768	8,106	45,874	241
	Total	248,710,000	774,375	405,319	1,179,694	474
England	White	46,946,751	36,300	–	–	77
and	Black	898,025	4,910	–	–	547
Wales	Other	2,045,501	3,350	–	–	164
	Total	49,890,277	44,520	–	–	89

Note: UK numbers do not equal column total in original source.
Sources: Jankowski 1992, tables 2.1, 2.3, 5.6; Home Office 1991, table 7; Bureau of the Census 1992, table 16.

TABLE 2   *Ratios of Racial Incarceration Rates 1990*

	Black	White	Ratio
England and Wales	547	77	7.10
United States	1,860	289	6.44

Cross-national Comparisons

Racial disproportions in the United States among jail, prison, and juvenile inmates, awful as they are, are not radically different from those in Australia, Canada, and England and Wales.

The conventional cross-national comparisons of incarceration rates, limited and methodologically flawed as they are, show gross American incarceration rates to be much higher than those for other countries. Table 3, for example, shows one recent estimate of incarceration rates in 22 countries in the late 1980s.

Cross-national comparisons are best seen as crude order-of-magnitude indicators and not as anything more precise. Different countries handle and report pre-trial detainees and short- and long-term prisoners in different ways. In Canada, for example, sentences of two years or longer are served under the authority of the national prison system; sentences under two years are administered by the provinces. In the

TABLE 3 *Incarceration Rates for 22 Countries, 1989*

Country	Rate per 100,000
United States	426
South Africa	333
Soviet Union	268
Hungary	196
Malaysia	126
Northern Ireland	120
Hong Kong	118
Poland	106
New Zealand	100
United Kingdom	97
Turkey	96
Portugal	83
France	81
Austria	77
Spain	76
Switzerland	73
Australia	72
Denmark	68
Italy	60
Japan	45
Netherlands	40
Philippines	22

Source: Mauer 1990.

United States, pre-trial detainees and convicted offenders are distributed among federal, state, and local authorities. The US Bureau of Prisons handles all federal confinement, including pre-trial. In most states, the state prison system houses offenders sentenced to terms of one year or longer and county institutions house pre-trial detainees and under one year sentenced offenders. There are, however, exceptions. Some states, like Connecticut and Delaware, have unified state departments of corrections that house detainees and all convicted offenders. In other states, local jails house offenders serving longer sentences; Pennsylvania's county facilities, in which terms up to five years can be served locally, are the extreme case.

The organization of corrections in the United States presents problems for counting offenders. If, for example, a count of all confined convicted offenders is wanted, data must be obtained from the Federal Bureau of Prisons, 50 state departments of corrections, the District of Columbia, and upwards of 3,312 county jails.

The most accessible source of population data is a series entitled 'Prisoners in America', which is compiled and reported semi-annually and reports all confined offenders under the jurisdiction of the Federal Bureau of Prisons and the departments of corrections of the 50 states and the District of Columbia. Counts are provided for total populations on a census date (including detainees and short-term prisoners in unified systems) and prisoners serving sentences of one year or longer. Jail populations are less reliably known. There have been a number of special censuses (in 1972, 1978, 1983, and 1989) and since the early 1980s, an annual 'Jail Inmates' report, based partly on estimates, has been published.

104

The only feasible way to calculate national incarceration rates is to combine the census-date population data reported for a given year in 'Prisoners in America' and 'Jail Inmates'. So calculated, both aggregate and racially disaggregated incarceration rates climbed steadily between 1972 and 1991.

It appears that patterns of differential incarceration by race in Australia, Canada, England and Wales, and the United States are much more similar than differences in their gross incarceration rates suggest. As noted earlier, the ratio of black to white incarceration rates in England and Wales in 1990 was 7.10:1, slightly higher than America's 6.44:1. Differential incarceration of Aboriginal people in Australia makes these patterns appear modest. The Royal Commission into Aboriginal Deaths in Custody (1990) found that 'for Australia as a whole, adult Aboriginal people are 15.1 times more likely than adult non-Aboriginal people to be in prison, but they are only 8.3 times more likely to be serving non-custodial correctional orders'. Biles (1993b) shows that, among persons 17 years and older, Aboriginals were 18.2 times likelier than non-Aboriginals to have been incarcerated on 30 June 1991. Comparisons with Canada are especially difficult because most Canadian jurisdictions, including Ontario, have prohibited the collection and dissemination of racially disaggregated statistics, except concerning the native population. Data obtained privately, excluding Quebec, from the Canadian Centre for Justice Statistics, a division of Statistics Canada, indicate that in 1986–7 natives were admitted to correctional institutions at a rate of 2,662 per 100,000 native population, compared with 315 non-native admissions per 100,000 non-native population (Birkenmayer 1992). Although these are admissions rather than population data as for the other countries, the admission ratio of 8.45:1 native to non-native is not unlike the population ratios of the other countries.

There seems to be general agreement that violent crime rates are higher in the United States than in other developed countries and that property crime rates are among, but not invariably, the highest. World Health Organization and Interpol comparisons of officially recorded crimes show American crime rates that are much higher than other countries' (Kalish 1988). Cross-national comparisons of official crime records are, however, subject to even more measurement problems than are incarceration comparisons. Just as national governments increasingly look to victimization surveys for an independent measure of crime that is less subject than police records to variability in reporting and recording, efforts have been made to obtain cross-national victimization data. The most ambitious effort to date concluded that victim-reported crime in the United States was higher than in most developed countries but that, for some offences, American rates were lower than elsewhere, and that the differences between American and other countries' rates were much lower than is revealed by official-rate comparisons (Van Dijk, Mayhew, and Killias 1990; Van Dijk and Mayhew 1993).

When America's higher crime rates are taken into account, three findings stand out. First, relative to crime rates, America's incarceration rates are closer to other countries' rates than might otherwise be expected. Secondly, relative to white incarceration rates, or absolutely, America's black incarceration rate is shockingly high. Thirdly, relative to white incarceration rates, Australia, Canada, and England and Wales handle their most prominent visible minority groups no less differentially harshly than does the United States.

The overriding problem turns out not to be a unique American problem of overreliance on incarceration but a general problem in English-speaking white-dominant countries that minority citizens are locked up grossly out of proportion to their numbers in the population.

Sub-national Comparisons

Another way to look at comparative incarceration rates is to stop the analytical lens down to focus on sub-national incarceration rates. England and Wales make up one unitary legal system, unlike the federal systems of Australia, Canada, and the United States. I lack provincial data for Canada, but state-level incarceration data are available for the United States and Australia.

Table 4 shows racially disaggregated incarceration rates and racial ratios for males in 1988 for 49 states and the District of Columbia. These data encompass state prisons only and do not count persons confined in county jails or in federal facilities. Thus, these data are not comparable to the inclusive England data. None the less, England and Wales's white incarceration rate of 77 per 100,000, its black rate of 547, and its racial ratio of 7.10 are not greatly different from what those of a number of American states would be if adjustments were made for non-comparability of the data. A few American states have lower white male incarceration rates than in England and Wales, some have lower black male incarceration rates, and many have lower racial ratios.

Table 5 shows Australian national and state incarceration numbers, rates per 100,000 population, and ratios for Aboriginals and non-Aboriginals in January 1993. The national ratio of rates was 12.8, nearly double the black/white ratio in the United States.

These data, which because of their inclusiveness are more comparable than American data to those from England and Wales, show that England and Wales incarcerate proportionately more whites than most Australian states and proportionately fewer blacks than is the case with Aboriginals in Australia.

England and Wales's middling location in these measures relative to the United States and Australia suggests that disproportionate black incarceration is a much greater problem in England than is commonly acknowledged, an oversight made possible only by the small number of blacks in England's general population.

Explanations of Minority Over-representation

Among numerous questions presented by the preceding data on incarceration of members of minority groups, three stand out. What causes the broad long-term patterns of overincarceration of blacks? Why do some not conspicuously punitive jurisdictions—Minnesota, Wisconsin, Victoria—have racial incarceration ratios that are especially unfavourable to blacks? Why has racial disproportionality in American prisons worsened in recent years? Although these same questions appear to apply equally to Australia, Canada, England and Wales, and the United States, my comments here concern the United States; appropriately adapted they may also apply to other countries.

TABLE 4   *Ratio of Black-to-White Incarceration by State,*
1988

State	Incarceration Rates		Black/White Ratio
	White per 100,000	Black per 100,000	
Hawaii	190	530	2.79
Maine	104	311	3.00
North Dakota	63	199	3.14
Alaska	349	1,296	3.72
Tennessee	108	402	3.72
South Carolina	217	829	3.82
Mississippi	135	562	4.16
Idaho	157	712	4.52
Alabama	164	757	4.62
New Mexico	213	983	4.62
Georgia	148	686	4.64
New York	165	781	4.74
North Carolina	136	665	4.88
New Hampshire	90	472	5.22
Arizona	329	1,725	5.25
Montana	136	714	5.26
West Virginia	72	382	5.33
Indiana	155	830	5.34
Arkansas	139	745	5.37
Louisiana	159	903	5.68
Kentucky	146	829	5.69
California	218	1,266	5.81
NATIONAL	155	965	6.24
Virginia	116	738	6.38
Colorado	148	994	6.69
Nevada	279	1,954	7.01
Oklahoma	200	1,406	7.02
Florida	147	1,045	7.11
Missouri	145	1,033	7.14
Delaware	235	1,722	7.34
Maryland	114	873	7.67
Texas	109	874	8.05
Ohio	140	1,137	8.13
South Dakota	115	952	8.28
Michigan	145	1,224	8.46
Kansas	156	1,382	8.83
Oregon	180	1,657	9.22
Washington	86	856	9.97
Illinois	74	739	9.96
New Jersey	95	946	9.98
Massachusetts	72	775	10.82
Nebraska	98	1,099	11.24
Wisconsin	84	966	11.52
Pennsylvania	72	940	12.97
Wyoming	174	2,302	13.23
Rhode Island	132	1,752	13.24
Dist. of Columbia	150	2,143	14.31
Utah	105	1,503	14.35
Iowa	85	1,395	16.33
Connecticut	83	1,383	16.58
Minnesota	42	797	19.01

Sources: Proband 1991; Bureau of the Census 1992; Flanagan and Maguire 1990.

TABLE 5 *Aboriginal and Non-Aboriginal Incarcerated Populations, January 1993*

	Non-aboriginal prisoners	Rates 100,000	Aboriginal prisoners	Rates 100,000	Ratio of rates
New South Wales*	5,388	86.2	614	868.5	10.1
Victoria	2,123	47.4	121	728.9	15.4
Queensland	1,685	56.1	422	629.9	11.2
Western Australia	1,201	71.7	566	1,415.0	19.7
South Australia	938	63.9	169	1,056.3	16.5
Tasmania	251	54.9	16	183.9	3.4
Northern Territory	124	101.1	308	804.2	8.0
Australia	11,710	67.1	2,216	861.3	12.8

Source: Biles 1993a from Australian Institute of Criminology data.

Long-term racial disproportion

Much, not all, black over-representation in American prisons over the past 20 years appears to be associated with disproportionate participation by blacks in the kinds of crimes—'imprisonable crimes' like homicide, robbery, aggravated assault, rape—that commonly result in prison sentences. Alfred Blumstein some years ago (1982) analysed black and white incarceration patterns in relation to arrest patterns (and, from victim surveys, victims' identifications of assailants' races, when known) and concluded that 80 per cent of the disproportion appeared to result from blacks' participation in imprisonable crimes. The remaining 20 per cent, he speculated, included some mixture of racially discriminatory discretionary decisions and other, arguably legitimate, sentencing considerations like prior criminal record. Hood (1992) in his study of Crown Courts in the English Midlands similarly concluded that 80 per cent of black-white incarceration differences 'can be accounted for by the greater number of black offenders who appeared for sentence . . . and by the nature and circumstances of the crimes they were convicted of' (p. 205).

Blumstein's conclusion that involvement in crime, not racial bias, explains much of the black disproportion among prisoners in the early 1980s is consistent with most recent reviews of empirical research on discrimination in sentencing (Wilbanks 1987). Most analyses of the past 15 years using multivariate techniques do not reveal racial bias as a major predictor of sentencing outcomes.

Most likely, however, if Blumstein's study were redone today, his imprisonable crimes analyses would be less powerful (e.g., Hawkins 1986). As noted below, drug offenders make up a steadily increasing proportion of prisoners, and they are even more disproportionately black than are other felony offenders.[3] Although I see no reason to believe that court processing is more racially biased than in recent years, both the national policy decision to launch a War on Drugs and local police decisions to focus on street trafficking foreseeably increased black arrests, prosecutions, convictions, and incarcerations.

The absence of research evidence of invidious discrimination is not evidence of its absence. Bias no doubt remains common—sometimes as a matter of conscious ill-will,

[3] More recently Blumstein (1993) analysed 1991 data and concluded that 76 per cent of the variance could be explained on the basis of arrests (the decline resulted from black over-representation among the greatly increased numbers of those arrested for drug offences).

more commonly as a result of unconscious stereotyping and attribution by middle-class and white officials of special dangerousness to underclass minority offenders. Moreover, all but the most sophisticated studies can be confounded by cross-cutting biases that result in harsher treatment of some black offenders and less harsh treatment of offenders (generally black) whose victims are black. Another complication is that many of the arguably legitimate bases for distinguishing among offenders, such as the nature of a criminal record, systematically adversely affect blacks (whose average first arrest is at a younger age than the average first arrest for whites and who, controlling for age and offence, are likely to have accrued more prior arrests and convictions, which may themselves result from earlier conscious and unconscious discrimination against blacks). None the less, at day's end, there is relatively little empirical basis for concluding that all or a large portion of the long-term disproportion in prison numbers results from invidious racial discrimination in processing of cases once arrests have been made.

Variations in racial ratios

That Minnesota and Wisconsin, generally considered among America's most socially and politically progressive states, and leaders in setting enlightened sentencing and corrections policies, have the most racially disproportionate incarceration rates in the country may strike many as surprising. They achieved that dishonour not only in the data reported here but in earlier analyses using 1979 (Hawkins 1985) and 1982 (Blumstein 1988) data.

At least three considerations partly explain the seeming anomaly. First, in juris-dictions in which blacks constitute a small percentage of the population, like Minnesota and Wisconsin (and England), the minority population is typically concentrated in urban areas. Crime rates are higher in urban than in suburban and rural areas; that a preponderantly urban black population experiences higher rates of criminality and incarceration than do groups that are more widely dispersed geographically is to be expected. In states like Georgia, Mississippi, and South Carolina, blacks live through-out the state and thus come from low, moderate, and high crime areas.

Secondly, black Americans are likelier than whites to be unemployed, ill educated, and to have been raised in single-parent households and impoverished circumstances (Jaynes and Williams 1989). All of these things are associated with increased participation in crime and, not unnaturally, are also associated with heightened arrest and incarceration probabilities (Blumstein *et al.* 1986).

Thirdly, in states like Minnesota, Iowa, and Wisconsin that have relatively low incarceration rates, prison spaces are principally used for persons convicted of violent and otherwise especially serious crimes. If the black populations of such states are small in number, concentrated in urban areas, and socially disadvantaged, they are disproportionately likely to be involved in serious crimes. By contrast, in states like Georgia, Alabama, California, and Texas, in which imprisonment rates are high, reflecting incarceration of many persons convicted of less serious crimes, larger proportions of white offenders are imprisoned and racial disproportions are less.

No doubt racial discrimination, especially in unconscious forms related to stereotyp-ing and attribution of threatening characteristics to minority offenders, also plays a role in the extreme racial incarceration ratios in states like Minnesota. None the less, much

109

of the variation appears explicable in terms of crimes committed and previous criminal records.

The short-term worsening of racial ratios

Racial disproportion has worsened markedly in recent years, as is shown both by Figure 1 and by a series of recent analyses showing that one in four black American males aged 20 to 29 is in jail or prison, on probation or parole (Mauer 1990) and that in the District of Columbia (Miller 1992*a*) and Baltimore (Miller 1992*b*), 42 and 56 per cent, respectively, of black males aged 18 to 35 were under the control of the criminal justice system.

The recent worsening is the result of deliberate policy choices of federal and state officials to 'toughen' sentencing, in an era of falling and stable crime rates, and to launch a 'War on Drugs' during a period when all general population surveys showed declining levels of drug use, beginning in the early 1980s (e.g., National Institute on Drug Abuse 1991).

At every level of the criminal justice system, empirical analyses demonstrate that increasing black disproportion has resulted from the War on Drugs—in juvenile institutions (Snyder 1990), in jails (Flanagan and Maguire 1992, table 6.49), and in state (Flanagan and Maguire 1992, table 6.81; Perkins 1992, tables 1–5) and federal (US Sentencing Commission 1991) prisons. The experience in several state prison systems is illustrative.

Figure 2 shows black and white admissions per 100,000 same-race population to North Carolina prisons from 1970 to 1990. White rates held steady during the entire period. Black rates doubled between 1980 and 1990 from a higher starting point, increasing most rapidly after 1987. According to Stevens Clarke, the foremost scholar

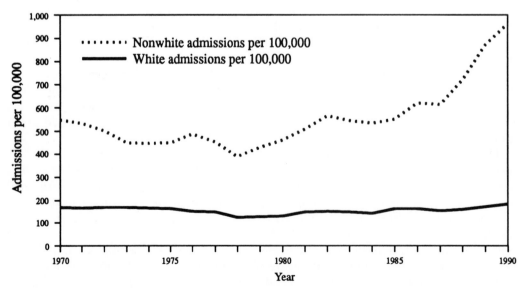

FIG. 2 Prison Admissions per 100,000 General Population, North Carolina, by Race, 1970–90 (Clarke 1992)

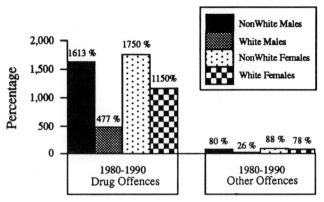

FIG. 3 Percentage Growth in Prison Commitments in Pennsylvania, by Race, Sex, and Offence, 1980–90 (Clark 1992)

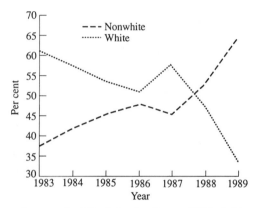

FIG. 4 New Drug Commitments in Virginia, by Race, 1983–9 (Austin and McVey 1989)

of North Carolina sentencing and corrections trends, the War on Drugs has increasingly targeted blacks: 'in 1984 about twice as many whites (10,269) as blacks (5,021) were arrested for drug offenses . . . By 1989, annual drug arrests of blacks had grown by 183 per cent, reaching 14,192; drug arrests of whites increased only by 36 per cent (to 14,007)' (Clarke 1992: 12).

Figure 3 shows increases in prison commitments in Pennsylvania for 1980–90 for drug and other offences by race and sex. Drug commitments of black males increased by 1,613 per cent during the decade; white males by 477 per cent. The pattern for females was similar, though the differences were less dramatic. In 1990, 11 per cent of Pennsylvanians were black; 58 per cent of state prisoners were black (Clark 1992).

Figure 4 shows white and non-white drug commitments to Virginia prisons from 1983 to 1989. Sixty two per cent of drug offenders committed in 1983 were white, 38 per cent were non-white. By 1989, those percentages had more than reversed; 65 per cent of drug commitments were non-white, 35 per cent were white. Drug commitments have continued to rise since 1989; current data would show worse racial disproportion.

111

Phrased most charitably to the officials who launched and conducted America's latest War on Drugs, worsening of racial incarceration patterns was a foreseen but not intended consequence. Less charitably, the recent blackening of America's prison population is the product of malign neglect.

Redressing Racial Imbalance

Problems of race and punishment in America are both more severe than is generally recognized and yet, controlling for crime rates, not all that much worse than in other English-speaking countries. Although increasing numbers of American blacks are moving into the middle-class, for a sizeable minority the traditional pattern of assimilation of in-migrants is not working. In any case, the immigration analogy patently does not hold for black residents of southern states. In the black urban underclass, rates of unemployment, illegitimacy, single-parent households, delinquency, and other correlates of social disorganization are far higher than in other population groups.

These patterns pose formidable—if obvious—policy problems. Concern for victims' rights to live their lives free from fear, assaults, and property loss obliges the state to respond to predatory crime and criminals. Because much crime is intra-racial, concern for minority victims necessarily occasions criminal justice system intervention in the lives of minority offenders. In so far as predatory crime is concentrated in the inner cities and predatory criminals disproportionately come from groups that lack opportunities, resources, and social supports, blacks are likely to continue to be disproportionately present among arrestees and defendants.

None the less, there are things that could be done to diminish racial disproportion. First, although the criminal law cannot acknowledge extreme social adversity as an affirmative defence, at all stages from prosecution to sentencing and parole, adversity can be recognized as an informal mitigating circumstance to justify diversion from prosecution and avoidance of prison in all possible cases and to justify provision of drug and alcohol treatment, remedial education, vocational training and placement, and supportive social services to minority and other disadvantaged offenders.

Secondly, designers of law enforcement policies should take account of foreseeable racial effects of alternative policy choices. Although American constitutional law sometimes distinguishes between actions taken with the purpose of discriminating against blacks, and actions taken for other purposes but with knowledge that they will systematically disadvantage blacks, policymakers should generally treat purpose and knowledge as moral equivalents (as they are in criminal law *mens rea* doctrines). The decision heavily to favour law enforcement over prevention and treatment strategies in the American War on Drugs, for example, was pre-ordained to affect young black males especially severely and for that reason alone (there are others) the 'War' should never have been launched.

Thirdly, policy makers generally should begin to look to delinquency and criminality as diagnostic markers of group social distress. Among recent immigrant groups, those in which offending is conspicuously more common than in other contemporaneous immigrant groups should be targeted for social services and supports. South-east Asian tribal immigrants in the United States like the Meo and the Hmong, for example, were less well-situated than the Vietnamese, many of whom were educated

112

urban dwellers, to succeed in America's capitalist economy. If second and third generation Meo and Hmong people demonstrate unusually high levels of criminality (it is too soon to tell), that will be powerful evidence that, as a group, they are having particular difficulty adjusting to life in a new country and, accordingly, that the state should allocate resources to help them overcome barriers to assimilation.

American blacks are the paradigm case of an identifiable subgroup that needs special aid in entry into full participation in American life. Fewer than 30 years have passed since discrimination against blacks in many settings ceased to be legal and full legal rights have only slowly, and as yet imperfectly, been institutionalized in day-to-day life. All American blacks suffer from the legacy of slavery and legal racism and many, especially southern agricultural migrants and their children and residents of inner city underclass areas, have suffered from inadequacies in education, employment opportunities, and health care. American social policy since the 1970s has not provided adequate educational programmes, housing, and income support to disadvantaged blacks, and their disproportionate participation in crime is in part the result. The War on Drugs has worsened the prospects for disadvantaged blacks by giving a majority of young urban black males criminal records, thereby diminishing prospects for jobs, marriage, and law-abiding material success. Conversely, the deteriorating life chances of underclass black males have made them less promising prospects as life partners of black women and are contributing to declining marriage rates and accelerating illegitimacy and single-parent households among black women.

Americans have a remarkable ability to endure suffering by others. Racially disaggregated incarceration patterns show that black Americans are suffering severely. Whether the recent presidential election will produce a more caring government and a more compassionate climate, prepared to deal seriously with the problems of disadvantaged American blacks, remains to be seen. If not, the intolerable racial disproportion in America's prisons and jails is likely long to continue.

REFERENCES

ALLEN-HAGEN, B. (1991), *Public Juvenile Facilities, Children in Custody 1989*. Washington, DC: US Department of Justice, Office of Juvenile Justice and Delinquency Prevention.

AUSTIN, J., and McVEY, A. D. (1989), *The Impact of the War on Drugs*. San Francisco: National Council on Crime and Delinquency.

BILES, D. (1993a), Personal correspondence with the author, 23 March.

—— (1993b), 'Imprisonment in Australia', *Overcrowded Times*, 4(3): 4–6.

BIRKENMAYER, A. (1992), Communication from the Chief, Corrections Program. Canadian Centre for Justice Statistics, Statistics Canada.

BLUMSTEIN, A. (1982), 'On the Racial Disproportionality of United States' Prison Populations', *Journal of Criminal Law and Criminology*, 73: 1259–81.

—— (1988), 'Prison Populations: A System Out of Control?' in M. Tonry and N. Morris, eds, *Crime and Justice*, vol. 10. Chicago: University of Chicago Press.

—— (1993), 'Racial Disproportion of U.S. Prison Populations Revisited', *University of Colorado Law Review*, 64: 743–60.

BLUMSTEIN, A., COHEN, J., ROTH, J., and VISHER, C., eds. (1986), *Criminal Careers and 'Career Criminals'*. Washington, DC: National Academy Press.

BUREAU OF JUSTICE STATISTICS (1984), *The 1983 Jail Census*. Washington, DC: US Department of Justice.

—— (1985), *Jail Inmates, 1983*. Washington, DC: US Department of Justice.

—— (1987), *Correctional Populations in the United States, 1985*. Washington, DC: US Department of Justice.

—— (1989a), *Correctional Populations in the United States, 1987*. Washington, DC: US Department of Justice.

—— (1989b), *Correctional Populations in the United States, 1986*. Washington, DC: US Department of Justice.

—— (1991a), *Correctional Populations in the United States, 1989*. Washington, DC: US Department of Justice.

—— (1991b), *Correctional Populations in the United States, 1988*. Washington, DC: US Department of Justice.

—— (1991c), *Census of Local Jails, 1988*. Washington, DC: US Department of Justice.

BUREAU OF JUSTICE STATISTICS (1992), *Jail Inmates, 1991*. Washington, DC: US Department of Justice.

—— (1992), *Statistical Abstract of the United States—1992*. Washington, DC: US Government Printing Office.

CALAHAN, M. W. (1986), *Historical Corrections Statistics in the United States, 1850–1984*. Washington, DC: US Department of Justice, Bureau of Justice Statistics.

CLARK, S. (1992), 'Pennsylvania Corrections in Context', *Overcrowded Times*, 3(4): 4–5.

CLARKE, S. H. (1992), 'North Carolina Prisons Growing', *Overcrowded Times*, 3(4): 1, 11–13.

FLANAGAN, T. J., and MAGUIRE, K., eds (1990), *Sourcebook of Criminal Justice Statistics, 1989*. Washington, DC: US Government Printing Office.

—— (1992), *Sourcebook of Criminal Justice Statistics, 1991*. Washington, DC: US Government Printing Office.

GILLIARD, D. K. (1992), *National Corrections Reporting Program, 1987*. Washington, DC: US Department of Justice, Bureau of Justice Statistics.

GLAZER, N., and MOYNIHAN, D. (1963), *Beyond the Melting Pot*. Cambridge, MA: MIT Press.

HACKER, A. (1992), *Two Nations: Black and White, Separate, Hostile, Unequal*. New York: Scribner.

HAWKINS, D. F. (1985), 'Trends in Black–White Imprisonment: Changing Conceptions of Race or Changing Conceptions of Social Control?', *Crime and Social Justice*, 24: 187–209.

—— (1986), 'Race, Crime Type, and Imprisonment', *Justice Quarterly*, 3: 251–69.

HOME OFFICE (1991), *The Prison Population in 1990*. London: Home Office, Statistical Department.

HOOD, R. (1992), *Race and Sentencing*. Oxford: Oxford University Press.

JANKOWSKI, L. W. (1992), *Correctional Populations in the United States, 1990*. Washington, DC: US Department of Justice, Bureau of Justice Statistics.

JAYNES, D. G., and WILLIAMS, R. M., Jr., eds (1989), *A Common Destiny: Blacks and American Society*. Report of the Committee on the Status of Black Americans, National Academy of Sciences. Washington, DC: National Academy Press.

JENCKS, C. (1992), *Rethinking Social Policy*. Cambridge, MA: Harvard University Press.

KALISH, C. (1988), *International Crime Rates*. Washington, DC: US Department of Justice, Bureau of Justice Statistics.

KATZ, M. (1989), *The Undeserving Poor*. New York: Pantheon.

KRISBERG, B., and DeCOMO, R. (1992), *National Juvenile Custody Trends 1978–89*. Washington, DC: US Department of Justice, Office of Juvenile Justice and Delinquency Prevention.

114

LANGAN, P. A. (1991), *Race of Persons Admitted to State and Federal Institutions, 1926–86*. Washington, DC: US Department of Justice, Bureau of Justice Statistics.

LEMANN, N. (1991), *The Promised Land—The Great Black Migration and How It Changed America*. New York: Alfred Knopf.

MAUER, M. (1990), 'Young Black Men and the Criminal Justice System', Washington, DC: The Sentencing Project.

MILLER, J. G (1992*a*), '42% of Black DC Males, 18 to 35, Under Criminal Justice System Control', *Overcrowded Times*, 3(3): 1, 11.

—— (1992*b*), '56 Percent of Young Black Males in Baltimore Under Justice System Control', *Overcrowded Times*, 3(6): 1, 10, 16.

MURRAY, C. (1984), *Losing Ground—American Social Policy, 1950—1980*. New York: Basic.

NATIONAL INSTITUTE ON DRUG ABUSE (1991), *National Household Survey on Drug Abuse: Population Estimates 1990*. Washington, DC: US Government Printing Office.

PERKINS, C. (1992), *National Corrections Reporting Program, 1989*. Washington, DC: US Department of Justice, Bureau of Justice Statistics.

PERKINS, C., and GILLIARD, D. K. (1992), *National Corrections Reporting Program, 1988*. Washington, DC: US Department of Justice, Bureau of Justice Statistics.

PROBAND, S. C. (1991), 'Black, White Incarceration Rates', *Overcrowded Times*, 2(3): 6–7.

ROYAL COMMISSION INTO ABORIGINAL DEATHS IN CUSTODY (1990), *Report*. Canberra.

SNYDER, H. N. (1990), *Growth in Minority Detentions Attributed to Drug Law Violators*. Washington, DC: US Department of Justice, Office of Juvenile Justice and Delinquency Prevention.

US NATIONAL COMMISSION ON LAW OBSERVANCE AND ENFORCEMENT (1931), *Report on Crime and the Foreign Born*. Washington, DC: US Government Printing Office.

US SENTENCING COMMISSION (1991), *The Federal Sentencing Guidelines: A Report on the Operation of the Guidelines System and Short-term Impacts on Disparity in Sentencing. Use of Incarceration, and Prosecutorial Discretion and Plea Bargaining*. Washington, DC: US Sentencing Commission.

VAN DIJK, J., and MAYHEW, P. (1993), *Criminal Victimisation in the Industrialised World: Key Findings of the 1989 and 1992 International Crime Surveys*. The Hague: Ministry of Justice.

VAN DIJK, J., MAYHEW, P., and KILLIAS, M. (1990), *Experiences of Crime Across the World: Key Findings from the 1989 International Crime Survey*. Boston: Kluwer.

WILBANKS, W. (1987), *The Myth of a Racist Criminal Justice System*. Monterey, CA: Brooks/Cole.

WILSON, W. J. (1987), *The Truly Disadvantaged: The Inner City, the Underclass, and Public Policy*. Chicago: University of Chicago Press.

CROSS-NATIONAL IMPRISONMENT RATES

Limitations of Method and Possible Conclusions

KEN PEASE*

Prison use is universally held to vary massively across countries (see e.g., Wilkins 1991). Such differences have attracted a range of explanations, from the notion that prison capacity drives prison use (see Blumstein *et al.* 1983 for a review and critique), to the notion that tolerance of inequality manifests itself in both income distribution and prison use (see Young 1986 for a review).

Cross-national comparisons of prison use are common in political debate on penal issues, usually to shame an administration into changed practice. However, the limits and meaning of such variations in use are not well understood. In particular, the rate of imprisonment per head of population has gained the status of the conventionally accepted form of presentation without having received the appropriate analytic attention. As Young (in press) notes, 'Cross national comparisons of prison rates are commonplace not only in the academic literature but also in political and popular debate on penal issues, particularly as a platform for lobbying on penal reform and the development of so-called "alternatives to custody".' Yet the study of comparative prison use is fraught with possibilities for misinterpretation. Those few studies which make national comparisons with an appropriate degree of circumspection yield results which are counter-intuitive. To take one example, the United States is usually characterized as being particularly heavy in its use of imprisonment. However Lynch (1987) makes estimates of 'the likelihood that a person arrested for robbery, burglary or theft in the United States, Canada, England, or the Federal Republic of Germany . . . will eventually be sentenced to imprisonment. When these arrest-based imprisonment rates are compared, the difference between the United States and the other countries in the use of imprisonment largely disappears' (p. 1).

The Arithmetic of Prison Use

The variables which describe prison use are deceptively simple. Admissions (receptions) represent the number of people entering prison during a particular period. Population indicates the number of people in prison at a particular time. Discharges are the number of people released from prison over a particular period. As long as there is no double counting of the measures (a condition less often met than might be

* Professor of Criminology at Manchester University. The work reported here comes from his collaborative work with Warren Young, of Wellington University, New Zealand, and from periods of work with the United Nations Crime Branch in Vienna.

Some of the data sets, and many of the ideas contained in this paper were gathered while the author was supported by the Economic and Social Research Council. This support is gratefully acknowledged. Many of the ideas and anxieties linked with this paper were shared with the late Professor Cathie Marsh, whose criticisms and encouragement were greatly appreciated. The author is grateful to Roy King and Mike Maguire for their constructive comments and tolerance of his tardiness.

supposed), it would appear that a simple relationship should hold between the variables, with population being the product of the number of receptions or discharges and the average length of stay. However, this is only an approximate relationship, and can in extreme cases be misleading, since the people featuring in the population in a particular year may not feature as admissions or discharges during the same year: thus any change in general sentencing levels will make the relationship less precise (see Perry and Pease 1992). The point may be illustrated by reference to convictions for murder. Most of the murderers in prison in 1993 will have been admitted to prison during previous years. Most of them will be discharged in the years after 1993. Thus changes in general sentencing levels will mean that the arithmetic linking population, admissions, and sentence length will be distorted. Other practical points of measurement have the same implication. For instance, average sentence length can be calculated only for those who have already been discharged. In particular, the average length of sentence served by those convicted of murder and sentenced to life will significantly misrepresent what an 'average' murderer may expect to serve. Of course, changes in general sentencing levels (and changes in prisoner life expectancy) can change the direction of this distortion. Comparison of prison use between countries which retain and use capital punishment and those which do not will mislead, since those executed will not make a long-term contribution to the sentenced prison population (although they may make a significant contribution to the remand population where due process is lengthy).[1]

Despite the practical difficulties of comparison, in principle the relationships between indices of prison use intra-nationally are simple, being of the same kind as relationships between stock and flow in every kind of activity from the sale of goods in a supermarket to strategies of animal conservation.

They enable intra-national analyses of change in prison use which exclude some possible interpretations (see for instance Worrall and Pease (1986)). They also allow descriptive statements of prison use (e.g., as in Council of Europe 1992). The problem of interpretation becomes acute when differences in prison use are expressed in relation to national population, particularly since the inference of underlying differences in punitiveness is seldom far from the surface.

The measurement of prison use in this way has particular dangers in that there is often common political interest across a wide spectrum to characterize national use of imprisonment as excessive. Imprisonment is expensive and apparently unproductive, and control of its use commends itself to politicians and officials in Justice ministries. Likewise, penal reformers have traditionally espoused the cause of limiting the size of the prison population, alongside that of improving the conditions in which prisoners are held.[2] In such diverse hands, the descriptive 'more than elsewhere' tends to slide into the moral 'too many'. In the last analysis, the question about the right amount of custody is a moral one, although it could be informed more than it now is by an understanding of the patterning of criminal careers. What should be avoided is the shrill assertion of national punitiveness on the strength of superficial interpretation. 'Fewer prisoners than elsewhere' could still be too many. 'More prisoners than

---

[1] There was ai Eurocentr c bias in the early runs of the United Nations Crime Surveys which marginalized the importance of capital punishment.

[2] There is no necessary linkage between the recognition of deplorable prison conditions and advocacy of their alleviation by reducing prison numbers. The hidden mediating variable is system cost.

elsewhere' could still be too few, according to taste. The academic's role is surely to break the issue down as far as possible for analysis, to enable a more informed debate to take place.

Punitiveness

In much of what follows, the notion of 'punitiveness' is somewhat glibly used. Some attention must be given to the term before proceeding. At base, it refers to the calibration of the diminished quality of life of those punished against another variable. The relevant other variable depends upon prevailing principles of sentencing. In crime-reductive sentencing, it may be thought of as crimes prevented (perhaps weighted by their seriousness). In retributive sentencing, the other variable is seriousness of offence. In the case of pure retributive sentencing, one unit of seriousness is responded to by $-n$ units of quality of life. 'n' is the measure of punitiveness. Most retributive systems are impure in allowing some offender characteristics to modify sentence. In these circumstances, punitiveness refers to the relationship obtaining between the 'seriousness' of a presenting offence/offender and the level of criminal justice response to it/them.

It will not have escaped the reader that none of the variables detailed above readily lends itself to measurement as the interval scale which makes direct measurement of punitiveness feasible. Practicable measurement of the concept can never be more than a remote proxy for true punitiveness. Indeed, there is every reason to suppose that the criminal justice process incorporates only extremely crude devices for ensuring a uniform method of converting distaste into sentence (see Fitzmaurice and Pease 1986). The simplification of punitiveness in the analyses which follow is as nothing to its simplification in the actions of sentencers supposed to be operating according to retributive principle.

Bringing the discussion slightly closer to international comparisons of criminal justice, we note that in functioning and *soi-disant* retributive systems, having to combine offence and offender reveals the next problem, namely that what invites opprobrium is some combination of the offending person and the offending act. This certainly varies intra-nationally over time, as the whole literature on sentencing law and reform indicates. These intra-national changes do not occur at the same time and with the same volatility in different countries. Thus there are bound to be international differences in what is seen to merit punishment, which will change over time. The presenting problem (offence/offender) is then translated into one of a range of criminal justice reactions, most of which entail a diminution of the quality of life of the person punished, of which the reaction reserved for the worst problems in most Western countries is imprisonment. The experience of imprisonment varies between nations, as any observer of prisons in different countries will attest. The range of conditions within a country's prisons varies greatly, as does the contrast with conditions encountered outside, the stigma of having been imprisoned, and the degree to which the information about having been imprisoned must be disclosed, with consequent possible reduction of work and other opportunities.[3] In short, how a pronounced prison sentence is

---

[3] Some of these complexities are captured by Downes's notion of the depth of imprisonment, and by King and McDermott's notion of the weight of imprisonment.

118

translated into a diminution of quality of life for a prisoner is very far from simple. If one operates a thoroughgoing crime-reductive criminal justice system, or a hybrid between retribution and crime reduction, the problems multiply. Some sanctions (notably social work interventions) are designed to improve the offender's quality of life.

In what follows the measurement of punitiveness is reduced to measurement of the number of cases dealt with by the imposition of a custodial sentence, and the expected duration of imposed custody. Imprisonment is the central severe sanction in Western criminal justice, for which reasonably complete statistics exist (Wilkins and Pease 1987). While this approach caricatures the measurement of punitiveness as described above, it none the less offers significant improvements over what now (implicitly) passes for such measurement. However, in recognition of the problems, punitiveness as measured will appear in the text from this point in inverted commas.

The Problem of the Denominator

The conventional form of comparison of national prison populations is as a number imprisoned per 100,000 population. Such a depiction is included as Table 1, amended from Council of Europe (1992). The amendment is for simplicity and is achieved by exclusion of those countries where notes qualify the meaning of the Table entries and by exclusion of some columns. This sort of depiction conflates differences in crime with differences in responses to crime. It has meaning only in showing the effects of some combination of national differences on rates of crime, rates of clearance of crime, and identification of putative offenders, processing of those offenders, and choice of final sanction. Any of those variables, singly or in combination, will produce differences in indices of prison use. As saying anything about national differences in 'punitiveness', Table 1 is useless.

TABLE 1   *Council of Europe. Prison Populations at 1 February 1990*

	Total prison population	Per 100k inhabitants	Unconvicted prisoners (%)
Austria	6,294	83	30
Belgium	7,001	71	52
Cyprus	225	40	2
Denmark	3,551	61	30
England and Wales	46,628	93	22
Finland	3,537	72	11
Greece	4,747	49	32
Iceland	101	40	3
Luxembourg	347	93	26
Netherlands	6,405	44	38
Northern Ireland	1,777	112	20
Portugal	8,730	85	31
Scotland	4,777	80	42
Spain	31,711	60	21

119

Given that size of prison population or number of admissions is the numerator, and one wishes to compare national 'punitiveness', population is an appropriate denominator only if people are imprisoned at random. No alternative denominator escapes all difficulties. Table 2 summarizes the list of possible denominators and the difficulties

TABLE 2   *Choice of Denominator and Confounds with 'Punitiveness'*

Denominator	Confounds with 'Punitiveness'
Convictions	Seriousness of mix of offences of which convicted
Apprehensions	National readiness to apprehend, and associated differing proportions of acquittals and cautions in lieu of court appearance (plus conviction confound)
Cleared crime	Clearance by means other than those which lead an offender to be available for processing, e.g., offences taken into consideration (plus conviction and apprehension confounds)
Recorded crime	Failure to clear crime (plus cleared crime, apprehension, and conviction confounds)
Total crime	Failure to report or record crime (plus recorded and cleared crime, apprehension, and conviction confounds)

associated with each. In general terms, this means that the measurement of national differences in 'punitiveness' is elusive. Restricting oneself to admissions under sentence as the numerator and convictions as the denominator and analysing separately by offence type is perhaps the closest one can get in a non-experimental situation to assessing national differences in 'punitiveness' of sentencing as defined by the imposition of custody. Substituting prison population as the numerator converts the measure to one of the sentencing and discretionary release segments of the process combined. Even with these limitations imposed, the analysis is only convincing with those offence types in which one can be confident that pre-trial diversion has not removed a significant proportion of offenders from the picture. If one wishes a measure of system 'punitiveness' including pre-trial diversion, apprehensions (or arrests) is probably the closest one can get to an appropriate denominator. It remains an unsatisfactory measure, since it ignores informal dealings with offenders in lieu of apprehension. Further, countries which are most scrupulous in recording the point of apprehension may spuriously look to be least punitive at the pre-trial stage, for no other reason than that the point of recording apprehension is earlier in those administrations than in others. This is the only alternative interpretation of the Lynch (1987) findings mentioned earlier, in a study which was exemplary in its carefulness.

In short, prison admissions/convictions is the closest to a plausible measure of sentencing 'punitiveness' in the imposition (excluding the duration) of custody, and prison population/convictions is the closest to a plausible measure of the 'punitiveness' of sentencing/discretionary release combined. Both are most persuasive when dealing with the most serious offences. Convictions/apprehensions is the least flawed measure of pre-trial diversion, without being persuasive. Prison admissions/apprehensions offers some insight into pre-trial and sentencing 'punitiveness' combined. Looking at the data in a variety of ways is the only prudent option for those wishing to make sense of international differences in prison use.

All the above techniques operate by secondary analysis of official data. One attractive alternative to such analysis which specifically addresses the severity of pronounced sentence involves presenting equivalent case information to decision-makers from a number of countries, and thereby to make direct comparisons of pronounced sentences. Data from the only attempt of this kind known to the writer is presented in the next section.

The 'Punitiveness' of Sentencing

The Criminal Law Committee of the International Bar Association recently attempted a worldwide overview of sentencing practice. The analysis below is taken from the mimeoed report of the exercise dated 1990.[4] The report gives no details of the identities of those who responded beyond that they were 'the representative legal practitioners of IBA countries' who were 'asked to assess ranges of sentences which should be imposed'. Nor is it clear how many countries were invited to participate. Twenty-four countries or regions responded, of which the Northern Ireland response consisted of general remarks only. Some of the replies look odd, as does the information in some of the 16 vignettes on the basis of which sentencing was invited. The offences included murder, armed robbery, drunk driving, and theft. The presentation below is modified from a previous analysis of these data (Pease 1992).

The value of the IBA data set is that it represents sentencing decisions made across 16 cases representing a wide range of offences upon precisely the same case information by people well qualified to make such assessments from a variety of countries.[5] Some conventions adopted here in its analysis are as follows.[6] Some respondents gave a (typically narrow) range within which the proper sentence should lie. The mid-point of the range was taken as the value. Suspended sentences were taken as non-custodial (which de facto they are, whatever the legal niceties). Custody lengths were rounded to the nearest full year, and all life sentences, death sentences, and determinate sentences over 20 years were arbitrarily set at 20 years. The four cases where eight or more countries did not provide a response were discarded from the analysis. Otherwise, where a value was missing, it was replaced by the median value of other countries' sentences for that case. This represents a conservative way of dealing with missing values.

To restate, the attempt was to generate a single scale of 'punitiveness' along which countries could be compared. First, the median sentence for each case across all countries was calculated, from which each country's sentence was subtracted to produce a different score. Difference scores were then summed across cases to yield a score of 'punitiveness' shown as Score 1 in Table 3. The disadvantage to this scoring system is that in principle it could be distorted by an eccentric sentence for a single case. This was one of the reasons why life and death sentences were set at 20 years. If the preferred sentence for armed robbery (to take an example at random) had been 50 years in one country, it would have swamped all the more realistic differences in the other cases and made the country concerned look extremely punitive. An alternative method, not liable to this problem, was used and the results set alongside Score 1. The method involves calculating the number of cases in which the individual country

---

[4] The Chairman of the Criminal Law Committee responsible is Peter M. Muller, Attorney at Law, Montgelas Str., 2, D-800 Munchen 80, Germany.

[5] Although the possibility must be acknowledged that the respondent is a maverick in sentencing.

[6] Other conventions were explored, and made no essential difference to the pattern of results reported.

121

TABLE 3   *Scalings of Sentencing*
'Punitiveness'

Country	Score 1	Score 2
Norway	−35	−6
Cook Islands	−13	−2
Canada	−9	−2
Denmark	−8	−2
Netherlands	−6	−1
Irish Republic	−5	0
West Germany	−2	−1
Scotland	−2	−1
Greece	−1	1
New Zealand	−1	−1
Hong Kong	2	−2
Kuwait	3	1
England/Wales	4	2
India	5	4
Western Australia	10	4
Spain	12	2
New South Wales	13	6
Kenya	14	1
Zambia	14	3
Nigeria	22	5
Texas	28	3
United Arab Emirates	33	7
Tanzania	40	8

imposes a sentence greater or less than the median, ignoring the size of the difference. Thus, if the median for a case were ten years, a country imposing 12 and a country imposing 20 would both have plus one towards the score presented as Score 2 in Table 3.

It will be seen from Table 3 that the pattern yielded by the two scales are similar, and gives confidence that Score 1 is not distorted by individual aberrations (confirming the impression gained while doing the analysis). The English/Welsh respondent thought longer sentences were more appropriate than did colleagues in other European countries, with the exception of Spain. The scale neighbours are Kuwait and India. It seems possible to classify countries into five groups. There are the very lenient (Norway and the Cook Islands), the quite lenient (Canada to the Republic of Ireland), the quite punitive (Western Australia to Zambia), and the very punitive (from Nigeria to Tanzania). The middle group (West Germany to India) are relatively neutral in this regard.

Table 4 gives a clearer idea of both the modesty of the differences in the central range and where they lie, by comparing Scotland, England/Wales, and the international median.

It will be noted that England/Wales was more punitive towards the offences of rape, serious assault, and tax fraud. In two of those cases, the international median was the same as the Scottish level, and in the third it lay between the two GB countries. Differences for these offences lie in the median length of custody. Looking at every line of Table 4, it is noteworthy that the differences between Great Britain and the average responding country always lie in length of custody, not the threshold of imposing

TABLE 4   *Scottish and English/Welsh Responses, and International Median*

Offence	England/Wales	Scotland	Median
Murder	Life	Life	Life
Rape	10	6	8
Indecent assault	0	0	0
Provoked assualt	0	0	0
Serious assault	4	2	2
Tax fraud	2	1	1
Pension book fraud	0	0	0
Theft	0	0	0
Domestic burglary	5	5	5
Armed robbery	5	6	6
Domestic assault	0	0	0
Breach of peace	0	0	0

custody. Wherever the international median response is non-custodial (0 in Table 4), the response is also non-custodial in both England/Wales and Scotland. This means that the British differ in the length of custody pronounced where custody is the international norm but not in the imposition of custody where that is not the international norm. Apart from being extremely inefficient, any British attempt to reduce the prison population by diverting short-term prisoners (Pease 1985; Bottomley and Pease 1986; McMahon 1992) apparently flies in the face of international practice as well as the arithmetic of prison use.

System 'Punitiveness'

In a system with many phases, the most appropriate form of analysis looks at the probabilities of transition between adjacent stages. An attempt to do this is presented as Table 5, being adapted from Pease and Hukkila (1990).

TABLE 5   *Suspects, People Prosecuted, and People Convicted per 100,000 National Population*

Country	Suspected	Prosecuted	Convicted
Bulgaria	402	347	291
Cyprus	983	127	–
Czechoslovakia	1,037	759	–
W. Germany	2,121	–	1,183
Greece	2,829	–	1,226
Hungary	802	582	570
Netherlands	1,770	1,523	–
Poland	836	836	428
Scotland	–	4,041	3,648
USSR	2,198	–	1,615
Yugoslavia	1,186	745	494

Source: United Nations Third Survey Data 1985.

It will be seen that the pattern of transitions is a complex one, and defies simplification into more and less punitive.[7] It will be noted that the 'filter' operates quite distinctively in different countries, with some countries (like Hungary) having nearly as many people convicted as prosecuted, while others (like Poland) having great attenuation of the population from the stage of prosecution to the stage of conviction. There are many caveats proper in a presentation of this kind, but the central point seems established that different countries operate markedly differently in filtering out offenders within the criminal justice process. It is analysis at this level, and in greater detail, that gives a more rounded picture of the way the system operates, in ways which can be caricatured as punitive or lenient. However, because the focus here is on prisons, and because it was argued above that the convictions/convicted population ratio approximates most closely to a measure of 'punitiveness' upon conviction, this is the form of analysis which will be pursued next.

Many jurisdictions have in recent years begun to legislate against what is sometimes known as 'bark and bite' sentencing, wherein prison sentences served bear little relationship to prison sentences pronounced. In England and Wales, for instance, the prison population under sentence[8] is between half and two-thirds the size it would assume if sentences imposed were sentences served (see Bottomley and Pease 1986). This serves to point up the fact that penal system 'punitiveness' and sentencing 'punitiveness' are only loosely linked, so that one nation may be more punitive than another in sentencing, but less punitive as a penal system.

An approach to the comparison of the 'punitiveness' of the penal system as a whole, involving the comparison of ratios of sentenced prison population to convictions in the same year,[9] can be done using the data of the Third United Nations Crime Survey. The analysis is done for those countries where the relevant data are available, except where they are clearly anomalous. Data are by preference from 1986, but earlier (1980–5) data are used if they are available when 1986 data are missing. Table 6 provides data

TABLE 6   *National Rankings of Prison Population per Conviction by Offence Type*

Crime type	England/Wales	N. Ireland	No. of Countries
Intentional homicide	2	3	14
Non-intentional homicide	4	5	15
Rape	11	13	15
Robbery	12	13	15
Assault	15	7	15
Theft	19	16	19
Fraud	11	9	12
All offences	20	15	30

[7] In fact the picture is more complicated than the table suggests, since countries have been omitted where data are anomalous in the sense that those appearing at a later stage in the process are more numerous than those appearing earlier. These anomalies can be understood in the light of system characteristics. However, it was preferred to restrict Table 5 to the more straightforward examples.

[8] Excluding life sentence and fine default prisoners.

[9] With the approximations that entails, described earlier.

124

for England/Wales and Northern Ireland, and states the number of countries on which the ranking was based. A ranking of one would mean that a country had the highest prison population per conviction. The lowest possible ranking would be equal to the number of countries on which the comparison was based. It will be noted that the home countries' penal systems are among the most lenient countries for all offences except homicide. Northern Ireland is also not lenient upon conviction for assault, a result whose further analysis may be informative.

The argument could be advanced that the apparent leniency is an artefact of the greater use made by other countries in diversion before conviction. The data showing that the system is lenient even for offences like rape make the interpretation unconvincing as a general account of national differences in system 'punitiveness'. The more plausible interpretation is that other countries modify sentence by discretionary release less than is the case for England, Wales, and Scotland. Table 6 provides a summary of national rankings of prison population per conviction by offence type, but individual comparisons may be of greater interest. In terms of prisoners per conviction, both England/Wales and Northern Ireland have around half the number of sentenced prisoners per rape conviction as France, and similar numbers to the former West Germany. Both home countries have little more than half as many prisoners per robbery conviction as West Germany, and a quarter as many as France. As stressed earlier, the prisoners per conviction statistic is liable to produce misleading results if applied to a rapidly changing system. In 1994 data will be released from the Fourth United Nations Survey. Should they reveal a similar picture to earlier surveys, the 'distortion through rapid change' interpretation can be discounted.

A Summary on 'Punitiveness'

The purpose of the discussion of punitiveness above is twofold. First, it seeks to discredit the measurement of international differences in prison use by the conventional means; i.e., by expressing prison population in relation to national population. Such measurement is useless for all practical and intellectual purposes. Secondly, it seeks to suggest ways of presenting and manipulating data which provide usable, albeit partial, insights into what is happening in different national systems. Within the second, and more constructive, part of the purpose, what is argued for is calculation of a number of indices, and calculation of the likelihood of transitions between adjacent states to yield a more sophisticated understanding of the calibration of responses to crime. While superficial statistical accounts do good service as bullets for politicians to fire, they do a disservice for the reasoned development of criminal justice. Furthermore, they do little in the long term to advance the cause of penal reform in the United Kingdom, despite short-term shame evoked by the spurious conclusion that we are the penal sadists of Europe. At the time of writing, the Home Secretary has just announced legislative changes which will (*inter alia*) allow courts to punish persistent offenders more severely because of their record. A penal reform movement which yokes the cause of improving prison conditions so rigidly to the reduction of prisoner numbers is seriously compromised in *both* these purposes by the public mood which forced the Home Secretary to make his announcement.

If compelled to take a position on the current severity of the English/Welsh system, it would have to be that pronounced sentences *may* be marginally more severe than

125

elsewhere in Europe, but that the severity of sentencing after taking account of the effects of discretionary release is, for all offences save homicide, lower than international practice generally, including those few European comparisons which are possible.

Remands: A Reappraisal

While the liberal consensus has been that English prison use has been too high by Western European standards, this has been less statistically marked for the remand than for the sentenced population. Put crudely, the superficial political interpretation invited by the figures has been that the United Kingdom keeps too many people in prison, but that the problem rests more with sentenced than remand populations. The 1985 Prison Information Bulletin of the Council of Europe, reproduced in Table 7,

TABLE 7 *Proportion of Prison Population on Remand 1985**

Country	Uncorrected remand (%)	Corrected remand (%)
Iceland	6	6
Cyprus	6	6
Ireland	6	6
Sweden	18	18
N. Ireland	19	24
Scotland	22	31
England/Wales	23	32
Austria	23	23
Switzerland	23	23
Denmark	23	23
W. Germany	24	24
Greece	24	24
Norway	25	25
Belgium	31	31
Malta	33	33
Luxembourg	35	35
Turkey	35	35
Netherlands	36	36
Portugal	37	37
Spain	50	50
France	51	51
Italy	64	64

* As presented in the original *Council of Europe Bulletin* (col. 2) and as corrected to take account of different status of prisoners eligible to appeal.

shows, in column 1, the percentages of the prison population on remand by country, which tends to confirm that impression. However, the figures are not comparable, since mainland European countries count a prisoner as being on remand after sentence until the last possible date for appeal against conviction has passed. In England and Wales, a sentenced prisoner is counted as such from day one of his or her sentence. To make the proper comparison between countries would require a detailed knowledge of the law on appeals against sentencing throughout Europe, knowledge which the author does not have. However, what is clear is that the English method of calculation overstates the proportion of the population under sentence and understates the proportion on remand relative to continental Europe. Column 2 of Table 7 recalculates the Council of Europe figures, reclassifying those serving the first four weeks of sentence in England and Wales (the period during which an appeal is possible) as remand prisoners, in order to facilitate more reasonable comparisons.

It will be seen that this markedly changes the observed composition of the prison population for England and Wales, and makes the remand population a more significant factor in determining the size of UK prison populations in comparison with others. It therefore also has the effect, not observable from Table 7, of reducing the contribution of the sentenced population. This makes the system severity of England and Wales rather less than in the more conventional presentation, and strengthens the tentative conclusions reached earlier in this paper.

International Comparisons: Playing to the Strengths

International comparisons allow many points of contrast or similarity to be identified. Of particular interest are cases where countries that one would take to be similar differ markedly in some penal practice. Such a contrast should never be taken at face value, but should be the starting point for more detailed comparison. The other category of comparison which may be thought especially interesting is where there is a change across most countries in most regions of the world.

As an instance of the first type of comparison, preference for different sizes of prison can be identified, for which data are presented as Table 8 (modified from Pease and Hukkila 1990).

TABLE 8   *Percentages of Penal Institutions by Size*

Country	0–99 places	100–499 places	500–999 places	1,000 + places	No. of prisons
Austria	11	78	11	0	32
Bulgaria	24	31	38	7	29
Denmark	83	16	1	0	63
W. Germany	28	50	18	4	153
Finland	19	81	0	0	16
Italy	73	24	2	2	385
Netherlands	62	38	0	0	60
Norway	83	17	0	0	46
Poland	8	60	19	12	213
Portugal	53	39	8	0	38
Switzerland	93	7	0	0	144
UK	10	67	20	3	100

Source: Responses to Third United Nations Crime Survey.

From this it will be noted that there is a Northern European preference for small institutions and an apparent mid and Eastern European preference for larger institutions. In this comparison, the United Kingdom seems closer to the mid-European than the Northern European pattern. Apart from this specific identification of an unexpected difference, the comparison as a whole is intrinsically interesting, given Farrington and Nuttall's (1980) identification of prison size as a possible factor leading to criminogenic effects for those housed therein.

Another comparison of interest concerns the composition of prison staff by function, which is presented as Table 9 adapted from Pease and Hukkila (1990).

TABLE 9 *Prison Staff in 1986, Total, by Function and Number of Prisoners per Staff Member*

Country	Manager (%)	Custody (%)	Treatment (%)	Prisoners per staff member
Austria	3	90	6	2.5
Bulgaria	6	58	13	6.1
Cyprus	5	90	3	1.2
Denmark	10	65	8	0.9
Finland	18	60	8	1.7
France	9	80	8	2.7
FRG	13	72	7	2.0
Greece	10	85	4	3.3
Italy	6	75	14	1.1
Netherlands	2	61	19	–
Norway	22	65	2	1.3
Poland	2	53	16	4.5
Portugal	1	68	7	2.3
England/Wales	14	72	8	1.8*
N. Ireland	11	66	3	–
Scotland	3	81	3	–

Source: Adapted from Pease and Hukkila 1990.
Note: The percentages do not sum to 100 because of the omission of 'other staff'.
* UK figure.

While there are obvious ambiguities surrounding staff not included in the table (designated as 'other staff' by responding countries), the table damages some possible preconceptions, such as the relationship between penal 'treatment' and the reputation for penal liberality. Bulgaria and Poland, for example, have a higher proportion of treatment staff in prisons than countries like Denmark and Finland. The Netherlands is the only country in the table with both a reputation for penal liberality and a high proportion of staff designated as having a treatment function. It does seem that countries with a liberal reputation are characterized more by richness of staffing (a large number of staff per prisoner) than a treatment ethos, at least as reflected in declared staff function. This kind of analysis of system function has more potential for informing change than those more commonly encountered. It could be taken further even within the limits of the United Nations Surveys and would hopefully form the basis of a new generation of cross-national comparisons. The development of the United Nations Criminal Justice Information Network[10] is likely to make secondary analysis of international data sets much easier than hitherto and is to be warmly welcomed. The close analysis of disparities in experience between relatively similar

[10] Information about UNCJIN and how to join may be obtained from Graeme Newman, UNCJIN Co-ordinator, School of Criminal Justice, SUNY, 135 Western Avenue, Albany, NY 12222, USA.

countries is also the motif of a forthcoming review of the literature and the addition of new analyses by Warren Young.

An example of the second type of comparison, where a surprising uniformity of change is found across nations, is that concerning the involvement of women in criminal justice as processed offenders. This reveals that over the years from 1975 to 1986, women comprised an increasing proportion of those officially processed but not an increasing proportion of those in prison (Harvey *et al.* 1992). This kind of analysis suggests something close to a worldwide movement in criminal justice. Further analyses of the same kind are to be undertaken comparing age distributions over time using United Nations Survey data.

Conclusions

The substantive views reached earlier in this paper are by no means to be regarded as settled conclusions. It does seem that the penal system in England and Wales is not punitive in some of the ways it was claimed to be. It does seem that discretionary release plays a huge part in moderating the extent of its intervention in the lives of convicted offenders so that less serious offenders are treated more leniently here than in many other countries. However, the purpose of the paper is not to express such views as determined fact (although the available evidence does point in the directions suggested) but to argue for more sensitive and imaginative use of comparative statistical data.

Cross-national comparison enlarges the repertoire of the nationally thinkable and is to be encouraged. Open-minded practitioners and applied academics visiting other countries return with notions of how to do things better or (which tends to the same end) motivated to think through the reasons for current national practice. Cross-national statistics of penal practice have proved of more doubtful benefit, not just because their undoubted distortions nullify their value, but also because their usual mode of presentation has (it is argued) been over-simple and misleading. Use of them has primarily been by those with a political or reformist point to make, and assertions made have been ignored or accepted by politicians and scholars, rather than forming the basis of a debate on their meaning and development. The availability of United Nations Survey data (information from the Fourth Survey will be available in 1994) makes possible a much wider and fuller secondary analysis of data allowing national comparison of penal practice. It is ardently hoped that use will be made of the data to inform national debate, and that more refined European or worldwide studies will be mounted to clarify and extend the lessons learned from the United Nations data. Some of the possible growth points in the United Nations data have been identified in this paper.

REFERENCES

BLUMSTEIN, A., COHEN, J., and GOODING, W. (1983), 'Influence of Capacity on Prison Population: A Critical Review of Some Recent Evidence', *Crime and Delinquency*, 29: 1–51.
BOTTOMLEY, K., and PEASE, K. (1986), *Crime and Punishment: Interpreting the Data*. Milton Keynes: Open University Press.

COUNCIL OF EUROPE (1992), *Prison Information Bulletin*, June 1992. Strasbourg: Council of Europe.

DOWNES, D. (1988), *Contrasts in Tolerance: Post-War Penal Policies in the Netherlands and England and Wales*. Oxford: Clarendon Press.

FARRINGTON, D. P., and NUTTALL, C. P. (1980), 'Prison Size, Overcrowding, Prison Violence and Recidivism', *Journal of Criminal Justice*, 8: 221–31.

FITZMAURICE, C., and PEASE, K. (1986), *The Psychology of Judicial Sentencing*. Manchester: Manchester University Press.

HARVEY, L., BURNHAM, R. W., KENDALL, K., and PEASE, K. (1992), 'Gender Differences in Criminal Justice: An International Comparison', *British Journal of Criminology*, 32: 208–17.

KING, R. D., and McDERMOTT, K. (forthcoming), *The State of Our Prisons*. Oxford University Press.

LYNCH, J. P. (1987), *Imprisonment in Four Countries*. Washington, DC: Bureau of Justice Statistics.

McMAHON, M. W. (1992), *The Persistent Prison? Rethinking Decarceration and Penal Reform*. Toronto: University of Toronto Press.

PEASE, K. (1985), 'Community Service Orders', in M. Tonry and N. Morris, eds, *Crime and Justice*, 4. Chicago: University of Chicago Press.

—— (1992), 'Punitiveness and Prison Populations: An International Comparison', *Justice of the Peace*, 27 June, 405–8.

PEASE, K., and HUKKILA, K. (1990), *Criminal Justice Systems of Europe and North America*. Helsinki: HEUNI.

PERRY, C., and PEASE, K. (1992), 'Controlling the Prison Population: Procedures for Anticipating the Effects of Alternative Strategies', *EuroCriminology*, 4: 69–82.

WILKINS, L. T. (1991), *Punishment, Crime and Market Forces*. Aldershot: Dartmouth.

WILKINS, L. T., and PEASE, K. (1987), 'Public Demand for Punishment', *International Journal of Sociology and Social Policy*, 7: 16–29.

WORRALL, A., and PEASE, K. (1986), 'The Prison Population in 1985', *British Journal of Criminology*, 26: 184–7.

YOUNG, W. (1986), 'Influences Upon the Use of Imprisonment: A Review of the Literature', *Howard Journal*, 25: 125–36.

—— (forthcoming), 'The Use of Imprisonment: Trends and Cross-National Comparisons', in M. Tonry and N. Morris, eds., *Crime and Justice*, XX. Chicago: University of Chicago Press.

WHY STUDY WOMEN'S IMPRISONMENT? OR ANYONE ELSE'S?

An Indefinite Article

PAT CARLEN*

This was going to be the article on *women's* imprisonment. I did not want to write on *women's imprisonment*—for two main reasons. First, because I've been wondering with increasing frequency exactly why women's imprisonment should be studied separately from men's. Secondly, because nowadays there seems to be an urgent need to study prisons primarily as forms of punishment, rather than as instances or representations of just about every other aspect of society (e.g. gender, racism, class, human survival, teaching pottery, drama, or poetry, etc.). Why not just write on 'imprisonment', or, more fundamentally, why continue to study prisons—women's or anyone else's—at all?

So I asked permission to transform the invitation to write a piece on women's imprisonment into an opportunity to try to unravel the questions about gender, punishment, abolitionism, and the iconography of 'the Prison' which had been teasing me for several months. This indefinite article is the result. It is divided into four parts.

The essay first discusses some of the problems of studying women's imprisonment separately from men's. The second bit of it analyses the circular and repetitive nature of prison studies in general. Part 3 suggests ways of both destroying the iconography of the prison and de-institutionalizing the prison research business. The final section calls into question the article's title and rationale, and implies that in a collection entitled *Prisons in Context* such interrogation might be a legitimate device for putting prison in its placeso long as such 'placing' is itself kept forever open to question.

Why Study Women's Prisons?

The most obvious reason for researching women's prisons separately from men's is that for most of this century women in penal confinement in Britain, North America, and Europe have been housed separately from their male counterparts. Prior to the 1970s, the composition of female prison populations, the disciplinary practices employed within the women's institutions, and the gender-specific needs of women prisoners were largely neglected by researchers. The situation was not remedied until women writing and campaigning in the last quarter of the century engaged in the unremitting research and investigative journalism which put issues of women's imprisonment on penal reform agendas.

Yet the focus of the research gaze has always been extremely dispersed. The women's prisons have become sites for studying (variously) everything from differential bailing

* Criminology Department, Keele University.

This paper has benefited immensely from the supportive, scholarly, and informative comments of Joe Sim and Richard Sparks.

patterns (Dell 1970), through the experiences of mothers and children in custody (Baunach 1985; Catan 1988), to the ways in which the disciplinary regimes of the women's institutions exacerbate the already-dire problems of the (primarily poor) women who experience them (Mandaraka-Sheppard 1986). Historical studies have accounted for the changing social and penal regulation of younger and older women (Haln-Rafter 1985; Dobash *et al.* 1986); studies in the zoo-keeping tradition have shown what quaint rigmaroles some institutionalized females can engage in (Ward and Kassebaum 1965); and organizational studies of women's prisons have successfully adapted Sykes's (1958) framework for analysing men's imprisonment to give insight into the pains of imprisonment for women (Genders and Player 1987). Additionally, there have been the predictable 'outside-in' theories claiming that women's prison regimes mirror the regulatory treatment of women outside prison (Carlen 1983), as well as the equally predictable 'inside-out' studies which show how disabling carceral effects spread crab-like beyond the prison walls, encircling both ex-prisoners and their (official and unofficial) judges in a psychological and material transcarceralism from which it is difficult to break free (Carlen 1988, 1990; Eaton 1993).

And the results of this new high profiling of women's imprisonment? At the interventionary level there has been a proliferation of campaigning groups in North America, Australia, and Europe, either struggling on behalf of all women prisoners, or representing the special interests and needs of, for instance, black women, foreign prisoners facing deportation at the end of their sentences, mentally-ill women, and 'mothers behind bars'. At a theoretical level, however, academic studies of women's prisons seem to have focused much more on racism, sexism, and the social regulation of all women than on the specifics of state *punishment* for female offenders. Claims to theoretical innovation seem mainly to have concentrated on 'adding in' demands in relation to race and class (see, for instance, Rice 1990). Or, alternatively, they have pointed to, and insisted upon, the capacity of women to resist oppression, and then have emphasized the existence of the many modes of resistance within the women's prisons (e.g. Shaw 1992). While I have a certain sympathy towards 'adding in' and 'insistence on resistance' positions, I wish to pause here and briefly consider some of their theoretical implications. They well illustrate a few of the different and difficult issues related to the pros and cons of:

1. making distinct theoretical objects of (a) *women's* imprisonment (i.e., theorizations of imprisonment characterized by conceptualizations which prioritize female gender constructs); and (b) *women's imprisonment* (i.e., theorizations of imprisonment which focus on the empirical phenomenon of women in prison but which may variously privilege race, class, or gender or other constructs in theoretical explanation);
2. abandoning theoretical rigour in the service of campaigning or wish-fulfilling rhetoric; and
3. seeking once more to theorize *imprisonment as punishment* without always already referring to something other than its punitive function, and/or always already inscribing its meanings in institutional sites other than the prison (cf. Foucault 1977: 22).

What I have called 'adding-in' demands are those made by theorists who claim, at the most general level, that a specific conceptualization does not adequately 'reflect'

132

the 'truth' of a specified empirical referent. Thus has it been with critics who, having pointed out that in many countries ethnic minority women suffer disproportionate rates of penal incarceration, insist that conceptualizations of a generalized *women's* imprisonment are inadequate—that the theoretical objective should be to theorize black women's imprisonment, aboriginal, or Native women's imprisonment—and so on. And at the level of prison reform or abolitionist campaigning such criticisms are most probably justified. A theory which has limited applicability to the experiences of a large sector of a specific female prison population may not be too useful in the short term. (Though even campaigners should 'add in' with caution. This is because, ironically, 'adding in' can often result in 'specializing out', when a multiplication of smaller and ever-smaller specialized campaigning groups weaken the impact of the larger, more generalized 'umbrella' organizations.) However, as a contribution to theory production, the 'adding-in' critique involves a realism which assumes that all theories should have a one-to-one relationship, or at least a verisimilitude, with an empirical referent. This is not a theoretical tenet which I hold. First because I think that the task of theory is to produce new knowledge and not mirror the old (cf. Lacan 1977: 171; Burton and Carlen 1979; Ulmer 1985: 88); and secondly (and almost conversely) because I believe that theoretical production still must initially essentialize certain empirical relationships as objects of knowledge which are not reducible to each other (cf. Fuss 1989). This is not to argue that material relationships are not *experienced simultaneously* or *separately* or *primarily* as being class-dominated, gendered, racially or culturally-specific, or racist. (It is only assumed that it is quite OK for any theorist initially to prioritize and essentialize one dimension of multidimensional empirical objects and theorize it separately.) Nor, furthermore, am I suggesting that any one dimension of penal oppression is always already more important than another. (A theorist may well choose to privilege gender, racism, class—or anything else—according to her own political values.) But it *is* to warn against any conceptual conflation and/or conceptual imperialism, which might result in theoretical closure. A similar warning might be timely in relation to the 'insistence on resistance' brigade.

A constant criticism of theoretical analyses which engage in a nominalist essentialism in order to recognize fully in theory that which must eventually be denied via political combat, is that they also deny agency to individuals. Thus theorization of the pains of women's imprisonment has sometimes been criticized for not 'adding in' prisoners' strategies of resistance and, in consequence, implying that the gaoled women are 'victims'. Unfortunately (and if, in common parlance, the word 'victim' is to retain any meaning at all) women prisoners are too frequently victims—and of more things than are usually dreamt of in either the empirical or theoretical universes of middle-class feminist criminologists. Full recognition of the complex power relationships and penal practices within which *women's imprisonment* is constituted as such is no more to *deny* women prisoners the power to resist than it is to *endow* them with that same power. For the effects of theories do not occur *sui generis*. They depend, rather, on the political calculations and conditions in which they are realized. None the less, it is imperative that theoretical explanation not be fashioned to fit the mish-mash of assumptions and interests whence prison-reform lobbies (women's or men's) usually draw their strength. Such a cross-section of ideals and ideologies, though often constitutive of the power of particular reform campaigns, should themselves be always open to question—and not incorporated into theoretical critique by analysts more concerned with being seen as

133

ideologically 'sound' than actually being theoretically 'open' and politically 'awk-ward'.

Finally, in this part, a further issue I wish to raise in relation to theorizing women's imprisonment separately from men's is the question as to whether the time has not come to effect some kind of 'federal' approach wherein 'women's prison' studies might inform and be informed by studies of 'men's prisons'. This question relates both to the 'adding-in' and 'insistence on resistance' issues already discussed, and also to the question of why study prisons at all.

Although the last two decades have seen the flowering of many campaigning groups intent on remedying the wrongs done to women prisoners, women's imprisonment is still with us and the numbers of women suffering penal incarceration have not significantly diminished. 'Adding in' women to the theoretical and political study of state punishment systems does not seem to have resulted in much incorporation of the findings of women penal theorists into the study of penality *per se* (hence the 'need' for this article on 'women's imprisonment'); while, as I have argued above, most 'adding-in', 'inside-out', and 'outside-in' studies of women's prisons have given more insight into the ways in which penal practices are related to other institutional forms than about the specifically penal powers, penal functions, and penal dimensions of such relationships. But has the study of men's prisons been much different? Would a federated approach to the study of men's and women's prisons be a progressive move? My answer to the first question is 'No'. To the second it is 'Yes, probably—at the present time'.

Through the Looking Glass—Or the Prisons We have Learned to Love

It could be argued that each decade sees a new focus or fashion in criminological research, and that 'prison studies' provided the fashionable focus of the 1970s. That decade saw the emergence of prisoners' rights groups in many countries, and also a resurgence of the abolitionist thrust which has been inherent in much radical critique since the birth of the prison (Bianchi and Swaanigen 1986; Mathiesen 1974). During the 1980s, however, the power of 'the prison' was re-asserted. A rich mixture of literary devices and ideological formations continued to inscribe the 'prison' as metaphor in a multitude of discursive practices. In England, moreover, the persistence of imprison-ment as a penal measure was ensured by Tory government 'law and order' policies, the craven expediency of the Labour party's position on crime and punishment, liberal critiques, and a short-term reformist approach—which latter has dominated both leftist campaigning on prison issues and liberal and leftist research. As a consequence, the hold of 'the prison' over the popular punitive imagination has been strengthened. Today, at the beginning of the 1990s, it is distinctly *un*fashionable to talk of a 'world without prisons' (cf. Dodge 1979; Carlen 1993; Sim forthcoming).

Innumerable autobiographies, literary accounts, and sociological writings testify to the perennial power of 'the prison' as metaphor. At the extremes, 'prison' has been both romanticized as a prime site for the engendering of human resistance in the face of oppression (e.g., Cohen and Taylor 1972, 1978); and invoked as the stock metaphor to best describe the state of psychologically oppressed people who have never experienced the actual pains of penal incarceration. (See, for instance, Morton 1992: 5 for an observation likening the currently unhappy state of the Princess of Wales to that of a prisoner in Holloway—Britain's largest prison for women!)

The extremely dubious notion that 'all human life' is encapsulated in 'the prison' most probably accounts for the popularity of the numerous films and TV soap operas based on fictionalized drama and documentaries of prison-life; as well as for the 'prison's' popularity with a range of social scientists wishing to use it as a crucible within which the microcosm of macro-social process can be studied. British psychiatry, indeed, is indebted to 'the prison' for its own institutionalization (Gunn *et al.* 1978); psychologists have claimed that by studying prisoners we can learn also about ourselves (Sapsford 1983: 115); and, most recently, a deconstructionist study of prisoners' writings has attempted to raise issues about 'how the prison experience might be read' (Davies 1990: 3)! Central to the transcarceral fascination which 'the prison' exercises on those who have no notion of, or who deny, its brutal reality, is the liberal marketeer's premise that (other people's) constraint is a necessary condition of ('our') freedom. During the last decade, moreover, the liberalism of 'prison' metaphorics has combined with the short-term compromises of prison reformers and prison researchers to atrophy the impact of more radical critiques.

One of the responses to 1970's Utopianism in criminology and abolitionist penal politics was a protest that however theoretically and politically correct radical critiques might be—and whatever Utopian programmes might be able to achieve in the long-term—in the short-term they did very little to help actual prisoners in the here-and-now. Campaigning groups therefore turned their attention to achieving short-term objectives and to working with, rather than against, prison administrators. Most researchers took, perforce, a similar line. After Cohen and Taylor (1975) had returned a prestigious research award, rather than have their investigations compromised by modifications of research design proposed by prison administrators, a number of other British academics argued that maybe it was better to keep the 'prison-research' door open, than to give officials an excuse to bar researchers from prisons altogether. Subsequently, prison researchers and prison administrators in Britain have colluded in liberal critiques of imprisonment. These, as I claimed earlier, imply that although prison conditions in Britain are generally horrendous, this state of affairs is an unintended consequence of policies and social relationships existing beyond the remit of the prison, rather than as being integral to the logic of prisons as very specific and unique sites for the official delivery of retributivist suffering. When prison-induced pains *are* recognized, they are most usually depicted as being regrettable but inevitable adjuncts of enforced confinement, organizational control mechanisms, or 'bad apple' prison officers. They are not evaluated as the carefully-achieved products of a most cherished site of state punishment. Two analytic perspectives in vogue in the 1980s lent theoretical respectability to such politically-neutered analyses. The left realism of Jock Young (1987) and his associates argued for the production of non-Utopian theories which would have direct policy pay-offs. Deconstructionists (sometimes called 'post-modernists') argued for an anti-essentialism in theory which was taken by some to entail, also, completely relativist positions in relation to penal politics.

Thus, at the end of this section, I have to conclude that although the 1980s saw a slight increase in the campaigning and serious research attention accorded to women's prisons, the overall approach to the academic study of prisons in Britain during that decade lost much of the radical edge which had characterized it both theoretically and politically in the 1970s. Now, as the end of the century approaches, prisons are still seen but through a glass darkly; and their forms and functions as very specific instances of state punishment are concurrently illuminated and obfuscated by the age-old myths of metaphor, the ever-new displacement of deconstructionist fragmentation, and the compromises of liberal optimism.

Breaking the Glass

Towards the end of an extremely imaginative article on 'Utopias in Criminological Thinking', Peter Young also asks 'Why do criminologists pay so much attention to the use of imprisonment, to the analysis of its emergence, and to the ever-present penal (read prison) crisis?' (Young, P. 1992: 434). Young's focus, though, is different from mine. Whereas he is intrigued by the disparity between the dominance of 'the prison' in criminological thought and its relatively rare usage in modern times, my concern is that while criminologists seem nowadays endlessly to focus on (and represent) prisons as being either functional or disfunctional to a seamless web of social control (of, for instance, 'net-widening', 'warehousing', 'disciplining' or 'transcarceralism'), they concomitantly peripheralize the study of 'prison as punishment'. Does that matter? And if it does, what should be done about it?

First, a disclaimer. At no point in the foregoing do I intend to imply that prisons should *not* be interrogated as being other than places of punishment. But I do think that it matters that empirical prison research (in Britain at least) is not currently investigating and theorizing prisons as deliberate and calibrated mechanisms of punishment inflicting state-legitimated pain. And pain of such magnitude that prisoners routinely suffer psychological damage, routinely suffer from prison-induced physical ill-health, and are frequently driven to suicide (Sim 1990). Until prisons are again studied from that viewpoint they will not be seen in context. Indeed, and as I argued above, in one type of deconstructionist analysis they will not be seen at all, but will disappear within a kaleidoscopic palimpsest of 'Other' discourses! Or, in empirical (liberally compromised) studies—conducted by researchers whose access to prisons and permission to publish are alike conditional upon governmental approval of the projects' methods and findings—prisons may well be shown as being the vile places they are, but that vileness will be explained as (or even deconstructed into!) an unintended consequence of the less-than-ideal social conditions existing outside prison.[1] Such studies, together with other analytic writings on prisons, have given excellent theoretical insights into generalized modes of social regulation and do, in passing, often analyse the pains of imprisonment (see, for instance, Scraton *et al.* 1991). But usually they still fail to theorize the prison as being a state mechanism for legitimated pain delivery (with, of course, the exception of Christie 1981). In Britain this theoretical deficit may currently be having serious effects on penal politics and policy. Further- more, and, as Richard Sparks (1993, and here) has argued, the reluctance of theorists

---

[1] Research access to British prisons is only obtained after a research project's objectives and methods have received Home Office approval. All Home Office funded prison research has to be 'approved' prior to publication. Several researchers into British prisons have been threatened with libel suits or with prosecution under the Official Secrets Act. Even when Home Office funded prison research findings *are* approved, the vetting process can take an inordinately long time, thus delaying publication and thereby blunting the impact of findings which can conveniently be officially labelled 'outdated' when they are eventually published.

themselves to focus on the prison's punitive function may in part be responsible for the scarcity of jurisprudential or moral input into privatization debates.

So what is to be done? And where do women's prisons come in?

To break out of the institutionalized mould wherein it is now accepted that empirical prison studies can either be of the liberal exposé type or provide sites of infinite opportunity for deconstructionist theorists to make something of prison other than it is, at least some theorists might like to engage in the twofold strategy of: refusing to see the prison as an inevitable condition of freedom; and essentializing prison as a mechanism for the state's delivery of retributivist pain. The first part of the strategy would lead to a complex of abolitionist principles, one of which would challenge the state-monopoly of control over all prison research; the second would necessitate raising those unspeakable questions which cannot be posed within the compromised framework of official approaches to imprisonment.

All criminologists seeking research access to prisons are required to collude in the liberal myth that, 'We *all* want prisons to be more humane places, don't we?' Yet, given the state of some British prisons, it might be more theoretically productive to say the unsayable—that it is an equally reasonable assumption that *no one* really wants prisons to be any 'better'—and then pose questions as to the modes whereby prisons exactly and systematically impose the excesses of punishment which they do. Such questions might include the following:

How successful are prisons in returning prisoners to society in a worse state of physical health than they were in prior to their imprisonment? How are these degrees of success achieved?

How successful are prisons in returning prisoners to society in a worse state of mental health than they were in prior to their imprisonment? How are these degrees of success achieved?

How successful are prisons in returning prisoners to society with a variety of emotionally disabling symptoms which they did not have before they went to prison? How are these degrees of success achieved?

How successful are prisons in engendering extremes of tension, fear, and mental anguish in prisoners? How are these degrees of success achieved?

How successful are prisons in making the most of *any* pains already suffered by prisoners prior to their sentence? How are these degrees of success achieved?

If people go to prison *as* punishment and not *for* punishment—as official ideology would have it—why are prisons not more like three-star hotels?

Why are there so many studies of police officers' ideological and working practices, and so few similar studies of prison officers?

Who controls the research access to, and research agendas of, the privatized prisons?

And so on. Sure: class, gender, race, and racism should still be studied in relation to imprisonment. And the views of prisoners and prison officers should still be taken seriously. None the less, let us for a time, at least, give empirical research priority to the prison's overwhelming power to punish. For this punitive power has a specificity which exists and persists independently of the best attempts of (some) prisoners to defeat it via strategies of resistance, and the best attempts of (some) prison officers to defeat it via humanistic zeal. It is a power which grinds both women and men and it grinds them independently of the gender-specific modes wherein it is activated.

137

I conclude, therefore, that, following recent attempts to consider prisons within the wider social contexts of, for example, gender, racism, and class, the time has now come for a move in the other direction—to analyse prisons in the much narrower context of the state punishment apparatus. From such a perspective the study of women's and men's prisons could usefully be federated to constitute a more focused analysis of prison penality. It is also to be hoped that some new and more fundamental questions might be asked.

Where Do These Questions Get Us?

At the level of theory they are innovative, fundamental, and could give prison research a much-needed shake up. In terms of the received wisdom relating to penal research politics they will most probably not get us very far—especially in any future access negotiations with prison authorities! But that is the point. Until researchers stop tailoring (or trimming!) their research proposals with a view to making them completely non-threatening to the powers-that-be, it is unlikely that much progress will be made in analysing the distinct specificity of 'prison as punishment'; or in working towards its abolition as such. Of course prisons provide excellent research sites for the study of the relations between macro and micro social process. Of course officials and campaigners need up-to-date information about what is going on behind the walls. Of course much goes on in prison other than punishment. Of course prison administrators and staff are decent people who care as much, if not more, about prisoners than many outside. Of course. But (and this is the article's main rationale), as *theorists* (and not primarily as investigative journalists, campaigners, or grant-grubbers) it does behove us every now and then to stop and ask, 'Where are present research trends getting us?' My fear is that present trends in the study of women's and men's prisons are getting us further and further away from understanding the power of the prison both to promise and deliver pain as punishment. Unless investigation of that most specific power is put back on the research agenda, studies of both women's and men's prisons will continue to produce either short-term-reformist exposés, or the deconstructionist diversions wherein important questions about the prison's punitive capacity lie are left unasked. The danger then is that unchallenged, triumphant, and transcarceral, the power of The Prison to punish will increase, both in and out of context—indefinitely . . .

REFERENCES

BAUNACH, P. (1985), *Mothers in Prison*. New Brunswick, NJ and Oxford: Transaction Books.
BIANCHI, H., and SWAANINGEN, R., eds. (1986), *Abolitionism*. Amsterdam: Free University Press.
BURTON, F., and CARLEN, P. (1979), *Official Discourse*. London: Routledge and Kegan Paul.
CARLEN, P., (1983), *Women's Imprisonment*. London: Routledge and Kegan Paul.
—— (1988), *Women, Crime and Poverty*. Buckingham: Open University Press.
—— (1990), *Alternatives to Women's Imprisonment*. Buckingham: Open University Press.
—— (1993), 'Underclass, Crime and Imprisonment', Bonger Lecture, Bonger Institute, Amsterdam.

CATAN, L. (1988), *The Development of Young Children in HMP Mother and Baby Units*. Falmer: University of Sussex.

CHRISTIE, N. (1981), *Limits to Pain*. Oxford: Martin Robertson.

COHEN, S., and TAYLOR, L. (1972), *Psychological Survival*. Harmondsworth: Penguin.

—— (1975), 'Prison Research: a Cautionary Tale', *New Society*, 30 January 1975.

—— (1978), *Escape Attempts: The Theory and Practice of Resistance to Everyday Life*. Harmondsworth: Penguin.

DAVIES, I. (1990), *Writers in Prison*. Oxford: Blackwell.

DELL, S. (1970), *Silent in Court*. London: Bell.

DOBASH, R., DOBASH, R., and GUTTERIDGE, S. (1986), *The Imprisonment of Women*. Oxford: Blackwell.

DODGE, C. (1979), *A World Without Prisons*. Lexington, MA: Heath.

EATON, M. (1993), *Women After Prison*. Buckingham: Open University Press.

FOUCAULT, M. (1977), *Discipline and Punish*. London: Allen Lane.

FUSS, D. (1989), *Essentially Speaking: Feminism, Nature, Difference*. London: Routledge.

GENDERS, E., and PLAYER, E. (1987), 'Women in Prison: The Treatment, the Control and the Experience', in P. Carlen and A. Worrall, eds, *Gender, Crime and Justice*. Buckingham: Open University Press.

GUNN, J., ROBERTSON, G., DELL, S., and WAY, C. (1978), *Psychiatric Aspects of Imprisonment*. London: Academic Press.

HALN-RAFTER, N. (1985), *Partial Justice: State Prisons and Their Inmates, 1800–1935*. Boston: North Eastern University Press.

LACAN, J. (1977), *Ecrits*. London: Tavistock.

MANDARAKA-SHEPPARD, A. (1986), *The Dynamics of Aggression in Women's Prisons, in England*. London: Gower.

MATHIESEN, T. (1974), *The Politics of Abolition*. Oxford: Martin Robertson.

MORTON, A. (1992), *Diana: Her True Story*. London: Michael O'Mara.

RICE, M. (1990), 'Challenging Orthodoxies in Feminist Theory: A Black Feminist Critique', in L. Gelsthorpe and A. Morris, eds, *Feminist Perspectives in Criminology*: 59–69. Buckingham: Open University Press.

SAPSFORD, R. (1983), *Life Sentence Prisoners*. Buckingham: Open University Press.

SHAW, M. (1992), 'Issues of Power and Control: Women in Prison and Their Defenders', *British Journal of Criminology*, 32/4: 438–53.

SIM, J. (1990), *Medical Power in Prisons*. Buckingham: Open University Press.

—— (forthcoming), 'The Abolitionist Approach: A British Perspective', in R. Dobash, A. Duff, and S. Marshall, eds, *Penal Theory and Penal Practice*. Manchester University Press.

SPARKS, R. (1993), 'Are Prisons Part of the Public Sphere?: Penal Politics, Privatization and the Problem of Legitimacy'. Paper presented to a conference on 'The Public Sphere in Free Market Societies', University of Salford, January 1993.

SYKES, G. (1958), *Society of Captives: A Study of Maximum Security Prisons*. Princeton, NJ: Princeton University Press.

ULMER, G. (1985), 'The Object of Post-Criticism', in M. Foster, ed., *Postmodern Culture*. London: Pluto.

WARD, D., and KASSEBAUM, G. (1965), *Women's Prison: Sex and Social Structure*. Chicago: Aldine Publishing Co.

WOOLF, LORD JUSTICE AND TUMIM, JUDGE STEPHEN (1991), *Prison Disturbances April 1990*. London: HMSO.

YOUNG, J. (1986), 'The Failure of Criminology: The Need for a Radical Realism', in R. Matthews and J. Young, eds, *Confronting Crime*. London: Sage.

YOUNG, P. (1992), 'The Importance of Utopias in Criminological Thinking', *British Journal of Criminology*, 32/4: 423–37.

INSPECTING PRISONS

The View from Strasbourg

ROD MORGAN and MALCOLM EVANS*

In many European jurisdictions, Britain included, the absence or ineffectiveness of domestic remedies against what critics judge to be unacceptable prison conditions or decision-making procedures has meant that attention has turned increasingly to international agencies, both inter-governmental and non-governmental. Penal pressure groups seek more and more to bring international comparisons and scrutiny to bear on domestic policy. Council of Europe data regarding the number of prisoners per head of population in different jurisdictions have become a regular feature of British penal pressure group fact-sheets and critical texts (Cavadino and Dignan 1992: 13): in these league tables England, Scotland, and Northern Ireland generally fare badly as do other aspects of British penal policy when subjected to comparative analysis (see, for example, Rutherford 1984; Downes 1988; Feest 1988; Graham 1988). In 1989 a pressure group, Penal Reform International, was founded with critical comparative analysis as its *raison d'être*: significantly, PRI's Secretary General is the Director of NACRO, Britain's largest and most influential penal pressure group.

Because of legal, policy and counting differences, international comparisons of incarceration rates or the composition of custodial populations are difficult enough (see Pease 1991). Setting and applying custodial standards poses much more complex problems. In the same way that what is to count as acceptable conditions changes over time in relation to standards and expectations of life in the community at large, so cultural and economic differences between jurisdictions make it especially difficult to agree common standards and set reform priorities. This makes the Council of Europe Committee for the Prevention of Torture and Inhuman or Degrading Treatment or Punishment (CPT), the latest international agency to whose judgments appeal is being made, particularly interesting. Contrary to the first impressions created by its title, the CPT is not primarily concerned with torture: within Europe, fortunately, custodial conditions rather than torture chiefly concern the Committee. The CPT's work is critical, therefore, for the ongoing debate about what constitutes acceptable conditions in custody.

This article has three objects. First, to provide an overview of the international mechanisms and agencies which provide the context within which the CPT functions. Secondly, to describe the constitution of the CPT, its powers and *modus operandi*. Thirdly, to explain why the CPT is being listened to.

* Respectively Professor of Criminal Justice and Lecturer in Law, Department of Law, University of Bristol. Rod Morgan has on several occasions acted as an expert advisor to the CPT. This article covers material available to 1 April 1993.

International Mechanisms and Inspection Agencies

The United Nations

At the centre of any international map of agencies engaged in norm-setting or monitoring custodial conditions lie the various UN Charter and treaty-based organs. UN member states pledge themselves to observe and promote respect for human rights and fundamental freedoms (Charter, Articles 55 and 56). These rights and freedoms are not defined in the Charter but they are set out in the Universal Declaration of Human Rights (UDHR) adopted by the General Assembly in 1948. Article 5 of the UDHR proclaims: 'No one shall be subjected to torture or cruel, inhuman or degrading treatment'. The UDHR was not intended to be a source of legal obligation. Rather, it set out to establish 'a common standard of achievement for all peoples and all nations'. Two consequences flowed from this. First, states would only become subject to an obligation concerning the prohibition of torture, cruel, inhuman, and degrading treatment, if they chose to become a party to other international instruments which might subsequently be drawn up and which contained such an obligation. Secondly, since it did not oblige any state to do anything, the UDHR did not attempt to establish any mechanisms through which its standards could be enforced. Since 1948 much has changed, both as regards the applicability of the standard as a matter of legal obligation and the manner of its oversight and enforcement. The incremental developments that have brought this about have, however, spawned a network of nightmarish complexity.

First and foremost, the standard set by Article 5 of the UDHR is now recognized as having passed into the body of customary international law and, as such, applies to all states irrespective of whether they have become a party to an international instrument (Rodley 1987: 63–70; Meron 1989: 94–5).[1] If a state breaches customary international law in its dealings with another state, the state in breach is liable to the other under the normal rules of state responsibility. The problem, however, is that if State A violates customary international law by subjecting prisoners (who are nationals of State A) to torture or ill treatment, there is no one other state that has had its particular interests violated. Either no other state has the capacity to bring an international claim against State A or all other states have such a capacity—and international law has tended to eschew the possibility of states bringing an *actio popularis*. Although it is now generally accepted that the obligation reflected in Article 5 of the UDHR is an obligation *erga omnes*, and as such any state might seek to enforce it (Meron 1989: 188–208), the tendency is for this to take place either through the mechanisms developed by the UN or, when applicable, through the organs created by the various regional and international Conventions.

The UN has two distinct spheres of competence. First, it has developed a number of 'Charter-based' mechanisms which allow the UN to oversee compliance by all UN member states with their human rights obligations, premised upon their Charter

[1] Article 5 of the UDHR has been mirrored in Article 3 of the European Convention on Human Rights and Fundamental Freedoms (1950), Article 5(2) of the Inter-American Convention on Human Rights (1969) and Article 5 of the African Charter on Human and Peoples' Rights (1981) as well as in Article 7 of the UN-sponsored International Covenant on Civil and Political Rights (1966). In addition, torture has been the subject of the UN's Declaration of the Protection of All Persons from being Subjected to Torture and Other Cruel, Inhuman or Degrading Treatment or Punishment (1975), and the Convention Against Torture and Other Cruel, Inhuman or Degrading Treatment or Punishment 1984. The Organisation of American States has also adopted the Inter-American Convention to Prevent and Punish Torture (1985).

commitments. The procedure established under ECOSOC (the UN Economic and Social Council) Resolution 1503 (1970) enables a confidential examination of communications which appear to reveal a consistent pattern of gross and reliably attested violations of human rights to be conducted. Further, Resolution 1235 (1967) enables the UN Commission on Human Rights to debate situations publicly and investigate them (Alston 1992: 156). These procedures are of most use when systematic abuses of human rights are taking place as a matter of state policy. To be subjected to an investigation is more a statement of political denunciation by the international community than a means of seeking redress for violation.

Another weapon in the UN armoury is its 'theme procedures'. These have taken the form of either a working group or of a Special Rapporteur established by a resolution of the Commission to investigate and report back on particular human rights issues. A Special Rapporteur on Torture (SRT) was appointed in 1985 (Kooijmans 1991: 56–72). Although his mandate was originally limited to one year, it has subsequently been renewed, most recently in 1992, and will probably be extended further. The techniques used by the SRT include: requesting governments to provide information concerning individual cases; issuing urgent appeals to governments concerning individuals allegedly being subjected to torture or the risk of torture; and, when invited, visiting countries to have consultations with the authorities and NGOs. Finally, the Annual Report presented by the SRT to the Commission is in itself a source of pressure upon states, since it places a mass of detail concerning individual cases in the public domain. It also makes it easy to see which countries respond to requests for information and appeals for urgent action, and allows the public to make their own judgments upon the matter (Alston 1992: 177–9).

Although his mandate is limited to questions relating to torture, as opposed to cruel, inhuman, and degrading treatment or punishment, the SRT has taken the view that the distinction between the categories is a matter of degree: torture and other forms of ill treatment represent different points along a continuum and, as such, he is competent to consider questions relating to ill treatment which seem to fall into the 'grey area' between the two.[2] This is the great merit of the 'thematic procedure' approach—it is extremely flexible with regard to both the procedures it can develop and the interpretation of the standards applicable. Thus the SRT is able to draw inspiration from a variety of sources other than the UN Convention on Torture which, naturally, provides the starting point.[3]

The second aspect of the UN's function concerns its relationship with treaty-based mechanisms, two of which merit particular attention here. The ICCPR (see n.1) established the Human Rights Committee (HRC) to oversee the implementation of the obligations assumed by those states which became a party to it (numbering 113 at 31

[2] See 1st Annual Report, UN Doc E/CN.4/1986/15, paras. 22–3; 33–5; and Kooijmans 1991: 59–61. The 7th Annual Report includes several examples of letters requesting information about situations that seem to lie within the 'ill-treatment' end of the 'grey' area.

[3] These other sources include the UN Standard Minimum Rules for the Treatment of Prisoners (ECOSOC Resolution 663 C(XXIV) 1957 and Resolution 2076 (LXII) 1977), the Body of Principles for the Protection of All Persons Under Any Form of Detention or Imprisonment (General Assembly Resolution 1988) and the Principles of Medical Ethics Relevant to the Role of Health Personnel, Particularly Physicians, in the Protection of Prisoners and Detainees Against Torture and Other Cruel, Inhuman or Degrading Treatment or Punishment (General Assembly Resolution 37/194, 1982). While these sources provide guidance to all engaged in the progressive development of international standards, the SRT has, perhaps, a greater freedom than those who are more closely tied to the text of a particular convention.

July 1992). All state parties are obliged to submit reports to the HRC on the measures they have adopted which give effect to the rights contained in the Covenant. The HRC considers these reports and may make 'general comments', which are not directed at any specific country, concerning the application of particular Articles of the Covenant. The actual process of examination provides an opportunity for some rigorous examinations of particular situations (see Opsahl 1992: 397–419; McGoldrick 1991: 44–104). Article 10(1) of the Covenant provides that 'All persons deprived of their liberty shall be treated with humanity and with respect for the inherent dignity of the human person'. This is seen as an extension of Article 7 (prohibiting torture, etc.) and to form an element in a continuum. In 1992 the HRC updated its General Comments on both Articles 7 and 10, the latter of which drew attention to the relevance of the UN codes, which, while not legally binding, are thereby given an enhanced status.

The HRC also has the capacity to consider 'communications' concerning alleged violations of a state's obligations under the Covenant. This procedure is dependant upon a state party to the Covenant declaring that it is willing for the Committee to consider a complaint made against it by another state that has made a similar declaration (under Article 41 of the Covenant) or by an individual (under the provisions of the First Optional Protocol to the Covenant). Although both these procedures are in force, no inter-state complaint has been brought. The HRC has, however, dealt so far with approaching 500 individual communications, many of which have concerned the application of Articles 7 and 10. The views adopted by the HRC confirm that conditions of detention can violate both Articles but the extreme nature of most of the relevant cases—concerned with the situation in Uruguay in the mid-1970s—means that little light is shed upon the applicability of these Articles to more conventional situations (see McGoldrick 1991, chapter 9). Although not an organ of the UN, the HRC is closely woven into its structures, being funded by it and serviced by the UN Secretariat, and it submits an Annual Report to the General Assembly through ECOSOC.

The General Assembly also receives the Annual Report of the UNCAT, the body established by the 1984 UN Convention Against Torture. Like the HRC, it receives and considers reports submitted by state parties and communications from either states or from individuals under optional procedures contained in Articles 21 and 22 (as at July 1992, 29 of the 64 state parties had made declarations under Article 21, and 28 of these had also done so under Article 22). Unlike the HRC, the UNCAT can initiate investigations if it considers there to be 'reliable information which appears to it to contain well founded indications that torture is being systematically practised in the territory of a State Party' (Article 20). This procedure is confidential. In addition, states may choose to opt out of it when becoming a party to the Convention (Article 28). Despite its full title, the UN Convention is primarily directed towards torture, as opposed to ill treatment. Where ill treatment takes the form of abuse to the person, it is likely that this will not present too great a bar to the activities of the Committee. Where conditions of detention are at issue, however, it might prove more problematic.

Regional inter-governmental organizations

Regional human rights organizations have, like the UN, also devised systems and structures. The Inter-American Convention utilizes the Commission on Human Rights set up by the Organization of American States (OAS) and establishes a Court of Human

Rights. Under the Convention the Commission can hear complaints from citizens of any state party, but may only consider inter-state complaints if both (or all) states concerned have accepted the competence of the Commission to do so. The Commission also exercises a general supervisory function in relation to the obligations in the Charter of the OAS. Cases may also be referred by the Commission or by a state party concerned—but not by an individual—to the court established by the Convention, provided that all the states concerned in the case have made a declaration accepting the jurisdiction of the court. To date only 14 of the 23 states which are a party to the Convention have done so.

This system closely resembles that established by the European Convention on Human Rights under the auspices of the Council of Europe. The European Commission on Human Rights, however, has automatic jurisdiction over inter-state complaints and not over individual petitions. Petitions submitted by individuals may only be considered by the Commission if the state whose acts are called into question has made a declaration under Article 25 of the Convention accepting its jurisdiction. Cases may also be referred to the European Court of Human Rights, either by the Commission or by a state party concerned, provided that the states concerned have accepted its jurisdiction by making a declaration under Article 46 of the Convention. To date, all state parties have made declarations accepting the right of individual petition to the Commission and the compulsory jurisdiction of the court.

Both the OAS and the Council of Europe have drawn up regional conventions concerning torture. Like the UN Convention, however, the Inter-American Convention is primarily aimed at acts of torture, as opposed to conditions of detention. It does not establish any new monitoring body. The European Convention for the Prevention of Torture and Inhuman or Degrading Treatment or Punishment is of a fundamentally different nature. Although it derives its purpose from Article 3 of the ECHR, the purpose of the convention is to establish a Committee which 'shall, by means of visits, examine the treatment of persons deprived of their liberty with a view to strengthening, if necessary, the protection of such persons from torture and from inhuman or degrading treatment or punishment' (Article 1). The CPT, therefore, is the first body developed from within the international body of human rights law-making that has the monitoring of conditions of detention as an important part of its function. Although the CPT occupies only a small niche within the panoply of international human rights mechanisms, it represents a crucial evolutionary step within that lineage, a step other bodies already wish to emulate. The UN Commission on Human Rights is currently considering drafting an additional protocol to the 1984 Torture Convention that would establish a body with similar powers, and the CPT, by focusing upon the extent to which prison conditions may amount to violations of Article 3, demonstrates that many of the mechanisms mentioned above may yet become more pertinent to those seeking remedies for situations which have traditionally not been regarded as within their purview. It follows that the work of the CPT is attracting close scrutiny.

The International Committee of the Red Cross (ICRC)

The ICRC is uniquely placed between the inter-governmental organs and the NGOs. It has an inspectoral role regarding compliance with the four Geneva Conventions of 1949 (relating to field forces, combatants at sea, POWs and civilians in time of war respectively) and two additional Protocols of 1977 (relating to victims of international and non-international conflicts respectively), all of which unequivocally prohibit the infliction of torture, ill-treatment, or reprisals on persons protected by the Conventions. The ICRC has a mandate to visit POWs and civilian detainees in places of detention and does so with the agreement of parties to conflicts: the Geneva Conventions impose no obligation in this respect. Further, given the current resurgence of nationalism, the rise of religious fundamentalism and the risk of civil wars in the former Warsaw Pact nations and elsewhere, it is important to note that the ICRC seeks access to prisoners in conflict situations not covered by the Geneva Conventions. In domestic circumstances which do not degenerate into open warfare, but which involve violence between more or less organized groups and governments leading to the taking of emergency powers and widespread use of the army or police, the ICRC may offer its services: the Committee is concerned with persons arrested for offences with 'political connotations'. It is in precisely these circumstances that large numbers of persons are likely to be detained and labelled 'terrorists', 'collaborators', 'subversives' etc., with a high risk of their being tortured or otherwise ill-treated (ICRC 1988: 9–37; Gasser 1988). Among the countries in which the ICRC has visited detainees in extra-Convention situations is Northern Ireland.

The ICRC describes its purpose in visiting detainees as follows: 'to prevent torture, to prevent "disappearances" and to work for overall improvements in the material and psychological conditions of detention' (ICRC 1992: 4). However, the Committee 'allows itself the widest possible latitude for taking action': it 'generally does not use the word torture, preferring the broader term "ill-treatment", which is less offensive for the authorities but basically fulfils the same function'. It concerns itself with 'deliberately squalid material or psychological conditions, brutal acts . . . disciplinary rules designed to break the spirit' and so on (p. 5). The fact that the ICRC has to negotiate to obtain access to detainees also determines the methods it adopts. The Committee will only undertake visits if certain conditions are agreed to (access to all detainees, in all locations, permission to interview detainees freely without witnesses, permission to draw up lists of prisoners and to repeat visits and, if necessary, to distribute material aid) but it maintains a scrupulous neutrality. It does not involve itself in any way in the political problems underlying the conflict nor does it comment on the reasons for detention or inquire about the purpose of interrogation. Most importantly the ICRC undertakes to observe absolute confidentiality: it reports publicly on where it visits but not what it finds; its findings are transmitted only to the authorities concerned. The Committee claims that this working method is 'not a sign of timidity or a wish to conceal ill-treatment', but is a precondition to gain access, making 'the ICRC's "interference" more palatable to the detaining authorities' (p. 9). This approach has, the ICRC maintains, enabled it to visit over half a million detainees in some 100 countries since 1918 without a single government complaining that its security has been compromised (p. 11). The work of the ICRC has recently expanded rapidly. Between 1980 and 1985 the Committee saw 150,000 detainees in over 600 places of detention. In 1991 alone it visited 150,000 detainees in 1,927 locations.

Amnesty International

Best known of the international human rights NGOs is Amnesty International. Amnesty is mandated to: seek the release of prisoners of conscience; oppose detention of political prisoners without fair trial; oppose the death penalty, torture, or other cruel, inhuman, and degrading treatment of all prisoners; and oppose extra-judicial execution or 'disappearances' (Amnesty International 1991). It also opposes hostage-taking and deliberate and arbitrary killings by armed opposition groups. Amnesty's International Secretariat, based in London, comprises a large number of researchers organized in regional world sections, engaged full time in monitoring and publicizing human rights abuses within Amnesty's mandate. Data gathered from individuals and groups in the countries where the abuses are taking place are occasionally supplemented by investigatory missions, if the countries concerned will grant access to territories, institutions, or victims. When Amnesty judges that the information it has gathered suggests a *prima facie* cause for concern, it takes this up directly with the government or other authority responsible and through campaigning and other methods mounts pressure for remedial action to be taken. This generally involves publishing the evidence of abuse, often in the form of case studies which provide information about individual victims.

The widespread use worldwide of imprisonment of people by reason of their political, religious, or other beliefs, and the extensive use of the death penalty and torture, means that these campaigns have largely absorbed Amnesty's energies and resources. Amnesty has understandably been reluctant about straying too far into the question of custodial conditions that might amount to cruel, inhuman, and degrading treatment (Cook 1991: 173–4). It has not been the top priority and the issue raises difficult problems of definition and cultural relativity, which are potentially open-ended as far as an international campaigning organization is concerned. It follows that Amnesty largely concerns itself with prisoners rather than prisons and generally comments on conditions only if their consequences demonstrate clearly that they are cruel, inhuman, or degrading. For example, in 1980 Amnesty published its concern about the use of solitary confinement or small group isolation for prisoners suspected or convicted of politically motivated crimes in West Germany, principally the 'Rote Armee Fraktion'. The published dossier provided details on the deteriorating mental and physical condition of four prisoners, allegedly the consequence of prolonged isolation and sensory deprivation. The prisoners were not adopted by Amnesty as 'prisoners of conscience' but the organization pressed the German authorities to adopt a more humane mode of custody (Amnesty International 1980). Similar pressure was applied to the US Federal Bureau of Prisons in 1988 regarding conditions judged to amount to mental torture in the high security unit for women at Lexington, Kentucky (Amnesty International 1988). As a result of these cases Amnesty has developed its own working guidelines from which to assess the use of solitary confinement. Amnesty does not oppose solitary confinement *per se*, but it contends that prolonged solitary confinement 'can have serious physical and/or psychological effects and may in such circumstances constitute cruel, inhuman and degrading treatment or punishment' (Amnesty International 1985: 23).

Human Rights Watch organizations

Following in Amnesty's wake are a growing number of Human Rights 'Watch' organizations (Africa Watch, Americas Watch, Asia Watch, Helsinki Watch, Middle East Watch) which are in turn spawning more focused projects. Of the latter the most relevant for present purposes is the Prison Project formed in 1988 under the aegis of

Helsinki Watch, but which cuts across the five regional divisions of Human Rights Watch to focus on prison conditions world-wide. The Project is publishing a series of monographs on prison conditions in particular countries: included in the list of European national studies, for example, is one on the United Kingdom published in June 1992 (Human Rights Watch 1992a). These prison-specific surveys supplement those Watch publications on human rights generally which may make reference to conditions in detention (for example, a 1991 Helsinki Watch report on Northern Ireland made detailed reference to alleged ill-treatment of detainees at police detention centres). Like Amnesty, the Human Rights Watch organizations have largely to rely for information on media reports and on individuals and groups corresponding from the countries concerned. The Prison Project seeks to supplement such information with first-hand inspection visits by staff and experts commissioned for the purpose. Such persons have no right of entry to either countries or institutions, however, and it appears that access is often denied or made difficult, particularly in jurisdictions where there is alleged to be most cause for concern. For example, a recent report on Turkey was produced without a visiting delegation gaining access to a single prison (though the Turkish authorities are said possibly to have granted permission too late for the delegation to benefit from it—see Human Rights Watch 1989: 3) and the one visit to a prison made by a recent delegation to Spain is said to have been made possible by the intervention of a Penitentiary Judge in the face of a refusal to grant access by the Ministry of Justice (Human Rights Watch 1992b: vii–ix). Whether these difficulties could to some extent have been avoided is a question impossible to judge from published reports. It is conceivable that government departments might have doubts about the methodology the Project employs, quite apart from any mistrust they may have for a human rights organization about whose mandate, funding, and personnel they may know little. We return to this issue below. What is clear is that the Prison Project takes up every conceivable aspect of prison conditions.

Other organizations

Other NGOs, too numerous to mention, make important contributions to the debate about custodial conditions both by monitoring the treatment of detainees and publishing what they find, and by supplying information, formulating proposals, and generally lobbying those inter-governmental organs that have formal powers. For example, both the International Association of Penal Law and the International Commission of Jurists (ICJ) have contributed substantially to UN deliberations on aspects of custody (Rodley 1987: 235–6): both organizations also undertake investigatory work. Some NGOs have consultative status with the ECOSOC of the UN—the World Council of Churches, the Bahai International Community, Pax Romana, the International Federation of Human Rights and the Inter-Parliamentary Union, in addition to Amnesty and the ICRC, for example. From the footnote references in Rodley's exhaustive study of the development of international law in this field it is clear that the use of custody and conditions in custody are the concern of a large number of organizations. It is also apparent, as we shall see, that many of these same organizations contribute to the work of the CPT.

148

The CPT: Constitution and Modus Operandi

The European Torture Prevention Convention is, as we have seen, different from the similarly titled UN and OAS Torture Conventions. It establishes a Committee, the CPT, which, through a system of visits, aims to 'strengthen by non-judicial means of a preventive nature' (preamble to the Convention) the obligation of Article 3 of the European Convention of Fundamental Human Rights and Freedoms. The Convention is based on the principle of co-operation. It is concerned with torture *and* inhuman or degrading treatment or punishment, and because the CPT is not a judicial body (and has no sanctions other than the possible publicity of its findings at its command), it is under no pressure to define the boundary between the two forms of ill-treatment. It can concern itself generally with examining 'the treatment of persons deprived of their liberty with a view to strengthening, if necessary, their protection' against either form of ill-treatment (Article 1). Further, as the first annual report of the CPT made abundantly clear, the Committee is not bound by the case law of the European Commission or Court of Human Rights: it may employ that case law as a reference point, but it may seek guidance from 'a number of other relevant human rights instruments' (Council of Europe 1991*a*: paras. 5–6). Two other distinctions between the CPT and the European Commission and Court are worth highlighting. The latter exclusively comprise lawyers: the CPT may, either through its membership or the experts it employs, draw on medical doctors, criminologists, penal administrators, etc., as well as lawyers. Second, whereas the Commission and Court act only if petitioned, the CPT intervenes through visits which may or may not have been preceded by information from any number of possible sources.

Twenty-three European countries have so far signed and ratified the Torture Convention and are therefore entitled to have a member on the CPT. It is anticipated that Poland, Hungary, Bulgaria, the Czech Republic, and Slovakia will shortly sign. CPT members are elected by a political body, the Committee of Ministers of the Council of Europe. This ensures that the governments of the member states are able to exercise some political control over the complexion of the Committee, a compromise dictated by the sensitive nature of its task. CPT members are not government representatives, however. They serve in an individual capacity. They 'shall be independent and impartial' (just how independent when they depend on governments for re-election is an interesting question) and they 'shall be chosen from among persons of high moral character, known for their competence in the field of human rights or having professional experience in the areas covered by this Convention' (Article 4). The Committee is supported by a secretariat based in Strasbourg and both when preparing for and conducting visits may be assisted by experts recruited as and when the Committee considers it necessary.

The work of the CPT revolves entirely round its visits, preparing for them, conducting them, drafting reports on them and following them up through dialogue with party governments. Visits are of two kinds, periodic and *ad hoc*, 'as required in the circumstances' (Article 7). A party to the Convention must permit visits 'to any place within its jurisdiction where persons are deprived of their liberty by a public authority' (Article 2): this means such places as police stations, psychiatric hospitals, refugee camps, immigration detention centres and military barracks, as well as young offender institutions and prisons. Though a state may argue for the postponement of a visit on certain specified grounds (Article 9), this provision is exceptional: the presumption is that subject to notification the party will provide full information about places of detention and will allow visiting delegations full access to them and confidential access to all persons detained in them (Article 8). The CPT decided that the initial order of periodic visits should be determined by lot. Four such visits were made in 1990, five in 1991, seven in 1992 and eight are planned for 1993: it follows that by the end of 1993 every party state will have been visited once and one state, the United Kingdom, will have been visited twice. There have been two *ad hoc* visits to date, both to Turkey, in 1990 and 1991 respectively. Since Turkey also received a periodic visit in late 1992, it has so far received most CPT attention. *Ad hoc* visits may be arranged at the request of states that they be visited 'in order to investigate allegations and to clarify the situation' (Council of Europe 1989: para. 49). There is no evidence that the Turkish Government sought visits and thus the reasons for them must be a matter of speculation. It seems probable, however, that among the NGOs with which the CPT reports 'having entered into contact' (Council of Europe 1991*a*: para. 42) is Amnesty, which has in recent years published a stream of reports alleging torture and other forms of ill-treatment of detained persons in Turkey. If, as seems likely, the CPT decides that periodic visits should in future be decided not by lot but according to the Committee's assessment of need, then the current distinction between periodic and *ad hoc* visits will become less clear-cut.

Also of interest is the Committee's future interpretation of the Convention requirement that parties be notified of visits. This is currently satisfied by the CPT announcing well in advance periodic visits planned for the year ahead and informing the government concerned of the precise dates about two weeks before the delegation arrives. Finally, a few days before the visit commences the government is sent a provisional list of institutions to be visited. A balance clearly has to be struck between allowing countries to prepare for visits and making unannounced visits which might prevent abuses being covered up. The list of places which the delegation intends visiting is 'provisional': unannounced visits are made. Nevertheless the current three-stage notification procedure gives parties more detailed notice than Article 8(1) requires.

Reports on visits, including any recommendations the CPT considers it necessary to make, are confidential to member states. Only 'if the Party fails to co-operate or refuses to improve the situation in the light of the Committee's recommendations', may the CPT decide, by a majority of two-thirds of its members, 'to make a public statement on the matter' (Article 10). This is the Committee's only sanction, so far used once, with regard to Turkey in December 1992 (Council of Europe 1992*a*). This rule of confidentiality might have meant that few CPT reports saw the light of day, something which led some commentators initially to think that the work of the Committee would have little impact. Publication of CPT reports, with the permission of their state recipients, has become the norm, however. To date eight reports have appeared, on Austria and Denmark—the first countries the CPT inspected, agreed to publication and provided a precedent which other countries have followed—the United Kingdom, Malta, Sweden, France, Switzerland, and Finland.

Reports are slow to appear and thus, since 20 visits have been made, it is difficult to assess how many countries have decided that their reports should not be published. The CPT has so far taken between four (Malta) and nine (Sweden) months to adopt reports, and the time taken appears to be getting longer in spite of the CPT's stated objective that

150

they be sent to parties within six months of visits (Council of Europe 1992*b*: para. 23). Parties can then decide on one of four courses: allowing the report to be published almost immediately, whilst giving themselves the option of publishing their response later (Denmark, Sweden, and Finland); drafting their response and publishing both documents simultaneously (Austria, the United Kingdom, France, and Switzerland); sitting on the report and later allowing it to be published (Malta); and keeping everything confidential. If the first course is pursued then by definition the reports appear almost as soon as the CPT can produce them—so far after about nine months. If the Austrian and British precedents are any guide then the second course means publication after approximately 16 months, though other countries may take longer. It is not at all clear, for example, why Malta waited until October 1992 to publish, without publishing any response of their own, the CPT report they had received in November 1990 on a visit conducted in July 1990. With the exception of Turkey—which, following the CPT public statement of December 1992, we can reasonably presume had decided not to publish the CPT reports on visits in September 1990 and October 1991—we cannot be certain about the intentions of the other country visited over 18 months ago, that is Spain.

Reports are clearly written with a view to publication. Each provides: an overview of the work of the CPT; details of the visit, including places visited and groups met with; information regarding the relevant domestic legislative and administrative provisions; the delegation's findings regarding the conditions of custody and the treatment of persons detained; and, finally, the CPT's 'recommendations', 'comments', and 'requests for information', with regard to each of the institutions or type of institution visited. The distinction between a 'recommendation' and a 'comment' or 'request for information' is procedurally important, for it is only if a party fails positively to respond to 'recommendations' that the CPT may invoke Article 10(2) and make a 'public statement'.

The CPT: Gathering Credibility

It is ironic that the first member of the Council of Europe to ratify the Torture Convention was Turkey (in February 1988), the country which, if the strictures of Amnesty and other human rights NGOs are any guide, might have been expected to be most resistant to involvement of the CPT. Certainly Amnesty's repeated claims that the use of torture in Turkey is widespread (see Amnesty International 1992 for a recent statement) appear to have been endorsed by the subsequent decisions and findings of the CPT. As we have seen, Turkey, alone of the countries that have so far ratified the Convention, has been visited more than once and has been the subject of a public statement (Council of Europe 1992*a*). The CPT had 'reached the conclusion that torture and other forms of severe ill-treatment were important characteristics of police custody' after its first visit to Turkey in 1990 (para. 4) and justified its decision to make a public statement on the basis of 'the continuing failure of the Turkish authorities to improve the situation' (Council of Europe 1992*a*: para. 2). The public statement is extraordinarily damning. In it reference is made to CPT doctors having found injuries on prisoners consistent with their having been tortured and of the 1992 delegation having discovered torture rooms with torture equipment *in situ*. Why did Turkey apparently rush to ratify a Convention which has generated such embarrassment?

151

The Turkish Government has reportedly enacted legislation since 1988 which has made it more difficult for officers alleged to have ill-treated suspects to be proceeded against (Council of Europe 1992*a*: para. 26) and it has failed to publish CPT reports. It is likely, therefore, that the Turkish Government was keen to ratify a Convention the critical impact of which it anticipated would be small. By contrast the symbolic consequence of ratification might be vital. Turkey is an applicant for membership of the EC. Given Turkey's poor human rights reputation, its willingness to ratify the Torture Convention might be taken to signify a desire to reiterate and enhance its claim to be thoroughly European. The Convention presented an opportunity to join a club the membership of which it could not afford to refuse.

This reasoning undoubtedly explains why the Torture Convention has been ratified by all longstanding Council of Europe members and why former Warsaw Pact countries are waiting eagerly in the queue. The Council of Europe provides impeccable parentage for a family of nations at the heart of which is an economic community promising substantial benefits. This is not to deny honourable human rights intentions to most politicians and administrators keen to receive CPT attentions: it is simply to suggest that the CPT operates within a political context offering unparalleled associational attractions. Were it not for this political context, the CPT might not be concerning itself with torture, as opposed to custodial conditions, at all. By the same token it seems unlikely that a CPT-like structure will in the foreseeable future flourish within the UN: the European nations already have their own mechanism which they will not wish to be undermined or duplicated; and there is as yet no compensating attraction within the UN likely to persuade most nations outside Europe that they should ratify a Convention with the capacity to embarrass them. It might be observed that 19 of the 64 states currently party to the UN Torture Convention are already party to the European Torture Convention.

Two other politically-determined structural factors exert a powerful influence on the nature and effectiveness of the work of the CPT: the generosity of the Committee's budget and the quality of the Committee's membership. The former determines the size of the CPT Secretariat, the number of meetings and visits that can be sustained, and the use that can be made of experts. The latter determines the expertise, vitality, and commitment of the Committee itself. Clearly the two factors are interrelated. Were the Committee wholly composed of energetic experts there would be less need to employ outsiders. Conversely, a generous budget would enable a good many membership shortcomings to be made up. To date the evidence suggests that the Committee is moderately well-endowed with appropriate members and has been able to make up the deficit by drawing upon strong Secretariat support and outside expert assistance.

Of the 22 CPT members (San Marino has not nominated a candidate for membership): ten are lawyers, four are doctors, three are politicians, and one each is a civil servant, diplomat, academic, psychologist, and cleric. Some members fall into more than one of these categories. These descriptions say little about members' expertise, however. For example, some of the lawyers have little expertise or prior experience of human rights, the criminal justice system or the law relating to custody. One of the doctors has no particular knowledge or experience relevant to either police stations, prisons, or mental hospitals. By contrast the cleric was for many years a prison chaplain and the civil servant was at one time a senior prisons administrator. It is difficult, therefore, to assess the degree to which the membership can be said genuinely to have been chosen for their known competence as required by Article 4(2). It is clear that a minority of members have substantial relevant expertise. For example, the President, Professor Cassese (Italy), is an internationally recognized human rights expert who has written widely on the subject. Both the Vice Presidents—Professors Bernheim (Switzerland) and Sorensen (Denmark)—are doctors, one a psychiatrist with extensive experience of prison medicine, the other a surgeon, a member of the UNCAT and an active worker for an internationally recognized treatment centre for torture victims. There are at least half a dozen other members with experience which may be less obviously extensive but which is none the less considerable and relevant. This means, however, that about half the members come less than well equipped to assist with the onerous work of the committee.

The age distribution of the membership might also be considered a handicap. Only three members are under 50 years whereas no fewer than eight members are 65 or over of whom two are over 70. Indeed the most recently appointed member, Mr Oehry (elected November 1992, for Liechtenstein), is, at 72 years, the oldest member of the Committee. Though several of the older CPT members have invaluable experience, this age profile cannot be advantageous when it comes to organizing visits to police stations when they are busiest in the middle of the night, or conducting gruelling inspection tours for almost a fortnight at a time.

Whatever deficiencies the composition of the CPT membership may be judged to exhibit has so far been compensated for by the provision of an efficient Secretariat and the extensive employment of expert assistance. This has been made possible by the 'firm financial basis' provided by the Council of Ministers (Council of Europe 1992b: para. 14). The Strasbourg Secretariat which, *inter alia*, prepares briefs on the countries to be visited and drafts reports afterwards, includes three lawyers and another administrator with a criminal justice background. Moreover, in addition to the expert assistance the Committee initially gathered in order to prepare members for their task (Council of Europe 1991a: paras 35 and 37), the CPT has to date employed, on an *ad hoc* basis, 17 different experts drawn from nine countries to assist with visits. These experts have been medical doctors, psychiatrists, and persons with practical experience of penal or police custody in roughly equal proportions. It is now the custom for visiting delegations to comprise four or five members of the Committee plus two members of the Secretariat and two experts, the precise number depending on the duration of the visit, which in turn depends on the size of the country or its population. Initial visits to large countries (Germany, the United Kingdom, France, Italy, etc.) have lasted 11–13 days and visits to smaller countries (Denmark, Portugal, Cyprus, Switzerland, etc.) 6–8 days. Sweden and the Netherlands were judged to fall between these two stools, whereas the visit to San Marino was undertaken in one day by a small group breaking off from a delegation to Italy.

It is obvious that, with the possible exceptions of Liechtenstein and San Marino, it would be impossible to inspect all places of detention in a country within the compass of a single brief visit. In that sense all visits, whatever their duration, involve sampling. What is clear is that the CPT has set its face against what we might term 'penal tourism'. A few institutions are looked at in depth and samples are drawn geographically and by type. A typical 12-day visit—we may take that to the United Kingdom in 1990 as an example—may involve five residential institutions and as many places for short-stay detention. In the United Kingdom all the places of detention visited were physically

153

proximate in two areas, London and Leeds, and, slightly unusually, only two types of institution, police stations and adult prisons, were selected. No attempt, for example, was made to cover Northern Ireland or Scotland, nor to visit psychiatric, including the special, hospitals, or holding centres for illegal immigrants, or young offender institutions. CPT visits are focused. In this respect they are more akin to the short visits of inspection conducted by the English Inspectorate of Prisons (HMCIP) than, for example, the Prisons Project of Human Rights Watch. HMCIP teams, whose mandate is very much broader than the CPT, take two days to carry out a short inspection of a single prison. By contrast, on those few occasions when Human Rights Watch have been allowed full access to institutions and prisoners, their agents have ranged widely. In 1989, for example, the Prison Project delegation, comprising two persons, was able to take advantage of the openness of the new regime in Poland, a country whose prisons were previously closed to them (Human Rights Watch 1988: 5) and 'visited some 15 prisons and police lock-ups throughout the country' in eight days (Human Rights Watch 1991: 4).

The focused nature of CPT visits reflects the systematic methodology the Committee is developing. CPT reports describe each of the institutions visited in considerable detail including, typically: the amount of accommodation, the prisoner population, cell sizes and furnishings, sanitary arrangements, the daily routine, time spent in cells, opportunities for exercise, access to facilities, etc. In some areas the CPT provides more precise data than HMCIP. For example, though the Chief Inspector wishes the Prison Service to formulate standards governing floor area per person, volume per person, temperature, window area, natural ventilation, lighting and noise levels (HMCIP Annual Report, 1992: 9) he does not yet provide all the data on these issues that he might (he appears never to report how large cells are, for example). This relatively precise evidential groundwork by the CPT allows the Committee to move to findings the basis of which is relatively clear. Thus commentators may quarrel, as the British Government has (Council of Europe 1991b: para. 6), with the CPT conclusion that some conditions in Brixton, Wandsworth, and Leeds Prisons in August 1990 amounted to 'inhuman and degrading treatment' (Council of Europe 1991c: para. 57), but there is no doubt as to the criteria the CPT employed to arrive at that conclusion. The matter is clearly stated. A cumulative view is taken similar to the 'totality of conditions' approach adopted by the US courts (see Morgan and Bronstein 1985). Thus conditions that might not in themselves be inhuman and degrading become so if combined with others. The building blocks for the conclusion in the British case were: overcrowding (of which the worst cases were three prisoners sharing cells measuring between 8.2 and $8.6m^2$ designed for one); lack of integral sanitation (with the consequence that prisoners answered the calls of nature in plastic pots without privacy in front of cell mates); and lack of out-of-cell activity (at worst up to 22 and a half hours per day spent in cells). 'Each alone would be a matter of serious concern . . . the three elements interact, the deleterious effects of each of them being multiplied by those of the two others' (Council of Europe 1991c: paras. 36–57). Very similar reasoning and conclusions are to be found in the more recently published report on France with respect to the prisons at Marseille-Baumettes and Nice (Council of Europe 1993: paras. 93, 97, and 102).

The CPT has set out some of the standards it will apply to penal custodial conditions (Council of Europe 1992b: paras. 44–60). The Committee pays particular attention to overcrowding, but has not adopted a precise space standard: what is acceptable clearly depends on usage. Thus the 6m^2 cells in Kumla Prison, Sweden were 'not particularly spacious', but they were well equipped and, given that the prisoners 'spend a significant proportion of the day outside their cells', were judged 'adequate' (Council of Europe 1992c: para. 73). By contrast, the cubicles measuring 1.45m^2 in Stockholm's Central Police Station, though used only for brief periods, were considered 'too small for even the shortest term detention' and the Committee recommended that they be 'either enlarged or dismantled' (para. 18). The Swedish authorities subsequently announced that the cubicles would cease to be used until renovated (Council of Europe 1992d: 5).

Closely related to cell size are (as the report on the United Kingdom makes clear) the twin criteria of access to lavatories 'without undue delay at all times (including at night)' (Council of Europe 1992b: para. 49) and 'purposeful activity' outside cells. Here the CPT has come close to adopting a minimum standard: the Committee considers that prison authorities should aim to ensure that prisoners, including remand prisoners, spend eight hours or more outside their cells daily. That this is the minimum to be aimed at is made clear by the expectation that 'regimes in establishments for sentenced prisoners should be even more favourable' (Council of Europe 1992b: para. 47). Part of the time out of cells must include the opportunity to take daily outdoor exercise, ideally for at least one hour: outdoor exercise must be available to 'all prisoners without exception (including those undergoing cellular confinement as a punishment)' (para. 48).

As regards other aspects of penal detention the CPT is cautious, setting out broad principles but seldom quantifying their operationalization. For example, prisoners' contacts with the outside world, particularly with their families, should be promoted, but no minima for contact are set out (Council of Europe 1992b: para. 51). Or, to take the controversial issue of solitary confinement, the CPT appears to have adopted a stance almost identical to Amnesty. The Committee recognizes that solitary confinement may be resorted to for various reasons, including the request of the prisoner, but maintains that the measure 'can have very harmful consequences' and 'can, in certain circumstances, amount to inhuman and degrading treatment': accordingly solitary confinement 'should be as short as possible' (para. 56). In some respects statements of principle nevertheless provide a relatively unambiguous standard to be applied. For example, both prisoner complaints and prison inspection arrangements should include agents independent of the prison authorities (para. 54) and prisoner disciplinary systems should provide for prisoners to be heard and for 'appeal to a higher authority against any sanctions imposed' as of right (para. 55).

The significance of this relatively precise methodology might be illuminated by drawing a comparison with the approach adopted by Human Rights Watch in their reports regarding prison conditions. Even putting on one side those occasions when Human Rights Watch has necessarily to rely on second-hand information difficult to verify, their reports occasionally seem to lapse into unsubstantiated—or inaccurate— generalizations. For example, its most recent report on Poland (which contains an impressive variety of information), indicates that the new Polish prison rules mandate a minimum of 32.1 ft^2 floor space per prisoner and that this standard is currently 'met in Polish prisons . . . with some exceptions' (Human Rights Watch 1991: 13). Yet it visited only 15 of the more than 200 prisons that reportedly exist in Poland and the delegation appears to have found the standard breached in all three of the prisons visited for which cell measurements are provided. Perhaps the most graphic illustration of the over

155

ambitious approach of Human Rights Watch compared to the CPT concerns the former's comments on health and medical conditions. In 1988, when Human Rights Watch was allowed no access to Polish prisons or prisoners, the organization was nevertheless able to conclude: 'As one would expect, health conditions are very poor among prisoners, and medical care is grossly inadequate, sometimes verging on the criminally negligent' (Human Rights Watch 1988: 17). In 1991, having been given total access, including freedom to talk to prisoners in confidence, the conclusion was that: 'The quality of medical care is something difficult to assess from prison visits' (Human Rights Watch 1991: 23). This is very true and makes it doubly important that visiting delegations include a doctor, which the Human Rights Watch delegation did not.

Similarly, their recent report on the United Kingdom draws extensively upon newspaper articles and uncorroborated accounts rather than upon documentary evidence gathered during their visits to the institutions to which they had access. This may be partly explained by the ambitious programme undertaken: the delegation visited eight large prisons in as many days, taking in London, the Midlands, and Northern Ireland. Even more disquieting, however, is the tendency to rely upon statistics compiled by the penal pressure groups rather than official Prison Service statistics when these would more accurately and authoritatively establish several points to which Human Rights Watch rightly draws attention. This skews the tenor of their reports towards critical journalism rather than measured investigation and, as such, is unlikely to form the basis of a constructive dialogue with the authorities nor to be of much value to campaigning domestic human right groups. By contrast the CPT, quite apart from its Treaty base, international authority, and political advantages, seems to be devising a coherent approach towards the development of appropriate standards which reflect the complex interrelationships of the factors involved. This in turn provides a solid base from which it is able to approach and influence governments.

Conclusion

It is too early to conclude how much impact the CPT recommendations are having on the governments in receipt of the Committee's reports. Too few reports have so far been published, in only five cases have government responses been made public and even in these cases the CPT findings are but one ingredient in a stream of policy consciousness: one would need to know a great deal more about the domestic contexts to judge the influence of the CPT contribution. What is clear is that the CPT has established co-operative dialogues with parties to the Convention and the work of the Committee is being taken seriously by the governments concerned. Even in the case of Turkey, about which a public statement has been issued, the CPT is engaged in what it describes as an 'ongoing dialogue' which is in several respects—*vis-à-vis* prison matters, for example—said to be 'progressing satisfactorily' (Council of Europe 1992*a*: para. 22).

The fact that most parties have so far permitted publication of CPT reports, and that all have taken the trouble to produce responses, some of which have been published, suggests that they are keen to demonstrate that they regard a clean bill of health from the CPT as an imprimatur of some significance. Further, though it is often difficult to disentangle from government responses which policy initiatives were already in hand and which stemmed directly from CPT recommendations, the indications are that CPT attentions are a spur to change. For example, the introduction by the Austrian authorities of a comprehensive police 'custody record' appears not to have been in the policy pipeline (Council of Europe 1991e: 5) before the CPT recommended the measure (Council of Europe 1991d: para. 69). In Sweden, as we have seen, the Government immediately acceded to the CPT recommendation that certain cubicles for prisoners in the Stockholm Police Headquarters be no longer used. The Swedish authorities also appear to have been spurred on in their pre-existing review of prosecutors' powers to restrict the conditions within which remand prisoners are held, restrictions which the CPT judged to be excessive without the right to appeal against them to a court (Council of Europe 1992c: para. 68). It is not without significance that when asked for his view on the changes proposed by the CPT the Swedish Prosecutor-General said he did 'not consider any changes . . . to be justified in objective terms', but he did not 'oppose the transfer of the right to decide on restrictions to the courts' because 'involving the courts harmonizes better with Sweden's international commitments' (Council of Europe 1992d: 25). We must assume that these international commitments now include respecting the view of the CPT. Finally, though the British Government rejected the appellation of 'inhuman and degrading treatment' with respect to Brixton, Leeds, and Wandsworth prisons, measures were none the less speedily taken to end the practice of holding three prisoners to a cell (Council of Europe 1991b: 1). It is doubtful that the CPT would have approved of the principal method by which this was done—namely, transferring Home Office prisoners in large numbers to police cells—but the fact that it was done is further evidence of the potency of CPT influence.

References

ALSTON, P. (1992), *The United Nations and Human Rights: A Critical Appraisal.* Oxford: Clarendon Press.

AMNESTY INTERNATIONAL (1980), *Prison Conditions of Persons Suspected or Convicted of Politically Motivated Crimes in the Federal Republic of Germany: Isolation and Solitary Confinement* (EUR 23/01/80). London: Amnesty International.

—— (1985), *Discussion Paper: Solitary Confinement and other Maximum Security Detention Practices in Western Europe and Canada Related to AI's Mandate.* London: Amnesty International, International Secretariat.

—— (1988), *Conditions at the High Security Unit for Women at Lexington Federal Prison, Kentucky, USA.* London: Amnesty International.

—— (1991), *Statute of Amnesty International—as amended by the 20 International Council, Yokohama, Japan.* London: Amnesty International.

—— (1992), *Turkey: Torture, Extrajudicial Executions, 'Disappearances'* (EUR 44/39/92). London: Amnesty International.

CAVADINO, M., and DIGNAN, J. (1992), *The Penal System: An Introduction.* London: Sage.

COOK, H. (1991), 'The Role of Amnesty International in the Fight Against Torture', in A. Cassese, ed., *The International Fight Against Torture.* Baden-Baden: Nomos Verlagsgesellschaft.

COUNCIL OF EUROPE (1989), *Explanatory Report on the European Convention for the Prevention of Torture and Inhuman or Degrading Treatment or Punishment.* Strasbourg: Council of Europe.

—— (1991a), *1st General Report on the CPT's Activities Covering the Period November 1989 to December 1990* (CPT (91) 3). Strasbourg: Council of Europe.

—— (1991b), *Response of the United Kingdom Government to the Report of the CPT on its visit to the United Kingdom from 29 July 1990 to 10 August 1990* (CPT/Inf (91) 16). Strasbourg: Council of Europe.

—— (1991c), *Report to the United Kingdom Government on the Visit to the United Kingdom from 29 July 1990 to 10 August 1990* (CPT/Inf (91) 5). Strasbourg: Council of Europe.

—— (1991d), *Report to the Austrian Government on the Visit to Austria from 20 May 1990 to 27 May 1990* (CPT/Inf (91) 10). Strasbourg: Council of Europe.

—— (1991e), *Comments of the Austrian Government on the Report of the CPT on its Visit to Austria from 20 to 27 May 1990* (CPT/Inf (91) 11). Strasbourg: Council of Europe.

—— (1992a), *Public Statement on Turkey: Adopted on 15 December 1992.* Strasbourg: Council of Europe.

—— (1992b), *2nd General Report on the CPT's Activities Covering the Period 1 January to 31 December 1991* (CPT/Inf (92) 3). Strasbourg: Council of Europe.

—— (1992c), *Report to the Swedish Government on the Visit to Sweden from 5 to 14 May 1991* (CPT/Inf (92) 4). Strasbourg: Council of Europe.

—— (1992d), *Response of the Swedish Government to the Report of the CPT on its Visit to Sweden from 5 to 14 May 1991* (CPT/Inf (92) 6). Strasbourg: Council of Europe.

—— (1993), *Rapport au Gouvernement de la Républic Française relatif à la visite effectuée par le CPT en France du 27 octobre au 8 novembre 1991* (CPT/Inf (93) 2). Strasbourg: Council of Europe.

DOWNES, D. (1988), *Contrasts in Tolerance: Post-War Penal Policy in the Netherlands and England and Wales.* Oxford: Oxford University Press.

FEEST, J. (1988), *Reducing the Prison Population: Lessons from the West German Experience.* London: NACRO.

GASSER, H.-P. (1988), 'A Measure of Humanity in Internal Disturbances and Tensions: Proposals for a Code of Conduct', *International Review of the Red Cross*, Jan.–Feb.

GRAHAM, J. (1988), 'The Declining Prison Population in the Federal Republic of Germany', *Home Office Research and Planning Unit Research Bulletin*, 24: 47–52.

HELSINKI WATCH (1991), *Human Rights in Northern Ireland.* New York: Human Rights Watch.

HER MAJESTY'S CHIEF INSPECTOR OF PRISONS (1992), *Report of Her Majesty's Chief Inspector of Prisons April 1991–March 1992.* London: HMSO.

HUMAN RIGHTS WATCH (1988), *Prison Conditions in Poland, June 1988.* New York: Human Rights Watch.

—— (1989), *Prison Conditions in Turkey, August 1989.* New York: Human Rights Watch.

—— (1991), *Prison Conditions in Poland, January 1991.* New York: Human Rights Watch.

—— (1992a), *Prison Conditions in the United Kingdom, June 1992.* New York: Human Rights Watch.

—— (1992b), *Prison Conditions in Spain, April 1992.* New York: Human Rights Watch.

INTERNATIONAL COMMITTEE OF THE RED CROSS (1988), 'ICRC Protection and Assistance Activities in Situations not Covered by International Humanitarian Law', *International Review of the Red Cross*, Jan.–Feb.: 9–37.

—— (1992), *Visits by the International Committee of the Red Cross to Persons Deprived of their Freedom.* Geneva: ICRC.

KOOIJMANS, P. (1991), 'The Role and Action of the Special Rapporteur on Torture', in A. Cassese, ed., *The International Fight Against Torture.* Baden-Baden: Nomos Verlagsgesellschaft.

McGOLDRICK, D. (1991), *The Human Rights Committee: Its Role in the Development of the International Covenant on Civil and Political rights.* Oxford: Clarendon Press.

MERON, T. (1989), *Human Rights and Humanitarian Norms as Customary Law.* Oxford: Clarendon Press.

MORGAN, R., and BRONSTEIN, A. (1985), 'Prisoners and the Courts: the US Experience' in M. Maguire, J. Vagg, and R. Morgan, eds, *Accountability and Prisons: Opening up a Closed World.* London: Tavistock.

OPSAHL, T. (1992), 'The Human Rights Committee', in P. Alston, ed., *The United Nations and Human Rights: A Critical Appraisal*. Oxford: Clarendon Press.

PEASE, K. (1991), 'Does England and Wales use Prison More than Other European Countries?' Paper presented to the British Society of Criminology Conference, York.

RODLEY, N. (1987), *The Treatment of Prisoners Under International Law*. Oxford: Clarendon Press.

RUTHERFORD, A. (1984), *Prisons and the Process of Justice*. Oxford: Oxford University Press.